Intuition is not enough

Designed as a guide for trainers and academic staff as well as for practitioners working with the most disturbed children and young people, *Intuition is not Enough* explores the connections between the challenges of practice and of learning. The book introduces the 'matching principle' – the principle that, in order to be successful, training for any field of practice should 'match' or reflect key aspects of that practice in terms of personal experience as well as academic content.

Based on the work of a unique course at the University of Reading, the book includes accounts by staff and students of this special way of working – its rationale, content and process. The authors demonstrate how the developmental principles underlying therapeutic work with young people can influence the design and practice of training, how those who have experienced this form of training have been able to apply their learning in their own professional practice and the struggles they have encountered in doing so.

The book's clear and accessible style will appeal to practitioners and trainers at all levels and in a wide range of professions and it will be especially helpful for those responsible for designing and running courses in the fields of social work, social care, counselling and psychotherapy.

Adrian Ward is a senior lecturer in the Department of Community Studies at the University of Reading. **Linnet McMahon** lectures in Therapeutic Child Care at the University of Reading and is also a play therapist, supervisor and trainer.

Intuition is not enough

Matching learning with practice in therapeutic child care

Edited by Adrian Ward
and Linnet McMahon

London and New York

First published 1998 by Routledge
11 New Fetter Lane, London EC4P 4EE

Simultaneously published in the USA and Canada
by Routledge
29 West 35th Street, New York, NY 10001

© 1998 for the collection as a whole, Linnet McMahon and Adrian
Ward; individual chapters, the authors

Typeset in Times by Routledge
Printed and bound in Great Britain by Clays Ltd, St Ives PLC

British Library Cataloguing in Publication Data
A catalogue record for this book is available from the British Library

Library of Congress Cataloging in Publication Data
Intuition is not enough: matching learning with practice in therapeutic
    child care / edited by Linnet McMahon and Adrian Ward.
        p.   cm.
    Includes bibliographical references and index.
        1. Psychiatric day treatment for children – study and teaching.
    2. Child psychotherapy – residential treatment – study and teaching.
    3. Social work with children – study and teaching. 4. Problem children
    – counselling of.   I. McMahon, Linnet.   II. Ward, Adrian, 1953–
    RJ504.53.I57   1998
    618.92'8914–dc21
                                                            97-34706
                                                            CIP

ISBN 0–415–15661–0 (hbk)
ISBN 0–415–15662–9 (pbk)

To my mother and father, with love (A.W.)

Contents

Contributors

Deborah Best is a teacher in a secondary school unit for pupils with emotional and behavioural difficulties

Paul Cain is Lecturer in Philosophy, Department of Community Studies at the University of Reading

John Diamond is Head of Residential Therapy at the Mulberry Bush School

Teresa Howard convenes median groups at the Group Analytic Society and is qualified as a family therapist and architect

Linnet McMahon is Lecturer in Social Work at the University of Reading.

Adrian Ward is Senior Lecturer in Social Work at the University of Reading.

Ros Wheeler is a Lecturer at Caldecott College, Ashford, Kent

Preface

This is a book about learning: personal, professional and academic learning, and how these different types of learning are connected with each other. It has emerged from our own learning as we worked on running one training course in particular, the MA in Therapeutic Child Care at the University of Reading. Since 1990 this innovatory programme has been providing post-qualifying training for child care workers, social workers, teachers and others. It originated from a collaboration between the University and the Charterhouse Group of Therapeutic Communities, which is an association of schools and other facilities providing psychodynamic and educational support to emotionally disturbed children and young people. The MA has become established as a leading course for those working therapeutically with children and their families, especially those in residential, day care and groupwork settings. Our work on this course has led to the writing of this book through two routes: first, a need to produce theoretical material for the study of therapeutic child care; and second, from our developing interest in the processes of teaching and learning and in how these processes can be made to 'match' with practice.

A single MA course such as this can only hope to reach a small number of people directly, whereas the need for training and staff development in this field is very great. We found that we were frequently being asked for course materials both by those in child care practice who could not attend the course, and by those running other training and staff development programmes elsewhere. At first, we could only send out copies of our course handbooks and reading lists, plus a few reprinted articles, as there was little recent material in print. When originally preparing the course we had faced a considerable problem in assembling the content; in a sense we had had to draw on learning in several disciplines and in none. The extant disciplines included social work, psychology, psychotherapy and special education, although each of these only dealt indirectly with the residential and day care settings which were our own focus. Meanwhile the specific disciplines of residential and group care for children appeared to be less well represented in the literature: not very much had been published, and much of what there was had appeared either in books which were now out of print or in journals normally found only in university libraries. The literature was thus somewhat scattered, hard to find and full of gaps. In order to begin filling some of these gaps, we started to write and publish papers about our work, and encouraged our students to do likewise. When we first envisaged writing this book, our aim was simply to collect these papers on therapeutic child care and write with a primary focus on child care practice. However, as our work developed, so too did the focus of this book.

We found that, through our work on this programme, we ourselves were learning. We were discovering more about how the processes of learning and teaching operate, and about how staff and students can work together at enhancing these processes and at acknowledging and trying to overcome the problems which inevitably arise. It was difficult work, and we had much to learn. We met every week as a staff team to reflect on what was happening, on what sense we could make of it, and on what we might need to do in order to maximise the learning for all. Some of us kept journals of our own work, just as we encouraged our students to do, and we were able to draw upon these when the time came to write up our work. We realised that, through some of the methods which we were using, such as Opening and Closing Meetings, and an 'Experiential Group', we were hearing more than trainers usually do about the actual experience of those attending the programme: about their hopes, fears, excitements and anxieties, and about how these affected both their professional work and the quality of their learning about it. Indeed, we sometimes wondered whether these particular students had a more intense experience of these feelings than other students on professional training courses, but we do not believe this to be so. It was just that we had more direct access to such experiences than is sometimes the case.

Throughout this learning we became increasingly aware that what was distinctive about the course was that it built so firmly upon what we called the 'matching principle': the principle that the process of learning should match with the process of practice. While our main motive for running the course had always been to improve the quality of services to children in the child care system, our motives for writing the book now included a wish to propose and explore the matching principle, and indeed this has eventually become the primary focus of the book. As we talked with colleagues from other disciplines, we realised that similar questions arise in other forms of professional training, and indeed that people such as Donald Schön have theorized about, for example, the subject of how people learn about 'reflective practice'. However, it turned out that our experience was taking us beyond what we had read about elsewhere, and that, for example, what we meant by reflective practice was rather different from what Schön meant, so there was further conceptual work to be done – which is what we have attempted in this book.

Eventually we began to collect together the material on child care practice with the other material on the processes of professional learning, so that we could explore the connections between them more carefully, and so that we could make the results more widely available. The book still contains a large amount of material on child care practice and its theoretical base, but this is all set within the framework of the discussion of the matching principle. It is therefore addressed both to those whose primary interest is in the practice of therapeutic child care and to those whose interest is in the processes of adult education and professional training. This may be viewed as ambitious, but we have preferred to aim higher rather than lower, and we hope that, as one of our readers, you will find that this approach is of some value, whatever your professional background and special interest.

Acknowledgements

We acknowledge our debt to the members of the Therapeutic Child Care course who in their different ways have brought themselves and their work to the course and from whom we have learned so much.

Particular thanks to Michele Alfred, Mark Adams, Steve Bromage, Viv Dacre, Dave Fernyhough, Nyasha Gwatidzo, Margarete Lucas, Rebecca Nwaozuzu, Simon Peacock, Matt Vince, John Turberville and Janet Vale, who have allowed us to quote from their work.

During the original planning of the course we greatly appreciated the support of many colleagues in practice, especially John Whitwell, Michael Jinks, Richard Rollinson, Melvyn Rose, Christine Bradley, Caroline Whitehead, John Cross and Brian Bishop. This support was all the more valuable in coming from people who have each worked so hard to provide better care and treatment for troubled children. We are equally grateful for the encouragement and financial support provided by the Peper Harow Foundation, The Charterhouse Group, The Caldecott Community and the Tudor Trust.

We have also appreciated the continuing support of our colleagues in the social work team at the University of Reading, in particular the team leader, Doug Badger, who encouraged us in developing the course at a time when there were other great demands on the team.

Introduction

How can training really connect with practice? Surely training – and 'theory' – will always be distant and removed from the sheer grind and turmoil of everyday professional practice, whether this is in social work, teaching or any other setting? There has always been a dilemma about how to bring closer together the apparently different worlds of college and workplace and recent trends towards modularisation, distance-learning and workplace-based training seem to offer one way of resolving this dilemma. They do so by breaking down training programmes into small components, delivering them (literally) through the post or other media and in some cases expecting people to complete their studies without ever leaving the workplace and without entering a separate 'place of learning'. On the other hand, it is questionable as to whether all forms of professional practice are best studied in this way. Especially at the level of post-qualifying training for therapeutic work, which will be our focus in this book, there is a risk that the 'medium' of distance may conflict with the 'message' of involvement. Indeed, we will be proposing that in such intimate and intricate work as therapeutic child care, there are more appropriate ways of tackling the dilemma of the distance between training, theory and practice than by increasing the distance.

Our argument will be based upon what we are calling the 'matching principle': that in all professional training the mode of training should reflect or 'match' the mode of practice in terms of process as well as content. 'Let the training match the practice' might indeed be a motto for the design of all training courses, but what do we mean by 'matching' in this context? This book attempts to answer that question by means of a case-study approach, concentrating upon an analysis of one particular mode of practice: that of therapeutic practice with children. By closely modelling some aspects of training upon key features of the relevant practice settings, we aim to show how we have been able to provide learning opportunities which do seem to have enabled practitioners to achieve genuine improvement in the service they offer.

We are especially interested in the field of 'therapeutic child care', by which we mean that broad range of therapeutic work undertaken with children and young people in non-clinical settings, such as children's homes and other residential facilities, family centres and educational 'withdrawal units', as well as in foster homes. These settings are of particular interest because the need for training and for a new approach to training in such places is so great. Although they provide help and support for many of the most deeply damaged and troublesome children in the UK, very often this help is provided by staff who have had little access to the specialised training they require and who receive very limited support and advice in their work. We have been involved for some years in providing post-qualifying training for these staff, but we are very aware of the lack of opportunities nationally for such training. We are therefore keen to add to the possibilities of improved training for them, partly by stimulating some debate about how such training might be planned and delivered and partly by offering our ideas on the complex relationship between practice, training and theory. In the process we are also aiming to provide a means of learning about child care to benefit such training.

Beyond this particular context, however, we also want to propose that *all* professional training should involve some degree of 'matching'. We argue that, in order to maximise the potential for learning, the student's experience of the training process should have a 'felt' connection with their experience of practice. It will be seen in Chapter 6 that our emphasis is upon matching for *process* as much as for content and by this we mean unconscious as much as conscious process. Our assumption is that any matching must therefore begin with an analysis of process and content in the relevant field of practice, so in the early chapters we shall be asking not just: '*what* do people do within this field of practice?' (which might be as far as we would get using a 'competency' approach) but also '*why* do they do it, what sorts of thinking and emotion are involved and what else is happening around them as they work?'.

The book offers an extended case study in the application of the matching principle, which we explore in more detail in Chapter 6;

and we return to the question about the broader application of this principle in the closing chapter. We are proposing this approach because, while the design of many training programmes does suggest some element of matching, many others suggest an absence of such connections and indeed some seem to offer a model which is quite at variance with the relevant mode of practice. In the world of professional education this aspect of the design of training programmes often seems to have been left to implicit or intuitive reasoning, or even purely to chance, rather than being decided upon for explicit and well-argued reasons. Our aim in offering this principle is to show that these decisions can be reached in a more rational and explicit way, although we do not so much claim to have 'invented' this principle, but simply to have uncovered and articulated it.

TRAINING FOR THERAPEUTIC CHILD CARE

In our field of therapeutic child care, it was initially hard to locate appropriate models for the *content* of a training programme, let alone for its process. This was because, although there was an extensive range of settings in which this practice is carried out, the staff of these settings did not necessarily identify themselves as coming under the same professional or conceptual umbrella. Some of them would identify primarily with social work and some with nursing, special education, group analysis or child psychotherapy. However, our own experience in practice (as a residential worker and play therapist) had suggested that across this wide range of settings could be found a large number of staff all attempting to achieve broadly similar therapeutic objectives with some deeply troubled young people and probably all needing to draw on each of the perspectives mentioned above.

The real difficulty was that, if these staff had had *any* previous access to training, this would have been within one or other of the above disciplines, but not usually geared sufficiently to therapeutic work in the group care context, which has somehow remained relatively under-conceptualised. We therefore set out to assemble and in some areas to create, a theory-base for this work which would span across the settings. In the first part of the book we give some indication of this theory-base, although there has not been space to be comprehensive.

We have drawn upon the literature we have found to be most

useful in our own practice in terms of explaining the behaviour and feelings of children and young people and especially how these connect with their relationships, families and others. Primarily, it is a psychodynamic approach, but whereas many psychodynamic writings focus mainly on clinical work, whether with individuals or with groups, our own focus has been very much on applying these understandings in non-clinical settings and using them to explore the connections between individuals, groups and the overall context of the group care setting. From within child care literature this means that we have drawn especially on the work of B. Dockar-Drysdale and D.W. Winnicott, whereas from the broader therapeutic literature we have also drawn on fields such as group analysis and the therapeutic community. Among the problems encountered has been the fact that, often, much of this literature, while it is exceptionally helpful in terms of understanding children's relationships with their families and others, overlooks other key aspects of children's experience, such as the reality of racism and gender stereotyping and the harsh context of poverty and oppression within which many families struggle. We are reminded continually of these realities by the accounts of their practice which our students report and we have tried to take due account of such factors in our work both in the training programme and in this book. However, we acknowledge that we have in fact only just begun this process and that there is much further to go in this respect.

THE PSYCHODYNAMIC APPROACH

We are aware that in using a psychodynamic approach we may encounter various objections: some find it 'ideologically unsound' or elitist because of its continuing gaps in addressing issues such as gender, race and social class and we are in some sympathy with this objection and wish to work further at filling in the gaps. Others, however, may object that they find this approach complex and daunting, partly because the terminology and concepts seem strange and often mystifying and partly because the task of working psychodynamically can appear very complicated and difficult to undertake. People are reluctant to dabble because of a reasonable fear of doing harm rather than good, or of getting out of their depth. We are in sympathy with this objection too and feel that it is a real and in some respects inevitable difficulty.

Psychoanalytic theory is complicated and sometimes hard to

understand, probably because it is attempting to explain complicated and confusing concepts, such as the nature of the emotional
experience of very young children and how it may connect both
with the child's relationships with its parents and with its later
emotional and psychological development. There is much about this
field which is hard to fathom. Beyond a certain point it cannot be
learned simply by reading the theoretical texts or by relying on
personal intuition to guide one's practice. One of our themes is that
the ability to think clearly depends on the ability to be clear about
your feelings: theory and personal experience therefore need to be
brought together to help people arrive at new ways of understanding. This book demonstrates some of the ways in which these
elements can be brought together. In the process it describes a
distinctive approach to professional training in higher education.
The focus is on how people learn in both therapeutic and educational contexts. Throughout the book the parallels between these
processes are explored and developed.

A further objection which we sometimes encounter to the
psychoanalytic perspective on training and practice is that some
people feel it is somehow too introspective and even self-indulgent.
In particular, our students sometimes have to contend with
colleagues or managers who dismiss this approach with references
to 'the "feely" end of social work' and to 'navel-gazing exercises'.
The reality, of course, is that working in this way requires the
greatest mental discipline and emotional resourcefulness. It is also
true that even some of those most concerned with social work for
troubled children can find it awkward at a personal level to deal
with the power of the feelings involved and with the necessary focus
on understanding the detail and dynamic of human emotions.
Being aware of such dismissive comments can make it hard for us
and our students to assert confidently the value of a strong focus on
the emotional world of children, but in some ways it makes it all the
more necessary. If the workers themselves feel awkward and inhib-
ited about it, then how much more difficult and humiliating must it
be for those children who have suffered abuse and neglect to face
talking about such things?

Connected with the above is the fact that a great deal of therapeutic work which is undertaken with children is never properly
acknowledged as such. Many of the practice examples described in
this book come from ordinary children's homes and family centres
managed by local authority Social Service Departments, rather than

from prestigious special units labelled 'therapeutic communities'. It is our experience that, given the right support and training, staff in these ordinary settings can achieve extraordinary results, even though at times neither their managers nor they themselves recognise the true value of this work. If senior managers are uncomfortable, as sometimes they appear to be, with viewing their children's homes and family centres as having therapeutic aims, our response would be, 'If they are not therapeutic, then what are they?'. We would argue that it is not possible to have a children's institution which is neutral in this respect: either it is focused on providing skilled and intensive help to children and their families, in which case we would argue for it to be set up as a therapeutic resource, or it is not.

OUTLINE OF THE BOOK

In Part 1 we focus on therapeutic practice and on some of the theoretical frameworks which we have found helpful. We draw on the ideas of Donald Winnicott and others to outline the concepts of the inner world and the 'holding environment' and look at their implications for therapeutic practice. There is a strong emphasis on the group care setting as a context for therapeutic work and on the 'therapeutic community' approach as a model for harnessing the overall context of team, place and people to the therapeutic task.

In Part 2 we begin with a discussion of the 'matching principle' and in the ensuing chapters we outline the detail of our use of this principle in the design and operation of a training programme, looking at what is required of both staff and students. We show how this approach addresses the connections between the personal, the professional and the academic and we include some reflections on this theme from students of the programme.

In Part 3 we include a number of examples of ways in which people who have experienced this approach to training have applied their learning back into the practice setting, both in therapeutic communities and in less specialised settings. Finally in Part 4 we bring together the many ways in which we have used the idea and concept of 'reflection' throughout the book and return to the theme of the matching principle, looking at how it can be applied to other forms of training. All practice examples in the book have been 'anonymised' to protect confidentiality.

HOW TO USE THE BOOK

We have aimed to create a logical journey through complicated terrain and to offer signposts and reminders along the way, so our hope is that the book will make most sense if you work through it from start to finish. However, we do recognise that some of our readers will have a main interest in the details of therapeutic practice in group care settings: if this is your main interest, you may prefer to read the book 'back-to-front', perhaps even starting with one of the shorter chapters in Part 3 such as 'Alice and her blanket' and working back through some of the other examples before turning to the theoretical frameworks which these authors have drawn upon (and which are introduced in Part 1). Others may have more interest in detailed suggestions about training for therapeutic work: if this is your interest, you may prefer to start in Part 2 with the various chapters on aspects of the MA programme before engaging with the theoretical background. We also argue, of course, that no book can provide all the answers anyway and we concede that there is something paradoxical about writing a book which argues that you cannot learn it all from books. We have learned to live with this paradox. We hope you will find a path of your own through our ideas. Whichever path you take, we hope you will enjoy the journey.

Part 1

A basis for thinking about therapeutic practice

Chapter 1

The inner world and its implications

Adrian Ward

How can we understand the needs of troubled children and young people? My aim in this chapter is to set out one way of doing so, drawing upon some of the ideas central to a psychodynamic approach to helping children and their families. This is not intended as a full account of the field, but as a brief introduction to some of the ideas which we will be drawing upon later in the book: those requiring more detailed discussion will be referred to other places where fuller accounts are given. Neither is this approach claimed as the *only* way of understanding and addressing children's needs: other approaches – and indeed other versions of this same approach – have been successfully used by many others and it can certainly be helpful to draw upon a wide range of ideas and techniques. Our argument is simply that this approach is one which we have found useful and productive as a basis for thinking about both how to help and how to provide training for those learning how to help. The central theme in this chapter is the concept of the 'inner world' in human experience and its implications for those who experience special difficulties in childhood. The next chapter will explore ways of trying to reach this inner world in therapeutic work.

CHILD, FAMILY AND OUTSIDE WORLD

We are probably all aware, from reflecting upon our own childhood experience, that every child develops with some sense of 'self' and identity and that a central part of this self is what might be called the 'inner world': the internal psychological and emotional picture which we evolve of the world and the people in it. This inner world consists of a mixture of the conscious and the less-than-conscious: thoughts and feelings, fears and imaginings, understandings and misunderstandings, dreams and nightmares, images of people and places and assumptions about their meaning or importance. It is gradually built up out of the experiences the child has from its earliest days and especially out of the learning the child achieves from these experiences. To the child this inner world is real and important, although some parts of it may be a secret and private world which is not disclosed to anyone. Equally, some parts of it may be hidden from the child itself, partly because some of the experiences upon which it is built are absorbed without their emotional impact being consciously understood at the time, but also because some experiences may be too painful or frightening to keep in mind at a conscious level and may therefore be kept somewhere out of reach – although still within the scope of influence.

One of the best ways of learning about the inner world – apart from talking with children and reflecting upon one's own experience – is to read biographies and autobiographies. Many such works skim over the earliest stages of childhood to get on to the racy days of young adulthood as soon as possible, but some of them dwell most revealingly on the early days. One such is the autobiography of Jean-Paul Sartre, who turns out to have been a precocious thinker and a valuable source for our purposes as he conveys a vivid picture of his developing inner world from quite a young age. In one passage, for example, he describes his childhood anxieties about death and dying:

> I saw death. At the age of five: it was watching me; in the evenings, it prowled on the balcony: it pressed its nose to the window; I used to see it but I did not dare to say anything. Once, on the Quai Voltaire, we met it: it was a tall, mad old woman, dressed in black, who mumbled as she went by: 'I shall put that child in my pocket'. Another time, it was a hole: . . . I was playing at horses, half-heartedly and galloping round the house. Suddenly, I noticed a gloomy hole: the cellar, which had been opened; an indescribable impression of loneliness and horror blinded me: I turned round and singing at the top of my voice, I fled.
>
> (Sartre 1967: 60)

However remote Sartre and his upbringing may seem now, his intense and sometimes bizarre memories of his early childhood conjure up some of the intensity of the inner world of the child.

If we reflect upon our own recollections of childhood events, most of us can provide evidence that children not only experience the world and the people around them, but also make their own active interpretations of these experiences. These interpretations sometimes hold great power for the child, so that it may feel impossible to reveal them to anyone else. Problems can arise for the child when these interpretations of the world around them are based on misunderstandings, or on inaccurate information, or when, as Sartre indicates, the child's own version of events and feelings differs from what other people try to tell them. For example, in one passage Sartre says that his mother insisted that he was 'the happiest of little boys', even though he knew this was far from true. Another version of this mismatch arises when the child knows a truth which others wish to deny or refuse to hear: what has sometimes been called 'the hopelessness of not being believed'. Most people can recall some childhood experience of being unfairly accused of doing something wrong, but in work with troubled children the question of believing what a child is saying may hold much greater significance, e.g. in sorting out the truth in cases of suspected sexual abuse.

Our inner world remains with us through adolescence and beyond, although some people feel that by the onset of puberty some of its magic has gone, to be replaced by an awareness of the impingement of reality (which may also bring periods of depression or cynicism as well as times of mature understanding and realisation). On the subject of magic, most people are probably familiar with the idea of the magical thinking of the young child, whereby inanimate objects are treated as living beings with thoughts, intentions and feelings. This is also closely linked with the young child's view of herself/himself as the centre of the universe and thus as the *cause* of all events whether good or bad. This latter aspect of a young child's thinking is crucial to bear in mind when assessing what sense a child has made of traumatic events.

For most of us these childhood feelings are manageable and healthy, even though they may cause us considerable pain or confusion at the time: but for children who have experienced the trauma of rejection, neglect, or abuse, their inner world is often in even greater turmoil than the 'real' world around them. Other children experiencing traumatic events may seek refuge in a 'magic' inner world in which people and events can be changed, destroyed or denied as the child tries to insulate itself from knowing and feeling the pain of the situation. The worker who attempts to achieve communication with the child's inner world is therefore operating in highly sensitive territory; here, timing, patience and an ability to demonstrate real empathy are essential.

The question arises as to when and how the inner world first develops in the child. Are we born with an inner world or does it gradually evolve? Most people's earliest conscious memories date from around the age of four or five; many people are aware of sensory memories from even earlier, but these memories are usually not specific or clearly located in time. The psychoanalyst D.W. Winnicott would say that the capacity to sustain the sense of an inner world develops during the first year or so of life, out of the child's experience of being 'held' emotionally as well as physically by the parent(s). He calls this whole experience the 'holding environment'. As the child's most primitive and 'unthinkable' anxieties are contained and understood by the parent and the child learns to trust the parent, so that the child gradually learns to recognise thoughts and feelings, and develops the ability to think, as well as the capacity to symbolise and to play. The term 'holding environment' refers both specifically to the people (i.e. usually the parents) who 'hold' the child and more abstractly to the quality of the relationship the child experiences with these people.

This journey from absolute dependence into an emerging sense of independence and autonomy is a most significant element in the development of the child's inner world. Winnicott argues that the child manages this transition partly by making use of familiar objects (such as a favourite soft toy, blanket or teddy-bear) as 'transitional objects', which he also referred to as 'the first "not-me" object'. The argument is that it is through becoming attached to some familar object such as this that the child starts to learn the difference between what is 'inner' and what is 'outer', what is part of 'me', what is 'not-me' and what is part of other people. The process of starting to use such objects, of becoming deeply attached to them and eventually of letting them go again, is one of enormous subtlety and individual variation and for this delicate process to evolve in its own time requires the security and almost the 'blessing' of what we have called the holding environment. Winnicott sees the use of this object as the child's first experience of play and thus critical in the child's emotional development, forming the root of the capacity in adulthood to be creative in other ways. He says that most children either use such an object or some other personal ritual or meaningful creation (perhaps an imaginary friend). On the other hand, while research confirms this to be true for many children, it also reveals that many children do not use such an object and the concept of 'transitional phenomena' may well turn out to be a culture-bound metaphor relating to child-rearing in white or western cultures. Many other cultures handle the parenting of young children very differently from the white British approach – and even that approach is hardly consistent or uniform. Therefore, we need to be careful about *how* we generalise about the whole area of early childhood development.

There are strong connections between Winnicott's views on the holding relationship and Bion's work on 'containment'. According to Bion (1962) it is through the process of containment that the infant's most unmanageable feelings and deepest anxieties are 'projected' into the parent so that, initially at least, the parent can feel them for him or her, before handing them back in a more manageable form, as if to say 'There: that's what you were worried about. I think you'll find you can cope with this now'. (The term 'projection' is used in psychoanalytic theory to refer to one means by which people – in this case the child – deal with unmanageable feelings: by unconsciously getting someone else to experience them.) Bion's view was that as the relationship develops and as the child becomes emotionally more resilient, the child will increasingly be able to manage its own emotions without needing to project them, and even when it does project them, the parent will increasingly be able to hand back these feelings and anxieties to the child. Of course, this is hard for the parent to do without patronising, over-protecting or under-protecting the child, but it is argued that in the great majority of cases the emerging strength of the relationship ensures that containment is a facilitative rather than an intrusive or destructive one.

We shall return many times in this book to the ideas of containment and the holding environment as important parallels have been drawn, on the one hand, between these experiences in infancy and the quality of experience which troubled children and young people may need later in life, and on the other hand, between such provision and the overall quality of 'holding' in the organisation and management of therapeutic work.

EGO INTEGRATION

Looking at the origins of the inner world makes it evident that these earliest days in its formation are of great importance, but also that for some children things have started to go wrong long before the emergence of a secure inner world. Winnicott writes extensively of the vital importance for a child's healthy emotional development of what happens between mother and child during the first year of life. We need to consider this process in order to be clear about what may go wrong since many of the young people in the care system seem to be those for whom things have gone wrong from their earliest days.

In what follows it is important to recognise that when Winnicott refers to 'the mother' we should also think of the others who may provide for infants' needs, including the father (or the mother's partner) and other relatives. As society has evolved since Winnicott's day – the middle years of the twentieth century – it has become more widely recognised not only that fathers and others can provide what Winnicott assumed the mother should always provide, but also, as we have seen, that patterns of family life differ extensively from one culture to another and the white Western nuclear family is by no means the only environment in which children can flourish. Society has changed, too, in that many single parents successfully provide for children in ways which Winnicott assumed could only be achieved by two parents in traditional roles. Despite these changes in the social and political climate, Winnicott's core understandings of young children's emotional development continue to be of central value in therapeutic work. Our focus is primarily upon the *quality* of the child's early experience and on the extent to which this experience enables the child to develop and sustain the sense of a coherent and healthy inner world. Where Winnicott refers specifically to the mother we shall do likewise, but in other parts of the book we may refer to the parent or to the primary carer. Equally we have followed Winnicott's convention of referring to the child as 'he', rather than the clumsy 'he/she', 'himself/herself'.

Winnicott saw the newborn infant's inner world as being a bundle of instincts, fears and sensations, which the infant cannot think about and therefore cannot differentiate. In other words, the infant cannot at first distinguish between himself and his environment (including his mother) and is subject to the gales and fortunes of internal and external physical sensations, as well as to swings of pure feeling – e.g. discomfort, pleasure, feeling warm or cold, full or hungry (although at first he will not even be aware of any differences between feeling cold and hungry – things will simply feel good or bad). Winnicott saw these as potentially very powerful, even frightening, feelings for the baby.

As we have seen, the role of the parent is summarised as 'holding': literally holding the child physically, providing appropriate comfort, nourishment, etc; but also holding in its deeper sense of 'managing' or containing the child's emotional experience for him until he gradually learns to understand and contain his own feelings. In this sense the child is emotionally 'merged' in with the parent and the parent gradually learns to make sense of the child's experience and mirror this back to him so that he can begin to make sense of it for himself.

The child gradually brings together (with help and holding) all of these fragmentary bits and pieces of experience to the point where he can begin to hold *himself* together – the process of ego-integration. The term 'ego' refers to this capacity to organise and make sense of one's experience: what Winnicott is saying is that we are not born with an ego, but develop one, usually during the first year of life. He argues that the baby is born with an in-built tendency to develop and mature and that this tendency, when matched as it is in most cases with 'good enough' parenting, takes the baby through these earliest stages to the point where integration has taken place.

Unintegration

Most babies do have good enough experience, do achieve integration and thus have at least the foundations for healthy emotional development, even though they – we – may subsequently encounter all sorts of other difficulties and develop various neuroses as childhood and adolescence take their course. However, a small proportion of babies have a much harder time of it and for various reasons do not manage to make a satisfactory beginning to their emotional lives. Ego-integration is a very important achievement and if you do not achieve it at the appropriate stage you are likely to remain in some version (or with some core elements) of the 'unintegrated' emotional state of the newborn.

The kind of things which prevent the process from happening are chiefly related to things which prevent the parents from offering good enough 'holding'. For example, if the mother or primary carer is always or usually so pre-occupied with her own emotional needs that she cannot notice and respond appropriately to those of the baby, there is little chance that the baby will be able to feel safely 'held'. Instead, he is likely to feel ignored, abandoned, dropped, but without the capacity even to think about what this means or to understand what is happening. If there is no one there to mediate and manage the baby's potentially chaotic experience, he is left prone to the full blast of primitive instinctual fears and anxieties, such as the fear of going to pieces or falling forever. This may sound dramatic and it *is* so: to remain in the unintegrated state is an extremely serious business because it means that the child has not achieved any sense of predictability and understandability in people, in the world in general, or especially in himself. This is equivalent to what Erikson (1965) describes as failure to achieve a sense of basic trust; it is the stuff of which psychosis is made. Several of the examples from practice presented in later chapters describe work with unintegrated children.

Consequences

If integration does not happen, the child is left either with a chaotic inner world, or with very little awareness of the difference between his own inner world and other people's feelings or external reality. In some cases the child evolves a hardened emotional 'shell' or 'false self', built on having learned to survive by always complying totally with others' needs rather than learning how to recognise his own needs. This false self protects him from any real involvement with people. Such a child is likely to carry on interacting with people on the basis of these highly problematic patterns until dramatic things start to happen, usually when the child reaches playgroup or school age and disruption begins. People will experience the child as wildly unpredictable, out of touch, coldly manipulative, or vicious and violent: in other words, they will see in the child what the child is probably seeing around himself, because he has no capacity to trust himself or anyone.

What is most serious is that such children are most unlikely to recover spontaneously without skilled help. They may therefore remain in this highly vulnerable emotional state through their adolescence and even into adulthood unless and until such help is available. Some of them, of course, will develop pockets of emotional and intellectual functioning so that they can get by at a minimal level, but their fundamental emotional emptiness will remain untouched and they will be prone to panic and disruption when placed under the sort of everyday social stresses which most people can handle without any trouble.

Many of the examples of therapeutic work which we will be discussing involve children of primary school age and in early adolescence. This is the age group with which we have the most experience and the group with which many of our students are working and it is our view that at this age children may be more amenable to therapeutic intervention than when they reach later adolescence. By this later stage, if their initial difficulties have not been successfully treated, young people are likely to have developed even more intractable behavioural problems and more sophisticated systems of defence both against achieving insight for themselves and against accepting help from others. Earlier difficulties will also now be compounded by the emergence of sexuality and associated issues. There will not be the scope in this book to discuss these specific difficulties in detail, since our aim here is to explore the impact of the earliest emotional experiences, rather than to offer a comprehensive account of therapeutic practice with young people of all ages and types. Our argument about the matching principle, however, would suggest that, if most of our students had been working with older adolescents, we would have needed to evolve different patterns and structures in the training programme.

RELATIONSHIPS AND THEIR IMPACT

The term 'inner world' is perhaps rather imprecise, because it is sometimes used to refer to different aspects of what is variously called self, ego and identity and even (somewhat confusingly) self-identity. In this book we use the term to refer both to the child's inner emotional experience and to the child's capacity to reflect upon that experience. To be able to know and reflect upon one's experience presupposes 'ego' (the organising capacity) and it is out of such knowing and reflecting that the child develops a sense of self ('this is me – this is who I am') and ultimately a more or less stable sense of identity ('I am this sort of a person with this partic- ular mix of ability, personality and history') and of self-esteem ('I feel good, bad, or indifferent about myself'). The inner world, in fact, might be thought of as the voice with which we say such things to ourselves, as well as the inner mental 'space' within which this voice is heard. It is hard to be more precise without getting so meta-physical that we start to lose a sense of the hard-edged reality of the inner world – a reality which becomes very apparent when we engage in therapeutic work with troubled children.

We now need to return briefly to the origin and development of the inner world. Part of the child's inner world consists of the images built up of the external world: images which have to be constructed upon the available evidence, i.e. the nature of the rela-tionships which he has with those closest to him. In the first place this will mean his experience of his parents or other carers, but it soon extends to siblings, friends, teachers and others, although for most children it is the immediate family context which continues to provide the strongest influences.

The child carries in his inner world a mental picture not only of his mother and thus of other women, other adults and of the world in general, but also an image of himself as reflected in his mother's eyes – as lovable or otherwise, valued and respected or otherwise. Meanwhile he will evolve another version of this picture in relation to his father and thus of himself as seen by his father and then of his brothers or sisters and of himself as they see him. What emerges will in some sense be a complicated network of personal images of self and other, although for most children it may not feel like a complicated network, it just feels like 'me' and 'my family'. At a literal level many young children spend a lot of time making real these images through drawing, play and other means. On the other hand, for those who experience serious disruption or distortion in these early relationships, the picture becomes so confusing that it is hard for them to sustain or value a sense of 'me' and hard even to contemplate holding any sort of picture in mind. In those extreme cases where there has been abuse of a physical, emotional or sexual nature, the whole pattern becomes grotesquely distorted and deeply painful. A child who has been abused by his father or mother from an early age has no reliable means of knowing who loves or hates him and therefore cannot know whether he is lovable or 'hateable': under pressure he will assume the worst. One young adolescent who had grown up through such turmoil gave herself an extra initial of 'H' for 'Hateful', which she was careful to explain meant both hated and full of hate. What started as a version of the charming naive world of the innocent young child has thus led us to contemplate the very opposite: the inner world as a state of both siege and civil war.

There are many types of experience other than the overtly abusive ones which can cause children distress and trauma. Central among these is the experience of loss and the grief associated with it. Such loss may arise through actual bereavement of a parent or sibling, or in less straightforward ways, such as when a child loses contact with a family member through divorce or separation, or through the child's own reception into care. In such circumstances children may also lose close friends, school teachers and other significant people. Other more metaphorical forms of loss may play a part, too, such as the loss of innocence, or of one's childhood.

A certain amount of loss is in fact inevitable in the sequence of development through childhood, as we develop on from total dependency towards relative independence and as people and places to whom we were attached become less powerfully imbued with meaning. Learning to cope with the occasional relatively straightforward loss, through the death of a grandparent for instance, or even that of a much-loved family pet, is certainly part of the average child's healthy development. What is harder to bear is repeated or sudden loss, or loss which is added to – or confused with – other traumatic experiences.

Especially painful for many children in the care system are the instances of what might be called 'compound loss' where a child has had to move from home into foster care and where foster homes or other subsequent placements have then repeatedly broken down, leaving the child each time with further damage and disillusionment. Like the spilled beads of a necklace whose string has broken, it can then seem to the child impossible to regather together experiences into any meaningful or positive whole. In these circumstances some children seem to become progressively numbed by each further loss and then resistant to the next attachment. This is presumably done (by some children consciously, by others less so) to protect the self from feeling further pain, on the principle that you cannot fully lose that to which you have not become fully attached in the first place.

Such defences are somewhat different to the 'false self' in some unintegrated children, however. Since unintegrated children have never experienced a full and meaningful attachment, they have not yet learned what real loss feels like, although they will probably have a powerful instinct for the strength of the feelings involved, despite the fact that they may not be able to acknowledge or show them. For unintegrated children, when something or somebody is lost they are more likely to experience rage for that which they have never had and envy for that which everyone else seems to have, rather than the 'simple' grief of personal loss. Even these feelings of rage or envy, however, may not be directly experienced or expressed by such a child. Rather they will often find expression by being 'acted out' in less direct ways and often apparently disconnected from the original feelings.

The issues of loss and questions about children's ability or otherwise to reflect upon it and to be helped to 'work through' it, arise frequently and powerfully in therapeutic work with troubled children and often in unexpected ways. For example, sometimes even an apparently minor change in a situation can bring a sense of loss in its wake and if the new circumstances do not feel right the sense of loss can become exaggerated and the earlier feelings re-enlivened months or even years later. This applies to all of us, including the staff and students working at understanding therapeutic work with children, which also means that it is always a 'live issue' in training. The themes of attachment and loss are further developed in the work of J. Bowlby (1980) and in an especially accessible and moving form in the films of the Robertsons (1967–71).

THE INNER WORLD OF THE FAMILY

Since our inner world develops from our experiences and since for most children this will mean experiences located within the family, it is clear that there is a strong connection between family and self. In another sense, however, we can say that each family has some sense of a collective 'inner world': a common view of itself as a family with customs, habits and sayings almost like a small tribe, and with all the accompanying assumptions, views of the world, etc. In many families this collective inner world is never spelt out or acknowledged, although (like the British nation) it may evolve a complex and intricate 'unwritten constitution', as if to imply 'this is the way that we do/say things around here'. This can be a very powerful pattern, often built up by parents or partners early in their relationship (and, of course, in some respects brought with them from their own families of origin) and then enforced through a code of rules and expectations, which may be formally spelt out, or which may be so deeply embedded in the patterns of everyday life that people are just expected to learn them as they go along. These patterns are thus also very influential in individual terms, as each child comes along and learns the pattern by living through it and gradually internalising it.

If these family patterns become destructive or confusing in their effect on the individuals, it is usually the individuals who suffer and seek help by one means or another: much of this book is premised on the model of providing help to one individual at a time from a troubled family. On the other hand, in many cases it may be more productive to focus on the broader family patterns, working with the family together in family work or family therapy rather than focusing all the helping efforts on one troubled individual. Our pre-occupation in this book with the individual (and usually within the group care context) should not be seen as implying that all efforts of help should be delivered in this mode. It is rather the case that we and our students have found ourselves having to work with what is available, which often means working predominantly with the individual family member and less frequently with the rest of the family. In some cases this is because family patterns have broken down completely and the child has to be separated for his own or others' safety. In other cases it may be because the family – or at least the parent(s) – have totally rejected the child.

BEYOND FAMILY: THE SOCIAL CONTEXT

Part of each child's inner world, then, will not just be static images of parental figures and others, but dynamic representations of the nature and quality of the interactions between these people and between the people and the child himself. In addition, he is experiencing his family life not in a vacuum but in a social context which may impinge very powerfully on the family's way of life. It is easy to see how such impingement may operate in the extreme cases such as where a family lives in a country which is in civil war, in the former Yugoslavia for instance, where the family may be literally under attack from former neighbours and forced to flee their home. It is less comfortable to recognise that some versions of such patterns occur in apparently peaceful and so-called civilised Western European countries such as the UK, although the evidence is very clear on this point. Many children grow up with their families living under the constant threat of racist abuse or assault, or of anti-semitic or other religious persecution. For these children, even if they do not directly experience such attacks themselves until later in their childhood, they are likely to internalise the model of a family living under siege, or of their skin colour, food, or dress habits being regarded as hateful or contaminated. The consequences for the inner world of such children are potentially very serious – this is why we still hear of black children scrubbing their skin to try to make it white and Asian children whose first words, learned as they look from their pushchair in the street, are 'go back to your own country'.

While the research evidence in this area is substantial (Milner 1983), it is a complicated area and one which deserves careful attention. For example, it should not be assumed that *all* black children will experience this confusion and ambivalence. It is clear that black children growing up in a predominantly *black* society, or with black parents who encourage strong and positive images of black identity are in a much more positive position. Milner also demonstrates that the (albeit slow) improvements for black people at a societal level are clearly reflected in the research findings on black children's identity: the trend appears to be towards black British children being clearer and more positive about their racial identity. On the other hand, we should be quite clear that black children in Britain still encounter racism at both a personal and an institutional level and that black children in the care system may find themselves in double jeopardy: not only separated from their family and whatever confirmation of identity and self-esteem they may have felt from them, but then further deprived of support with their black identity through finding themselves in an all-white or 'colour-blind' environment (Barn 1993). The lasting impact of a racist environment on the development of a young child's inner world and the task which this creates for those attempting to help such children, have been described by Andreou (1992) and Thomas (1992) among others.

Another vital element in the child's experience of the world through his family will be in terms of the physical and material conditions of his upbringing. Those experienced in helping troubled children and families through public agencies will confirm that a very large proportion of these families turn out to live in conditions of real and lasting poverty, with all that this means in terms of its effects, for instance, on housing conditions, levels of nutrition and educational deprivation. It is not that it is only poor children who have problems, of course, but that those families which do have to

cope with the vicious circles of both material and emotional deprivation can be very hard places for children to grow up.

Looking at the variety of family patterns and their connections
with broader patterns in society has led us to consider the relationship which there may be between broad societal influences and
individual development and the representation of this relationship
which evolves within the child's inner world. This is an area in
which psychoanalytic theory (or at least that branch of applied
theory which focuses on therapeutic work with young people) is still
under-developed and indeed this gap remains one of the biggest
challenges for those aiming to develop practice in this field. The
problem is that in some respects the theoretical model does not
quite match the reality of experience. One of our aims in this book
is to expand and explore the theoretical material in such a way that
it addresses the real concerns of practitioners more directly.

Understanding the world of feelings

The reason for thinking in terms of the inner world of the child is
that it gives us one framework for understanding the complicated
world of feelings in which those trying to help children and their
families must operate. There are many other possible frameworks,
of course and in fact the simple idea of the 'inner world' can allow
for many different theoretical perspectives on exactly how
emotional experience can be explained and therefore on how troubled children can be helped. For our purposes in this book,
however, we have mainly drawn upon the ideas of Winnicott and
certain other psychoanalytic writers in the British tradition, since
these are ideas which we have found useful in our practice both in
therapeutic work with children and in the educational setting. We
are aware that others may find different ideas more helpful and we
are certainly aware that there are gaps and limitations within this
approach itself, but we are realists and are not looking for any
complete answer: there is none.

For those trying to help troubled young people there are some
important implications of using this framework: first, it is clearly
the inner world that we need to reach if we are to communicate with
unhappy children about whatever is troubling them. In some cases
this may be relatively straightforward: the child knows something is
wrong, knows what it is and knows roughly what her feelings are
about it and sooner or later can communicate about these feelings

in a productive way. For many children and young people, wherever they are growing up, one would hope that most of their experience comes within this category: it is important that professional helpers should be aware of this aspect of normal experience, although for the most part they are unlikely to be called upon to offer sustained help in such circumstances.

Second, there will be some children who do have real problems in their inner world for a variety of reasons, including the experience of serious trauma in early childhood. These are the children whom we are more likely to be called in to help. They may be out of touch with the nature or strength of their own feelings, they may have an impoverished or confused inner world and therefore they may also be unable to express themselves through play or talking. Thus, they may be beyond the reach of help. In these cases, the question of the origin of the inner world becomes of great importance if we are going to understand what the child is struggling with and what has really gone wrong. A small proportion of these children will have experienced such great trauma from so early on in their infancy that they have not developed an inner world and are left in a state of more or less permanent confusion, distraction and despair. This last group are the 'unintegrated' children to whom we refer later in the book.

Third, we also need to understand our own inner world as child, adolescent and adult if we are going to appreciate that of the child with whom we are working. It is especially important that we should be able to empathise with some version of the child's inner world, but without becoming lost in their world in an over-identified way. Children who are so deeply troubled have often had to develop an extreme watchfulness because they are so anxious that further trauma might be inflicted upon them. Often, therefore, they are very adept at judging whether or not the person trying to help them really understands them at all or is 'just a professional'. This is one of the paradoxes in therapeutic work: you need to be absolutely genuine and authentic in your work and yet you also need to draw upon certain professional skills and concepts which might be seen as 'artificial'. The key to this paradox lies in the 'professional use of self': using one's own personal resources (including one's own emotions as well as certain skills and techniques) to achieve real communication. This is what we have called later in this book 'being real with people'. If you are going to 'use' your self, then you need to understand your self and it is for this reason that so much emphasis will be placed on the use of experiential learning (by which we mean in this context 'learning about yourself from your interactions with others') and on the overlap between the personal, the professional and the academic areas.

Fourth, if we accept Winnicott's argument that it is the inner world of the child that eventually develops into the faculties of imagination and creativity in the adult, then this creativity is also an important element in the 'use of self' which any counselling involves. It can be argued that many adults, social worker and client alike, have become out of touch with their inner creative resources and that they might benefit from rediscovering them. These are the resources which help us cope with stress, doubt and anxiety and which may help us find meaning and fulfilment in our own lives as well as in our efforts to help other people in such struggles. Frances Wickes, a Jungian analyst, develops this theme in her book *The Inner World of Choice* (1977) and another very useful book in this context is *On Not Being Able to Paint* (1950) by Marion Milner.

SUMMARY

In this chapter I have concentrated on the idea of the inner world of the child, looking at its origins and its development and at what happens if this inner world does not have the chance to develop into a secure sense of self. I have also outlined some of the external influences on the inner world and how these contribute to, but may also impinge negatively upon, its development. It is inevitable in a book such as this, focused on the helping process, that we should need to concentrate on the things which may go wrong and it may be as well to conclude with a reminder that for the great majority of children and families things do not go wrong: there is reality as well as reassurance in Winnicott's belief that parents do not have to be perfect and that most children receive 'good enough' parenting.

Chapter 2

Helping and the personal response
Intuition is not enough[1]

Linnet McMahon and Adrian Ward

If damage to a child's inner world can have such serious consequences, how can these children and their families be helped? It is
clearly going to be complex and delicate work, and we are used to
thinking of such work as happening in clinical settings, either
through individual or group psychotherapy, or perhaps through
play or family therapy. However, some of these children never get
access to such services at all, while others are so damaged that even
twice-weekly clinical sessions will never be enough. Many of them
are the children who find themselves in children's homes, family
centres and 'withdrawal' educational units, where staff work with
(and in some cases live alongside) them for long periods of time,
trying to engage with them and respond helpfully to their troubled
behaviour. Our focus here is going to be on the ways in which such
children can be helped in these non-clinical settings and our
starting-point lies in the everyday interactions which can be so challenging and problematic – since this is where the challenge arises to
produce helpful responses to challenging situations most powerfully, and in considering what resources these staff can draw upon
in their efforts to help.

Our argument is that for most people the resources they draw upon
in such circumstances will not be formal strategies or techniques, but
a more personal and intuitive response based on a mixture of
common sense and the pooled 'practice wisdom' which develops in
teams in such settings. We want to explore this intuitive element in
helping and to consider first how it may be helpful and constructive,
but also what its limitations are and how it needs to be informed by a

---

1 Practice examples supplied by: Deborah Best, Steve Bromage, Dave
  Ferneyhough, Rebecca Nwaozuzu and Matt Vince.

fuller understanding of the complexities of any situation. We shall draw on a number of examples from practice, provided by recent MA students all of whom are experienced practitioners in this field.

THE INTUITIVE WORKER

We start with two examples of workers using intuitive responses to situations arising in everyday life, beginning with a residential worker's account of working with a group of adolescents:

> In many of her conversations with staff, Jade (fifteen years old) claimed that another girl, Pat (a year younger), was receiving preferential treatment. On one occasion I noticed Jade breaking an egg on the floor. When I asked her to clean it up she replied that she had not broken it. On being asked again to clean up the mess she retorted 'It wasn't me, it was her!'. Instead of correcting her I asked, 'Do you always get blamed for the things that she does?' She replied 'Yeah, no one ever believes me. She gets away with everything'. From the ensuing conversation I realised that Jade was actually referring to her younger sister, with whom she had a poor relationship. Again intuitively, I asked Jade who out of the resident group of young people most reminded her of her sister and it was Pat. Following this incident Jade referred to Pat less and in fact began to develop a bond with her.

The worker here responds not to the explicit message of the words heard or the actions seen but to the implicit or latent content of the communication. In another example, from a children's home, the worker again responds not to the child's explicit statement but to the implicit message within what was said:

> A child who was sad that her key worker was leaving the unit trashed her room carefully and then lay on her bed, demanding 'Don't put the duvet over me'. Her key-worker intuitively understood that this meant 'Do' and gently covered her up, recognising her unhappiness and her need to be taken care of even though she was not able to ask for it.

In both cases these workers appear to be interpreting the meaning of current situations in the light of their prior knowledge of the young people's personal history and emotional needs. They are also, however, drawing upon their intuition in two significant ways: first to recognise the particular half-hidden meaning within what the child was doing or saying and second to decide upon an appropriate response. The aim of these responses is to enable the child either to acknowledge the source of their distress and thus begin to resolve it – as in the first example – or to at least accept some implicit (even if not verbalised) recognition of their needs – as in the second example. In both cases, too, the response which is offered is quite different from what a more conventional or regulation-led approach might suggest, but turns out to be probably much more beneficial to the child's long-term interests. This might be seen as the difference between therapeutic child care and 'ordinary common sense' child care. We will discuss the nature and aims of such responses more in Chapter 5 under the section of 'Opportunity-led work', but at this stage our aim is to draw attention to the largely intuitive basis upon which the worker often has to respond to such situations.

THE ORIGINS OF INTUITION

Since intuition clearly plays an important element in the workers' responses to the above situations, what is it and where does it come from? It seems to consist of a mixture of several elements: first the ability to pick up 'minimal cues' – subtle changes in tone of voice, patterns of speech, body language, etc., through which a young person may unconsciously communicate aspects of their anxiety. Second, the ability to process and interpret these communications, based on a personal identification (conscious or unconscious) with the young person's feelings or predicament. Third, as we saw above, intuition also contributes to the worker's decision on how best to respond to the young person. It can be seen in fact as a means by which the young person's and the worker's inner worlds come into contact with each other.

In line with the approach taken in Chapter 1, we would argue that workers' intuitive skills probably arise mostly from their own early emotional experiences. Even though in some cases these experiences may have been unsatisfactory in some respects, they will probably have been 'good enough' to provide the individual with the capacity in adulthood for the equivalent of primary maternal pre-occupation, 'the mother's intuitive understanding which makes her able to care for her infant without learning' (Winnicott 1950: 16).

The pre-occupied mother is seen by Winnicott as being so much in touch with her infant's needs that she can sometimes feel what is needed without thinking. This deep form of empathy has unconscious as well as conscious elements, enabling the mother to pick up subliminal cues, which she is not even consciously aware of noticing. Again as we saw in Chapter 1, the change since Winnicott's day is the recognition that it is not only mothers who can become pre-occupied with their babies; fathers and other carers may also do so. Similarly men as well as women may work intuitively with children: in the above example of work with Jade the worker was a man. In the context of professional child care, of course, such pre-occupation cannot be *demanded* of the worker and indeed it can only happen spontaneously – although we would argue that the capacity for intuitive communication *can* be developed and enhanced.

Since the roots of intuition probably lie in these early childhood experiences, it is also likely that some of the memories and feelings associated with such experiences will themselves reappear in the context of current work with young people. Indeed, many workers are aware of consciously drawing on their early memories to empathise with children experiencing similar situations. One residential child care worker described these feelings like this:

> When I'm supervising a contact visit I have a good insight into how the child may be feeling; before the visit anxious, scared, excited, worried or angry and afterwards – resentful, angry, disappointed, hurt or sad. I find it very draining having to support such a visit. Thoughts go through my mind about how difficult I found contact visits with my own mother when my parents separated. I suppose I unconsciously communicate to the children in my care my recognition of their difficult task and my encouragement and assurance that they will be able to manage it. Similarly at Christmas many children prefer and ultimately manage better on a quiet day. They find holidays painful and I can empathise with how isolated, forgotten, unloved and uncared for they may feel and how they grieve, wishing for things to change or to go back to how they might have been.

The important task for the worker in such situations, of course, will be to remain clear about whose feelings are whose. This will also require her to know when she is drawing consciously upon such memories and to recognise when she may be influenced by the more unconscious aspects of them.

EMPATHY OR MERGER

We therefore need to be able to understand our own inner world as child, adolescent and adult if we are going to be able to appreciate that of the child with whom we are working. Many intuitive workers with particular gifts in reaching disturbed children and young people have their own areas of emotional difficulty and even disturbance (Dockar-Drysdale 1990). This need not present an obstacle provided that the worker is willing to think about and work at the connection. In this context we have found that the selection of students for advanced training needs to be based both on their ability to identify and describe their practice and on their capacity to reflect on their childhood experiences and have some insight into the link between these and their current work.

At an intuitive level, a child care worker may become deeply involved in a relationship with a child and this may well be helpful to the child. The risk, however, is that what is intended to be empathy or a version of pre-occupation may unconsciously become unhelpful 'collusive merger', in which the inner worlds of child and worker become confused with one another. A teacher of children with special needs recalls a painful experience of such a confusion:

> At a time when I was rather new in my post I was not working with any other staff member. I was aware of seeing myself as 'radical' and able to understand expressions of rebellion. One day a graffiti poem was found inscribed on the rubbish bins outside. It was an interesting piece, albeit on the subject of 'taking spliff wiv me mate'. The author (who was in my group) confessed to me, on condition that I would not tell the other staff. I allowed her to copy the poem into her book and withheld the information from other staff. It meant that I became part of the delinquent activity and that I was then unable to use the incident to work constructively both because of her perceptions and my own sense of guilty collusion.

This worker describes how such a situation can be guarded against by the presence of a third person to act as catalyst, giving insight and support to the therapeutic relationship and helping to ensure that the deeply involved worker works in a conscious way, for therapeutic purposes, rather than in delinquent collusion. Supervision or consultancy, or peer support, can help an individual worker to retain the capacity for reverie, that is to think about what is happening in their own mind and how this connects with what is happening in the mind of the child. Working at the connections between the worker's own childhood experiences and the present situation in which resonances abound is the key to insight, but the process of unlocking these connections is often painful; some workers display immense courage but not all can bear to open the door too fast or too far.

The capacity for intuition, however, is not enough on its own. If people are going to develop and use their capacity for intuition they will need to be working within a 'facilitating environment' (Winnicott's phrase again) of organisational support. A different emotional climate in the school and a more formal structure of role support might perhaps have changed the following course of events which the previous worker describes.

On a cold and wet November morning Chris arrived in class almost an hour late, wearing a t-shirt, without jumper or jacket. He was rather breathless and his face was tense. At the time I was occupied with another child. I simply commented that he was late and asked if he was cold. 'Yes, my parents were having a row so I just came out'. That and his appearance, was enough to suggest something strangely wrong, but only for a moment. I was able to block an appropriate response by telling myself consciously that 'these people' are always having rows. Reflection later brought the realisation that I did not want to remember my own anxiety and fear about my own father's anger. At that moment my own lack of self-awareness rendered that intuition powerless.

There was no subsequent opportunity to raise the incident, except a casual comment to one colleague. A few days later the mother was strangled by the father and died. Even then there was no opportunity to explore and express my response, formally or informally. I wrote to Chris, privately, remembering that he had felt blamed for 'family problems'. An educational psychologist was asked to counsel Chris. Some weeks later I became ill and was away for several months. Intuition, disabled by anxiety and disallowed by the emotional climate and institutional structure, turned against the possibility of useful work.

THE INNER WORLD OF THE WORKER AND THE NEED FOR A THEORETICAL BASE

Dockar-Drysdale states that, 'Intuition informed is an essential tool: intuition uninformed can be a dangerous weapon' (1968a: 31). We have seen some of the limits to intuition and we now need to explore ways of informing it and building on it. The main way of doing so is by understanding more of the unconscious elements in communication and by reflecting on the meaning of these elements, drawing upon theory to help us in this.

Transference and counter-transference

Our understanding of a child's inner world derives from the child's communication with us, some of which is unconscious and consists of the child's 'projection' of feelings onto the worker. This projection of feelings (the transference) is based on the child's previous experience of significant figures in their lives, usually parents. The worker becomes aware of this process through reflecting on her own feelings about the child (the counter-transference). For example, with one child you may feel quite protective, with another angry that you (or they) are never good enough, while another may leave you feeling quite helpless or hopeless. These often turn out to be a reflection of the child's own feelings, based on their own learning from experience. Of course, we may also be bringing feelings derived from our own personal experience – another aspect of counter-transference. We need to distinguish these personal feelings (the personal counter-transference) from those feelings which stem directly from the child's transference (diagnostic counter-transference). Sometimes our own feelings resonate powerfully with the transference from the child, which may lead us to be extra sympathetic, or the opposite. For example, if we had to learn in childhood to stand on our own two feet very early, we might find a very clingy child extremely annoying to work with (probably because it risks bringing back long suppressed desires to be looked after). If a particular child tends always to make us feel a certain way, anxious, for example, when we would not normally feel this way in similar situations, then we can be fairly sure that this is related to the child's own feeling. Learning to tune in to the transference and to be aware of one's own counter-transference takes time and practice and it needs to be learned either under supervision or within a training context, so that there will be an opportunity to reflect on possible meanings and connections without jumping to conclusions or – still worse – imposing these on the child.

Reflection on feelings of transference and counter-transference provides a helpful way of bringing together the inner worlds of child and worker. The worker provides the 'inner mental space' in which the child's feelings can be borne, thought about and in due course passed back to that child in a more manageable form.

Difference and distance

Some of the factors which may inform our intuition may be less welcome or less constructive than others. For example, prejudicial stereotypes about people from groups perceived as different from our own may be lodged so firmly in our unconscious that we draw on them unthinkingly. Thus white workers' intuitive responses to black young people may carry a risk of incorporating racist assumptions about the capabilities or tendencies of these young people – assumptions which are endemic in society and may have been 'soaked up' in an unthinking way. Equally, male workers may make prejudicial assumptions about female young people and vice versa (e.g. Harris and Lipman 1984), female workers about male youngsters, and so on, in respect of other forms of difference such as sexual orientation, disability, religion and social class. Some of these assumptions may be held consciously, which presents one sort of challenge in overcoming them, but some will be held unconsciously (or somewhere between the two), which will make them much harder to acknowledge and overcome. It might be argued that the more differences there are between self and others, the more effort it will take to communicate effectively – and that this may happen whether or not we are consciously aware of the differences involved. Indeed, it may be particularly damaging if the worker imagines there is no difference when the young person perceives a powerful difference. Thus the risk of the well-meaning white worker who thinks it will be helpful consciously to adopt a 'colour-blind' approach to issues of ethnic difference, believing that 'we are all basically the same under the skin', whereas the whole life experience of a black youngster may have been blighted by poverty and disadvantage stemming from racist attitudes in society (see Chapter 4).

Intuition therefore emerges as rather more complicated than it may at first have seemed, since in drawing upon it we need to be aware of all the possible sources of bias and distortion, with an aim not necessarily of ruling them all out, but at least of being aware of how they may affect the communication. This is why people learning about this work need opportunities to reflect upon their own conscious and unconscious perceptions of 'difference', which will be based in part on their own developmental experience, so that they can reflect on ways of acknowledging and overcoming whatever stereotyped assumptions they may hold (see Chapter 10).

Using theory to inform intuition

Alongside this personal knowledge about oneself and one's own attitudes, a worker whose knowledge is also soundly based in theory and research is in a good position to use these to inform her intuition. The following example, from a residential therapeutic care setting for young children, reflects a common situation that requires an understanding response informed by knowledge both of what happens in the internal emotional world of a child and also of the effects of separation and loss. The worker contrasts his response with the likely response from an untrained worker:

> Joe has been here for over three years. I am Joe's keyworker and he has formed a very strong attachment to me and I to him. He can be dependent on me and I can make some adaptations to his needs. Joe would like to return home to his mother but is prevented from doing so by Social Services and by implication ourselves. His mother visits him once a month for a few hours on a Sunday afternoon. These visits always raise a range of feelings and emotions for him which often find expression in forms of aggression after his mother has left. Once after a visit Joe got very angry with another child, which soon developed into a fight. This other child is able to spend regular weekends at home with his mother. As I intervened in the fight Joe became extremely angry with me, which in turn made me feel angry.
>
> I then realised that Joe was projecting onto this other child and then onto me all the anger and frustration that he was feeling following his mother's visit. Because I was conscious of

my intuitive feelings and because of the attachment between us and my pre-occupation with him I was able not only to understand how Joe was probably feeling but also to be aware of the fact that I was also feeling *his* feelings. Dockar-Drysdale calls this connection between worker and child 'something more primitive than empathy'. I first made sure that I did not express my anger with Joe. I then found an appropriate time to acknowledge with him how angry he must be feeling, validating and giving him the opportunity to communicate his feelings verbally or otherwise, fulfilling the function that Bion talks about of becoming a container for Joe's feelings, holding onto them until he was able to reintroject them in a more tolerable form.

This worker reflected, commenting,

Suppose the adult involved had been an inexperienced member of the team who did not know Joe and his history and who certainly did not have an emotional attachment to him. This adult would feel angry with Joe but first might not understand the true origins of his anger and second would not have the information to put the anger in context. Their likely reaction might be 'This child is deliberately winding me up' or more commonly 'It's because he can't get his own way', leading to an emotionally if not physically punitive response. When I find myself in such a situation when I do *not* have an attachment to a particular child I am aware that this is going to influence not only my feelings about the child but also how the child is able to affect me. I realise I may not have a good enough understanding of the child's inner world and so will consciously think about the child's needs based on quite objective information in order to reach a response. There are of course times when I am tired, or ill, or under stress, when my response may be desperately flawed, wholly based on my own needs.

Many situations are far from clear cut and the intuitive response may not always be either helpful or even available. The following illustration from a senior worker in a therapeutic community for young people throws light on the difficulties such situations can present. Statements made by the unintegrated or disturbed young person may seem nonsensical or inappropriate. However, they often

provide the only vehicle they may possess to communicate an inner
need to the worker.

Nick, a young man aged seventeen, initiated a furious row with
me. He demanded a large sum of money for an evening activity,
but refused to explain (and later fabricated) what the activity
was. I did not feel unreasonable in refusing the money, but he
then switched to making another impossible demand. All the
time his demeanour and behaviour were becoming more aggressive and uncontrolled. When two of his friends came in he
escalated his attack on me for not giving him money to go out. I
was by this stage thoroughly confused by his illogical and outrageous demands and felt relieved when his friends said they would
fund him and encouraged him to leave with them.

It was only on his frightened and drunken return that I
realised that what his bizarre and confrontational demands were
trying to communicate was *not* 'Give me lots of money so I can
go out', but rather 'You have to keep me in, forbid me to go out,
because I don't feel safe and cannot say no'. He had tried to be
so outrageous that I would act punitively, thereby containing him
and his anxiety. Intuition had failed me and I had not sought the
space to employ any other technique. Nick had acted out his
need to communicate with me. Possibly his drunken return was
as much a form of communication as a consequence of his delinquent social relationships.

Soon after, an almost identical situation arose. Nick came to
see me seeking money for a night out. Intuition pricked, I asked
him to wait, looked around and discovered a group of his friends
waiting outside. Believing my good relationship with him would
suffice, I proceeded to address his unreasonable demand for
money with a logical adult interpretation of the situation – his
friends were pressuring him to go out, he knew he would get into
trouble if he did so and he wanted me to stop him. Nick adopted
an adult manner, told me not to worry, that was not the case and
he would not get into trouble. Later that night he returned late
and very drunk.

Nick hadn't needed or been able to accept my adult interpretation of his situation and this had forced him into a level of
communication from which his emotional development totally
excluded him. It was as if I had interrupted him to discuss
another matter that he had no interest in. 'Stereotyped intellectu-

alised responses from grown-ups leave these children in a desert'
(Dockar-Drysdale 1968a: 29). Rather the worker naturally and
necessarily must acknowledge the interpretation of the young
person's latent communication but must respond in terms of the
actual communication, without losing any of its emotional life.
Young people are often aware of the pain of their past but their
need is now. Thus with Nick his inability to say 'no' belonged to
his past; his present need was to be contained, protected and
offered something to replace the delinquent attraction of his
friends.

The therapeutic importance of such communications can be undervalued and the chance to build on them lost unless both individual
worker and the staff team as a whole are able to locate such interventions within a theoretical framework which will help them
understand what is happening and offer some guidance about what
to do next. We need to listen to our intuition, reflect on it before we
use it and use it in context by attaching it into our repertoire of
more conscious responses.

CONCLUSION

We have started our exploration of helping troubled children by
looking at the individual response which will always remain at the
heart of any helping effort, and especially at the element of intuition within this reponse. We have considered the risks of relying
solely on an intuitive response, but we have also seen some examples
of genuinely helpful and constructive helping based mainly on such
responses. One worker wrote, 'Intuition is individual and precarious
and it is not enough for me. I need to be self-aware, informed and
closely supported within a suitable environment if I am to make
good use of the intuition I have.' Bearing in mind that our focus is
primarily upon therapeutic work in the group care context, perhaps
it is the purely individual response which will never be enough on its
own. What is needed is a reliable framework, both theoretical and
practical, within which to locate this individual and/or intuitive
focus and a 'facilitating environment' in the form of a team and an
organisation attuned to supporting and enabling such work. In the
next chapters we will explore a possible framework and its application in a version of the supportive environment.

Chapter 3

Helping together
Using the group care context to reach the inner world

Adrian Ward

If we want to move beyond a merely intuitive response to reliable frameworks for helping troubled children and their families, what should these frameworks be? They will need to help us explain the connections between individuals' helping efforts and the overall work of the whole unit and to plan for making best use of these connections. In the first part of this chapter we shall be exploring these connections, especially in the context of group care settings and considering the powerful interplay of feelings (both in the workers and in the children) involved in therapeutic work in such settings. In the second part, we will focus on the use of one possible framework for making sense of this complexity: the concept of the 'holding environment'.

THERAPEUTIC CHILD CARE: FEELINGS IN THEIR CONTEXT

We use the term 'therapeutic child care' in this book to denote a range of therapeutic endeavours with children and young people, especially, but not exclusively, in the context of group care settings, such as family centres, residential homes and schools and therapeutic communities. We emphasise the group care context partly because it is in these settings that one can most clearly see the relationship between therapeutic work and its context, but partly because it is in these settings that many of the most damaged children and young people can be found. We therefore have another aim in this section: to clarify the (often under-exploited) potential of these settings for therapeutic work and thereby also to redress something of an imbalance in the literature.

Much of the literature on therapeutic work with children focuses either on clinical settings (drawing on the traditions of psychotherapeutic work with children, most notably at the Tavistock Clinic, but also elsewhere, e.g. Copley and Forryan 1987), or on field social work settings (drawing on the more recent tradition of what is often called 'direct work' with children, e.g. Aldgate and Simmonds 1988). While there is a wealth of useful and insightful material in this literature, there are some limitations in the ways in which the material can be used by those working in group care settings because the practice described is so firmly located in notions such as the 'therapeutic hour' and the sanctity of a specially equipped playroom. By contrast, workers in family centres and residential homes, while they may in some units have access to such facilities and may certainly run therapeutic groups and offer planned individual sessional work, are also likely to have to 'be therapeutic' in everyday life alongside the children at mealtimes, in the informal 'in-between times' and sometimes in random or informal groupings around the unit and at unplanned moments. It is the implications of this context for therapeutic practice that I wish to explore here, both in terms of practice and in terms of training. I am thinking in particular of therapeutic work undertaken by those employed within the group care setting itself, rather than that undertaken by visiting or sessional external therapists, although some of my comments may be of interest to these workers.

I have previously (Ward 1991: 46–7) identified the defining characteristics of the group care context in the following terms:

1 an emphasis on the co-ordinated use of time through rotas, routines, shiftwork, etc.
2 a particular focus upon 'opportunity-led' work arising from the extensive everyday involvement between staff and clients
3 the close interdependence required of the team
4 the complex network of relationships between the team and the group of clients
5 the public or semi-public nature of much of the work
6 and the planned use of space and the physical environment

These characteristics, or some version or combination of them, will be found in all group care units, whether or not the unit has an overtly 'therapeutic' task and I have explored the general implications of these characteristics for group care workers in more detail elsewhere (Ward 1993a). The central implication is that, to be effective, group care workers need to keep in mind the various elements of the context as outlined above while keeping a clear focus on the task in hand with any given individual or group, and to be able to move between different areas of pre-occupation without undue confusion or anxiety.

For those units which do have a therapeutic task, these characteristics impose a special context on the methods which may be used towards achieving that task. In some respects this may be experienced as a context which inhibits the therapeutic endeavour because, for example, it may appear harder to maintain what are traditionally seen as the appropriate boundaries around the therapeutic relationship. Thus, the worker may feel, 'How can I possibly remain clearly focused on helping this particular child when so much else is going on around me?'. On the other hand, if the context can be understood and harnessed towards the endeavour, it can provide a greatly enriched environment for therapeutic work. Now the worker may be able to say, 'What I am attempting with this child has parallels and overlaps with other things which are happening here – if these efforts can all be brought together we may stand a better chance of overall success'. Part of the task of management in such units will be precisely this business of promoting an understanding of the complexities and potentials of the system as a whole and enabling the team to maximise the potential. This management task has become more urgent with the decline of local authority children's homes and the burgeoning of foster care and would-be therapeutic residential units in the private and voluntary sector and simultaneously with the exponential growth of family centres, including those identified within the Children Act 1989 as 'therapeutic family centres'.

When people attempt therapeutic work in such units – even if they intend to confine the therapeutic work to (for example) planned individual sessions in 'special' playrooms, they are entering an intricate pattern of powerful relationships. At the heart of any therapeutic work will always be the relationship between a worker and a child: this is a relationship which, of course, is likely to evoke strong feelings in both parties, as seen in Chapter 2. In the child there will be a range of transference feelings connected with the child's experience of other significant relationships, especially his relationship with his parents or carers, where considerable stress, confusion, ambivalence or anxiety may be located. For the worker, in addition to being on the receiving end of this range of feelings from the child, there will be the range of counter-transference feelings both 'personal' (in the sense of associations which she as a worker may bring to any such piece of work from her own childhood or other experience) and 'diagnostic' (in the sense of feelings generated from this particular relationship with this particular child and which may indirectly tell her important things about the child's own inner world). These relationships occur in all therapeutic work and have been clearly documented in respect of clinical work: for the most part, clinical workers can focus exclusively on the experience of this individual therapeutic relationship without having to attend simultaneously to the broader context in which the work is set.

On the other hand, the therapeutic child care worker in a group care context will additionally need to attend to a much wider range of feelings, including those generated in the other children in the unit who may or may not be present during some of the significant interactions which she has with this child, as well as those feelings in her colleagues who again may or may not be present at key moments. Meanwhile she will also sometimes be party to other children's interactions with their 'key' or 'special' people and to children's comments to each other about their experiences and about the staff who are attempting to help them, as well as witnessing interactions between the child she herself is involved with and some of her colleagues, managers or supervisors. In addition, the worker may have to put this child to bed later that same day, or, in a family centre, escort that child back home with his mother and may subsequently have to complete a late shift or sleep-in duty! Furthermore, in settings such as family centres, the child's actual parent/s may be present in the next room, or witness to or part of some of the communication between child and worker, child and other children and so on. Some of these parent–child–worker interactions may be apparently trivial, some of them deeply significant; some of them may be conducted in verbal and rational ways, others in less direct and conscious ways and others again may be enacted in physical and other ways, even including threatened or actual violence at times. Such family dimensions will be familiar to sessional family therapists, just as some of the group dimension described above arises in the context of sessional group work: my argument, however, is that it is only in the group care context that all of these factors may arise together and interact with each other.

For example, in a family centre Julie, a senior worker, observed that Peter, a four-year-old attending with his mother and baby sister, frequently became agitated shortly before the end of the day.

For no apparent reason, he would often begin racing around the building towards the end of the afternoon, avoiding contact with grown-ups as far as possible before eventually colliding with a smaller child or tripping over a toy on the floor and collapsing in a heap, crying. This behaviour was in marked contrast to his apparently subdued and compliant behaviour at other times and Julie also noticed that Peter's mother, Ramona, would not intervene during his disruptive behaviour but would eventually shout angrily at him when he had fallen to the floor crying. Other children and parents, as well as staff, were affected by this behaviour but nobody intervened. There is often some confusion in family centres as to who is responsible for the children's behaviour, but normally Ramona seemed to have clear control over Peter and staff would not need to intervene unduly. After the third similar occasion, Julie asked Ramona why she thought this was happening but obtained little response. She consulted the rest of the team at a team meeting, especially with Carole, who was holding weekly sand and water play sessions with Peter. These sessions were intended to help Peter to express his feelings more, particularly in relation to his confusion about his father, who had suddenly left the family twelve months before, shortly before the birth of Peter's baby sister. Carole herself had noticed that in recent weeks Peter had tended to become agitated towards the end of his sessions with her, but she was not clear of any specific reason for this development.

Eventually another member of the team made a connection with a recent occasion when another child had referred to one of the drivers who escorted families home at the end of the day as 'Peter's daddy'. It emerged that this was a new driver and that on his first day, Peter had mistaken him from a distance for his own father and had naturally become very distressed when he realised his mistake. This incident had gone almost unnoticed at the time except by this other child and by Ramona, but it had reawakened some of Peter's distress about his father and caused great anxiety to his mother, who preferred to think that Peter had actually forgotten about his father.

Out of these realisations it was then possible for the play-worker, Carole, to pick up this theme with Peter in his subsequent play sessions and for the senior, Julie, to spend some time talking with Ramona about her response to Peter's feelings about his absent father and indeed about Ramona's own feelings about her absent husband. A few days later, at the weekly meeting of all the families and centre staff, a comment was made by another parent about Peter's difficult behaviour and Julie found an appropriate and supportive way to help Ramona explain to the rest of the group something of what had been happening for Peter recently. This helped to re-establish understanding between Peter, Ramona and the rest of the children and parents.

In this way, a potentially confusing set of apparently disconnected incidents and feelings were pieced together by the team and the resulting pattern was used as the basis for future work with different members of the family and eventually with other families attending the centre.

To an inexperienced group care worker, such situations might be something of a nightmare, apparently at risk of spiralling out of all control into an unproductive chaos: how can we possibly create something positive and therapeutic out of this mêlée? To an experienced worker, on the other hand, the potential within such scenarios for productive therapeutic work may be quite evident and the ways of achieving this potential relatively clear, if still challenging. The key to unravelling the situation described above was teamwork: observation and deduction on the part of different team members and the use of the team meeting to assemble the pieces of the jigsaw so that team members could then use the emerging pattern in their future work. I will return later in this chapter to the framework within which such teamwork may be understood and planned. For the moment, having outlined some of the implications of context, I would like to stay with the feelings of the worker engaged in the therapeutic task and the implications of these feelings for the way in which the context needs to be managed.

We should remind ourselves briefly of the nature of the experience that the children may bring to such settings: these are children who may have been abused physically, emotionally and/or sexually; they may have been let down or deceived time and time again, systematically ignored or brutalised and so on. Bearing in mind the damage that such experiences may have done to a child's inner world and thus to its ability to relate with people, there will be extreme stresses on the worker/s who attempt to become closely involved with such deeply disturbed children and their family dynamics.

The worker can expect to be continually mistrusted and mistreated by the child and experience feelings of confusion, disillusionment and despair. In other words, she will be made to feel a whole range of emotions equivalent to those the child may have felt, as the child attempts to understand his experiences by re-enacting them and learning about their effect by (consciously or unconsciously) inflicting them on anyone who tries to help. Indeed, just by indicating that they are trying to help, the worker may arouse strong reactions from the child, partly because she is trying again where others may have failed in the past, possibly exposing the child to the risk of further disappointment and pain, and partly because the child may unconsciously envy the worker's apparent 'togetherness' which endows them with the capacity to help. All of those engaged in therapeutic work with children will be exposed to complicated emotions such as these: those in group care settings will additionally encounter the parallel and criss-crossing tracks of other children and workers in their multiple relationships.

The impact of these stresses upon the worker is of particular importance, because it is largely through the worker's experience and handling of these emotions that she will discover ways of achieving contact with the child. If the worker is to achieve this contact, she needs to be relatively undefended in her relationship with the child, so that she is not constantly guarding herself against the child's strong feelings impinging upon her and so that the child can realise that it is indeed possible for someone to bear the pain and confusion. Such children often have an advanced ability to read others' emotions (they have had to develop this ability in order to survive) and they will certainly know to what extent the worker really is in touch with their feelings.

The worker therefore needs the support of a working climate which is similarly undefended. This means an organisation in which, first, people are clear about their task, individually and collectively, and second, people are in open and effective communication with each other about the means of achieving the task. This is so that, as in the example above, they are able to speculate jointly about the possible causes of puzzling behaviour or confusing emotions and work painstakingly towards achieving some understanding.

We must also consider what the worker *herself* brings to the situation. If it is such difficult and potentially stressful work, then why does she do it, beyond the immediate factors of apparent altruism and a wish to exploit her natural abilities? The answer is presumably that we are all motivated to do such work by a complex range of factors in our own lives, including perhaps some need of our own to rework and understand childhood experiences which may have some equivalence to the experiences of the children we are now trying to help. Thus, we may know from first-hand experience *something* of what it is like to be abandoned, ignored or misunderstood and we may be driven to find ways of somehow redeeming our earlier experience by proxy, through engaging with children in extreme circumstances who now need help.

This version of a motivation to help deeply troubled children is only one of many possible scenarios. Another might be explained as the drive to become the kind of helpful, understanding or powerful adult we wish we had known during our own childhood troubles. Such motivations, often lodged somewhere in our unconscious or just below the surface of awareness, may suddenly feel inhibiting or shaming when we first discover them in ourselves, but once recognised and explored, they can be used as a source of strength and inspiration. The aim is to draw upon such factors consciously rather than being driven by them unconsciously. It may be that, in the example above, Julie's original observation of Peter's troubled behaviour meant something particular to her which motivated her to pursue the issue until she understood it more fully, but equally, other colleagues may have had their own reasons for not noticing this pattern or taking it seriously. Strong feelings about the causes of childhood distress (and especially about absent fathers) are at times so pervasive and powerful in family centres that people may be unconsciously driven to believe that the work will only become manageable if they do not think about these feelings too much. This is, of course, a counter-productive defence in that it reproduces the pattern that in this case Peter's own mother had adopted.

To summarise, therapeutic child care involves offering sensitive and insightful support to troubled children and their families *in vivo*: in the midst of the turmoil of everyday life and amidst the anxiety which this turmoil generates. It requires of the worker an understanding of professional task and method plus an awareness of the overlap between personal and professional issues and of the ways in which this overlap may be worked with and interpreted.

THERAPEUTIC CHILD CARE AND THE HOLDING ENVIRONMENT

Given the nature of the therapeutic child care context described above, people need a way of thinking about this work that will help them to understand what is happening and to plan what they should be doing. My aim in this section is to outline in brief some ideas which I have found useful and to draw particular attention to one central concept: that of the 'holding environment'.

If children are to be helped in these settings, staff first need to be absolutely clear about what they are there to do. This means being clear about the primary task of the unit: the task that it 'must perform in order to survive' (Miller and Gwynne 1972), or in other words the task which it must be seen to be achieving if it is to continue receiving funding and maintaining a supply of suitable incoming work. In many child care units there is considerable difficulty in being precise and clear in defining the primary task: this is partly because people often confuse defining their task with describing their methods. Thus 'providing a warm homely atmosphere' (or even 'providing a holding environment') do *not* constitute the task of a unit, although they may be the means by which people try to achieve their task. Task must be related to outcome, which in the case of therapeutic child care, must always include planning for the child's future placement.

In a family centre defining the task will mean being clear as to precisely whom the centre is there to help: in the example given earlier, the primary task was to help families in which there was a risk that young children would be abused to become families in which there was less risk of abuse. In other family centres the task is more one of providing a local service of self-referred help and advice to all families within a neighbourhood. In some children's homes the task may be to help young people who have been rejected by their own family to achieve the transition to a safer living situation in which they will have a greater chance of a secure future. In other units the task may be more specifically formulated as, to help young people who have been sexually abused to recover sufficiently from their trauma so that they may be able to manage living either back at home or in a substitute family. I have only been able to give broad and general examples of tasks here, since each unit needs to undertake detailed work in clarifying and negotiating its task and even then, the task of the unit needs to be redefined in even more specific terms for each new young person and/or family.

Other difficulties in task definition arise from the need to reconcile the conflicting expectations placed upon units by families, employing organisations, inspectors and others, as well as from the range of anxieties which may be associated with therapeutic tasks (Menzies Lyth 1988). There is of course a great deal of work involved in arriving at a precise, accurate and agreed statement of the primary task of the unit and the work is never complete as the situation is always changing. It will be a responsibility of management to ensure that there is a consistent focus on reviewing and revising this statement of task through a process of consultation and staff meetings.

Once there is some clarity and agreement about task, people need to be clear about their *aims*: the sorts of services which they will need to provide if they are to achieve their task, e.g. a range of therapeutic interventions and pre-school experiences for the children attending a family centre, or in a children's home a combination of provision for ordinary daily living and for therapeutic support tailored to the needs of individuals and groups. They will also need to be clear about the specific *working methods* by which they will achieve these aims, which will include management methods as well as practice methods, and some that overlap between the two. Management methods include properly organised systems for the support and supervision of staff and a system for the co-ordination of communication between people at all levels in the organisation through a regular programme of staff meetings of various sorts. Practice methods include the details of work with individuals and groups of children, including the arrangements for 'key-worker' relationships where appropriate and for whatever planned sessional therapeutic work this may involve, as well as the plans for the daily 'living alongside' work. In the example given earlier, it was clear that the practice methods included the play therapy for the individual child and the counselling for the mother, as well as the attention paid by the staff to the families' experience of daily life within the setting and the potential significance of apparently minor events unfolding in the centre. An example of the overlap between management and practice methods would be the teamwork which was in evidence as people worked together at understanding the meaning of the child's behaviour.

If these methods of working are to be successfully implemented, attention will need to be paid both to the connections between primary tasks, aims and working methods, and to the skills, knowledge and values staff need to employ in carrying out the working methods. Given the complex patterns of interaction described above, it is especially important that a premium is placed upon high-quality communication throughout the organisation: open and genuine communication between staff at all levels, between the children and

their families and the staff and between all of those inside the unit
and those outside it. Such communication does not happen by accident, and by and large, it cannot happen through relying solely on
bureaucratic channels such as memos and noticeboards; nor can it
rely simply on having a schedule of staff meetings. It requires people
to give of themselves in communication, to receive awkward feedback at times and to take risks in talking about things which may feel
confusing and uncertain at first. It therefore depends on the development of a feeling of mutual trust and respect throughout the
organisation. If all of these things are to be achieved, there will also
need to be good leadership, to provide the overall management of the
unit and to help people to remain clear about both task and method
and to help them achieve good communication both with each other
and the young people while doing so.

It will be seen that what has been described here focuses mainly
on the ways in which people relate to each other, on the systems for
organising these relationships and on the central role of leadership
in devising and sustaining these systems. It therefore comes as little
surprise that a key finding from a recent national inspection of children's homes was that, in terms of the quality of staff relationships
with children, 'the effectiveness of staff in those homes where good
practice was observed was based on clear leadership, organised and
consistent ways of working and clarity of purpose' (Social Services
Inspectorate 1993: 31).

All of these aspects of the relationships between people in therapeutic child care settings can be summed up in the concept of the
'holding environment' (Winnicott 1965), a concept which, as we
have seen in Chapter 1, was originally applied to the care of babies
and young children, but which has been also usefully applied in a
range of other contexts, both in terms of everyday ordinary care
and nurturing, and in terms of therapeutic practice.

We saw earlier that the origin of the term lies in Winnicott's
emphasis on the connection between the quality of *physical* holding
and handling of the child during infancy and the child's experience
of a metaphorical holding of its *emotional* wellbeing. He argued
that what is being 'held' in the care of infants is not just the child's
physical body and its needs for warmth, food, washing, etc., but
also its incipient fears and anxieties and its needs for reassurance,
understanding and love. What parents convey to their children
through their sensitive holding is that such fears, although they may
feel real and create moments of genuine panic in the child, are

temporary and survivable and that the child itself can eventually learn to understand and dispel its own fears. Winnicott used the term 'holding environment' to refer to the totality of the parents' provision (for most children) of these physical and emotional experiences and he saw this holding environment as fundamental to the establishment in children of a secure and healthy personality. In this respect, then, the term 'holding environment' is primarily a way of referring to the quality and importance of the human context in which the young child begins its developmental journey.

Winnicott himself drew parallels between these experiences in infancy and the needs of some children later in their childhood who may not have experienced sufficient 'holding' during infancy and who may therefore have remained in an emotionally 'unheld' and chaotic state. The parallel extended further into the needs of adults in therapeutic relationships: here the emotional 'holding' is provided by the therapist through the medium of insightful and well-timed responses which convey to the patient the sense of being understood without being intruded upon. Finally the metaphor was extended to incorporate the total treatment environment, or the whole human and physical context in which care and treatment is provided for those in a range of settings, including the children's home and the family centre. As we saw earlier in this chapter, what needs 'holding' in these settings is not only the individual child and his or her own distress, but also the group of children and their interactions with each other and with their families, schools and broader networks, plus the group of staff, whose own strong feelings both as individuals and as team members, will be aroused through working with the children and their families. Since the staff need to provide emotional holding for the children, they will also need some element of holding in their own right if they are to feel sufficiently secure and resilient to provide for the children.

In each case, the aspect of 'holding' in a relationship will consist of a number of elements, including the following:

1 the provision of appropriate boundaries upon behaviour and upon the expression of emotion so that strong feelings can be expressed but do not get 'out of hand'
2 at the same time, an element of 'giving' and tolerance in relationships, so that people feel genuinely cared for and, where appropriate, looked after. If this element is not consciously aimed at, there is a risk that the holding environment can merely

become either a 'controlling environment' or a '*with*holding environment'
3 the appropriate containment of anxiety (see Chapter 1 and Bion 1962). This might mean conveying to the other person – 'I'll worry about that problem for the moment until you can find a way or an opportunity to manage it for yourself'
4 working towards maximum clarity in communication, which means making sure that any misunderstandings get clarified and resolved as soon as possible. People under extreme stress are highly likely to interpret things in quite distorted ways and for those prone to feeling 'unheld' these distortions will often consist of variations on the theme of being persecuted or in other ways undervalued

Some of these elements can be provided mainly in conscious and rational terms, whereas others will be conveyed through less conscious and direct means. Providing a holding environment for one troubled child is therefore a complicated task, involving a mixture of conscious and unconscious elements: providing such an environment for a group of troubled children and their families will be all the more complicated; and when we also take into account the provision of appropriate 'holding' for the staff team who are themselves engaged in the holding process, it will become evident why the task of leadership in such settings is such a complex and demanding one. In this context Eric Miller makes two interconnected propositions:

1 The quality of the holding environment of staff is the main determinant of the quality of the holding environment that they can provide for clients.
2 The quality of the holding environment of staff is mainly created by the form of organisation and by the process of management.

(Miller 1993a: 3)

Therefore, providing an appropriate holding environment for staff can be seen as the overall framework within which therapeutic care is provided for children and their families. In practice, the holding environment in a therapeutic child care setting is provided through the arrangements for one-to-one, group and inter-group relationships, as well as through the containment of these relationships through a network of arrangements for supervision, staff meetings, consultancy and management (see Ward 1995a). In addition, 'holding' will be conveyed through less tangible means such as the atmosphere of the place and the spirit in which the work is conducted, as well as through those more tangible means such as the quality of the physical environment. In everyday life in group care settings, there is sometimes a real and difficult challenge to be met in trying to maintain the quality of atmosphere in the face of the diversionary and even subversive interventions which may come both from troubled young people and their families and from anxious or exhausted staff. Here again we see the crucial role of good leadership.

One further element to add here which was not part of Winnicott's own formulation is the notion that in group care settings there can be an important element of mutuality in the holding environment – it does not all need to be a 'top-down' process. People (children as well as adults) can be encouraged and enabled to give as well as to receive in 'holding' and to gain further learning and development in the process. This ethos is at the heart of the 'therapeutic community approach' and finds particular expression through the use of the daily 'community meeting' of children and staff (see, for example, Worthington 1990), but is also found in other forms of groupwork, including analytic group work with children (T. Lucas 1988). This element is important in that it starts to redress the balance of what might otherwise become an impossibly burdensome model and in that it re-introduces the element of empowerment into these relationships, counteracting what might otherwise risk becoming patronising and encouraging over-dependency. It is also important in indicating that holding is far from being a static or 'reactive' mode of practice, since it can involve an urgent reaching out in order to try to achieve communication in complex situations as well as responding to difficulties which appear to require containment. 'Holding' can therefore include some element of 'self-holding' within the larger group and I would argue that it is especially through the use of the daily community meeting that the holding environment can be provided (see Chapter 4).

There is more to be said about the theory of the holding environment later in this book and others have argued its more detailed implications for practice in, for example, therapeutic communities for adults (Hinshelwood 1987) and special education and residential care (Greenhalgh 1993). In this chapter my intention has simply been to draw attention to this concept as a central one in the framework for understanding the critical importance of 'context' in therapeutic child care.

SUMMARY: THE INDIVIDUAL, THE GROUP AND THE COMMUNITY

In Chapter 1 we considered the child's individual development in terms of key relationships, family and outside world and in Chapter 2 we looked at the individual approach to helping. In the present chapter we have explored the broader context for helping which is created by the group care setting. Thus, any help for an individual is set within the context of the immediate group (the child's peers and the worker's colleagues), the institution as a whole and again the wider community (including the family and its own community and the professional agencies involved). In Chapter 4 we shall look at the difficulties which arise when trying to provide such help.

Chapter 4

The difficulty of helping

Adrian Ward

The problem with the idea of the holding environment is that it sounds too nice, as if all we have to do to help these very troubled young people is to put a large metaphorical 'hug' around them and all will be well. Of course, nothing could be further from the truth: this is exceptionally difficult, conflictual and stressful work, which is constantly unravelling into uncertainty and at risk of breaking down entirely into pandemonium. In this chapter we consider some aspects of why it is such difficult work, focusing particularly on anxiety and defences against anxiety. We shall start by adding further to our picture of the difficulties facing young people: we have already seen how the experiences of neglect, trauma and abuse may have affected the inner world of these children and how this impact can affect the task of those trying to provide help for them. Here we shall be looking at broader social issues which may complicate both their emotional difficulties and the task of those wishing to help them: issues of power and of prejudice.

THE SOCIAL CONTEXT: PREJUDICE AND POWER

If we start by looking at the situation of young people in residential care, the painful reality is that at times they are likely to feel extremely powerless. For many of these young people, important decisions about their present and future life are quite likely to have been taken without their feeling properly involved and consulted. For example, they may have been required to move away from their previous setting against their consent: however unsatisfactory that previous setting may have been at the time, it was at least a known and familiar place, where they may have begun to feel at home, but from which they have now been uprooted. In addition, there may be extra difficulties facing young black people in the care system, since they are likely to have been on the receiving end of racism in various aspects of their lives, both at an immediate level from individuals, but also more indirectly through organisations such as schools, the police and Social Service Departments. There is ample evidence of the structural disadvantage young black people face in society and increasing evidence of the extra impact which these difficulties have on those who are also having emotional or developmental difficulties at home.

Further negative stereotyping may affect some young people in terms of their social class, gender, sexual orientation and any physical or other disabilities. This general sense of powerlessness may add further to a sense that these young people may already have of disaffection and alienation from adult society and its values. When these conscious difficulties are added to the problems in the less conscious aspects of the young person's inner world, there may be real problems. Furthermore, a vicious circle may operate for these young people if they are then further misunderstood by the care system. This system is often staffed by people who may not themselves have experienced such prejudicial treatment – or not to the same degree – and who may not necessarily appreciate the full effects of the prejudices built into the system. Even where the staff have had some equivalent experiences in their own past, if they have not had adequate training, as is often the case, they may never have had the opportunity to recall and re-explore such experiences so that they can draw healthily and productively upon them rather than being haunted by them or unconsciously driven into re-enacting versions of them in their professional work.

Young people in this complex situation of powerlessness understandably will be prone to feeling 'got at' and misunderstood in everyday situations and therefore liable to express very strong feelings about instances of this. This may happen especially in relation to the minor incidents which can arise in the course of daily life because the young people may feel that at least *these* incidents can be brought back under their own control, even if the larger scale aspects of powerlessness are completely beyond their influence. This may help to explain why there can often be explosions of strong feeling about apparently trivial events in residential settings; it can also indicate, as we shall see later, how important it may be for staff to 'read' and respond to the message of despair or frustration which often underlies such explosions.

Thus young people who themselves often feel power*less* come to be perceived as very power*ful*, by provoking strong emotional reactions in those who encounter them at an everyday level. There will sometimes also be a link between these patterns and the early emotional experiences described in Chapter 1, because the young people may have learned how to produce these reactions in others through a combination of conscious and unconscious learning from experience much earlier in their lives. Especially relevant here may be the process known as 'splitting': in the theory of infant development (Klein 1959), splitting refers to the way in which the child may protect him or herself against acknowledging powerful feelings such as distress or anxiety by unconsciously allocating all 'bad' qualities to one person or relationship and all 'good' qualities to another (or to the self), rather than being able to manage a mature and balanced relationship in which ambivalence or anxiety is contained. Typically this might be expressed as an idealised 'good' mother and a persecutory bad father, or good self and bad parent and so on. What usually develops from this point is that, by responding with love and tolerance the parent helps the child to tolerate anxiety and ambivalence and thus eventually to develop a more secure pattern of relating to people.

The connection with the scenario of the troubled young person in the care system is that, whereas most people do develop rapidly in infancy through the phase of splitting into a more mature recognition of mutuality in relationships, others do not manage this and stay locked into the 'paranoid' mode of relating which splitting implies. Thus when a young person who has had disastrous early emotional experience encounters, or even imagines, a disapproving look on the face of one of his substitute carers, he may unconsciously feel that he can only survive by regressing back into a 'splitting' response. Rather like a much younger child, he may then behave as if to imply 'I presume that your disapproving look means that you hate me, which to me feels like complete annihilation, because I also hate myself – but I'll protect myself against acknowledging all this by making *you* feel awful'. Instead of tolerating feeling bad about him or herself, all the bad feelings are projected onto the adults providing care, sometimes very successfully so, as the carers (sometimes for their own reasons) start to experience a sense of ill-feeling, depression or despair which actually belongs to the young person. All these unconscious communications, as seen elsewhere in this book, may drive people's interactions without ever being acknowledged or verbalised.

Meanwhile, there may also be other more conscious reasons why the residential staff might describe themselves as feeling powerless. They may do so both in relation to their voice in the child care system in which they are working (where they may feel they do not have enough influence over key decisions about the children's lives or about other aspects of their work) and in relation to their everyday interactions with the young people (where they may feel that they have insufficient authority to control young people whose behaviour is difficult and challenging). In reality this is not as much of a paradox as it may appear, because both groups *are* powerless in relative terms, for there can be 'relative powerlessness' just as there is 'relative poverty'. Just as a person living on a subsistence level of welfare benefits in the UK can be living in genuine poverty even though their actual income is far higher than that of another person living in poverty in a third world country, so both the children and the staff in a residential setting can feel an equivalent sense of powerlessness, even though the staff member will always hold more *actual* power than the child does and probably in more areas of his or her life.

Nevertheless, this is potentially a fraught combination. Judging from the reported views of some of the young people and from some of the reports from official inspections of children's services (e.g. Social Services Inspectorate 1993), it appears that staff sometimes deal with their own frustration by exceeding or abusing the power they do have, e.g. by disregarding or undermining young people's views and wishes, or by paying insufficient attention to their needs and rights. In these situations, it can appear that the staff are taking revenge for their own sense of powerlessness upon the next most powerless group available, the young people themselves. It is therefore very important that those working in residential care are trained, supported and managed in such a way as to enable them to recognise and deal more appropriately with their own sense of powerlessness and to respond more constructively to the young people's needs. In other words, they need professional management in order to be able to develop and sustain their focus on their professional task.

This part of the professional task may be summed up as engaging with the young people's real needs: getting alongside them, understanding their needs and acting appropriately upon these in collaboration with the young people as far as possible. This will involve:

1 developing an everyday atmosphere of trust and respect, in which communication is encouraged and taken seriously;
2 finding ways of identifying and responding to opportunities for communication as and when they arise;
3 trying to work collaboratively with the young people, rather than talking down to them or overriding their wishes;
4 trying to help them resolve difficulties and disputes which may arise and to restore some sense of personal power and influence, without infringing other people's rights;
5 actively engaging the young people, both individually and collectively, in addressing issues of racism and other powerful prejudices and showing readiness to take challenging action against such forces, whether within the immediate context of the group care setting or beyond its boundaries in the wider systems of society.

Staff will therefore need to be able to demonstrate to the young people that they are willing to listen and ready to take the young people's views and feelings seriously, even though they may not always be able to act upon these views in the way that the young people would like.

The complication is that such communication is not always as easy as we would wish and that in fact it may be very hard at times for the young people to articulate their views in the way that they would like to, or in the way that might gain them the most sympathetic response. For example, some young people who are not used to being taken seriously, or even heard at all, may feel that they have to shout or enact their feelings physically in order to get their message across, while some others may have given up hoping that anyone will listen at all and may be extremely reluctant to say anything at a personal level, leaving staff with the frustrating task of trying to guess what they may be feeling or thinking. It can therefore feel very difficult to achieve in practice the task of working with young people in the collaborative sense described above, especially as some residential staff work in settings where they are not adequately prepared and supported for such work, although this frustration should not be used as an excuse for not aiming high. Chapter 5 describes one approach to this task which has been tried in some units.

DIFFICULTIES IN BEING REAL WITH PEOPLE

Despite the acceptance that an idea such as the need for engaging
with young people can gain in theory, there often seems to be
serious difficulty in implementing such ideas: it is as if something
gets in the way, even though people know of the importance of
direct engagement with those they are trying to help. For example,
one thing that many residential child care teams seem to have found
difficult is engagement with the families of the young people. A
rational explanation for this difficulty is sometimes offered by
pointing out that some residential centres are located far way from
the children's families, which can make for real logistical difficulties
– the truth of this situation is well supported by research evidence
(Millham *et al.* 1986). Another explanation sometimes offered is
that the families themselves are likely to have real difficulties in
communicating with others and this certainly may be true in some
cases. On the other hand, there may also be problems for the staff:
they may identify more with the children than with their families –
perhaps they feel especially protective of the children, sometimes for
reasons which may connect with their own childhood experiences
and their motivation for doing this work. If this is the case they will
have to make a special effort to overcome their own lack of confidence. On the other hand, some staff find they can work more
confidently with the parents than with the young people and they
may even avoid contact with the young people as much as possible,
because it can feel so difficult to spend much time with them.
Likewise, similar problems seem to arise in some family centres,
where some staff may identify more readily with the mothers
attending than with their young children and feel more confident in
helping adults than children, while in other centres, staff are very
confident in addressing the needs of the children but less so with the
children's mothers and even less so with the fathers. What emerges,
then, is the unsurprising finding that, although some people are
powerfully drawn to doing this kind of work, they may find some
aspects of it difficult and even threatening at a personal level and
often for unconscious reasons which are hard to fathom.

ANXIETY: KNOWING IT AND MANAGING IT

Why should it be so difficult for people to engage with each other?
The clue lies in the idea of the primary task (see Chapter 3) and in

the anxieties associated with the task. If we think about the real purpose of children's homes and other residential homes, or of family centres, or psychiatric units, we are always face to face with anxiety: the primary task of such units usually involves some element of engaging with those who have been rejected by society and who feel a profound sense of failure and inadequacy and helping them to regain some self-esteem and to recover as people. For the staff, there is often a high degree of anxiety associated with such a task: anxiety that the young people will go out of control and hurt themselves or someone else, that parents will injure or even kill their young children, that troubled adolescents will 'go mad' or kill themselves, etc. These are genuine anxieties and belong to society as a whole, but are implicitly taken on by staff when the organisation accepts the referral: this acceptance of anxiety comes about partly because at an individual level people's motivation to do this sort of work involves some readiness to engage with other people's emotional pain and partly because at an organisational level accepting the referral means taking on the anxiety that comes with the task.

However, these anxieties can be very powerful indeed and can operate at both an unconscious and at a conscious level. Staff can feel that, if they are to survive at all, they need to evolve some degree of defence against feeling the anxieties. The people living and working in such organisations not only have their own individual defences, they also tend to pool them into collective defences which they employ (largely unconsciously) to protect themselves against the deeper anxieties associated with their task. This is really a form of collective neurosis – as if to say, 'we can't cope with the implications of this, so we'll try not to think about it, but we'll busy ourselves with other things that we *can* cope with'. Thus, two important things happen at once: first, people get out of touch with the real anxieties and therefore with the real pain of the experience of those they are trying to help; and second, they also take on new (and largely distracting) secondary anxieties arising from the defensive activities. At one level, this is how people end up putting disproportionate amounts of energy into displacement activities such as folding sheets and blankets, filing endless report forms on inconsequential matters and setting down petty rules to which children must conform if they are to receive 'privileges'. The fact that some of these activities may have been embarked on as a defence against the real anxieties means that, however well such activites are implemented, there will still be something hollow and unrewarding about completing them.

At a broader level, this phenomenon also explains how it comes about that large organisations avoid defining a real primary task for institutions, because they cannot face the anxiety entailed in undertaking such tasks. In one sense this is quite understandable, since the situation of some of the young people needing help is often so dreadful as to be almost literally unthinkable, but in another sense, if the agencies as a whole cannot face these realities, it will be all the more burdensome and problematic for any individual worker or small team to try to do so. This difficulty may also explain how child care organisations sometimes arrive at policies which overlook the real needs of children, because they cannot face the anxiety involved in the proper management of a child-centred policy. A potent example of the latter has arisen during recent years over the issue of physical contact. Physical contact between children and between the children and their carers, has become more highly-charged than ever, with workers fearing the misinterpretation of their actions and the increasing awareness of sexual abuse both inside and outside institutions. This is a situation which understandably creates enormous anxiety for the employing organisations, but the ways in which this anxiety has been handled have varied greatly from one authority to another (see Ward 1990). Thus some authorities have drawn up rigid rules forbidding physical contact between children or between children and their carers, while others have taken a much more realistic line and refused to be driven into such a corner.

ENGAGING WITH THE TASK

Some of these defences arise at this wide level across whole departments, while others arise within institutions or teams, often because of the particular needs of influential staff members and especially those in leadership roles. It is therefore most important that people in these roles work towards maximum awareness of their own feelings in relation to their tasks and responsibilities and towards the open discussion within their teams of such feelings and their associated anxieties. I am not arguing against people having appropriate defences (such as withdrawing from the 'fray' at times in order to refresh and recompose themselves): what I am arguing is that people should aim to be aware of their individual and collective defences so that these do not obstruct or overwhelm their task.

This means that the task of leadership in such places is especially demanding: people need strong but sensitive leadership if they are to be helped to remain 'on task' and to stay in touch with their individual and collective anxieties about that task. They therefore need regular and reliable opportunities first to reflect in supervision upon their work and their feelings about their work; second, to communicate with each other in staff meetings about these thoughts and feelings and third, to gauge their own feelings against external reality through external management or consultation. The outcome of all this support and management should be that people are enabled to be 'real' and present at work in a very direct and personal way, not only as individuals but also as a team.

CONCLUSION

In this chapter we have looked at what is difficult and challenging about trying to help young people in the group care context, at the anxieties surrounding the task and at the defences which people tend to evolve (both individually and as teams) against feeling these anxieties. If the work starts to sound fraught and stressful, there is probably some accuracy in this, although there *are* ways of engaging with young people and engaging with the anxiety which can lead to more positive outcomes both for staff and for young people themselves. In Chapter 5 we shall look at one such approach in more detail – the therapeutic community approach.

Chapter 5

A model for practice:
the therapeutic community

Adrian Ward

If this work is fraught with such difficulty, is there any way of planning and organising it so that real progress can be achieved at all? In this chapter we will consider one model of practice which has been used successfully in some settings: the therapeutic community. It is a model which we will be drawing upon extensively in Part 2 of this book as we move into thinking about ways of helping people to learn about practice and then when we hear in Part 3 from practitioners themselves about how they have implemented such ideas in their own work settings. In this chapter I will outline some key characteristics of the therapeutic community approach, before discussing two details of practice more fully: opportunity-led work and community meetings.

THE THERAPEUTIC COMMUNITY

The idea at the heart of the therapeutic community model is one of equality between people and of the capacity in each of us to help and heal each other and to contribute to each other's development. This model is an appropriate one (although not the only one) upon which to base therapeutic work in a group care setting, because it is a model in which the connections between individual work and the context of that work have been productively thought about and it seems to offer an approach that can be adapted for different settings according to the needs and abilities locally. I will start this chapter, therefore, by outlining some aspects of this model, especially as it is used in the therapeutic communities for young people in the UK.

Defining characteristics

In one sense there is no such thing as '*the* therapeutic community' for children and young people, since every place claiming to be one turns out to be different from each other in important ways. These may be differences in terms of size, definition of task, or philosophy of practice and especially in terms of what actually happens in daily practice. There are also significant differences in origin, since the therapeutic community approach in respect of child care has a complicated and somewhat confused origin (see Ward 1996a and Bridgeland 1971).

However, despite these independent roots and individual variations, external observation does suggest that there is some common core of practice which can usefully be identified as the therapeutic community approach. This core would include:

1 an emphasis on the group care setting as a setting for the medium- to long-term treatment of emotional disturbance rather than simply as a place of temporary accommodation;
2 the use of psychodynamic rather than solely behavioural or cognitive theoretical frameworks to underpin the treatment philosophy;
3 a commitment to the value of the physical and personal 'environment' for its contribution to the therapeutic task;
4 a general emphasis on the value of groupwork as a medium both for therapeutic work and in some places for decision-making with the young people;
5 in daily practice with the young people, a commitment to a personal and involved style of working, in which the quality of the relationships between young people and staff is seen as playing a central role in the treatment process;
6 similarly, an emphasis on the potential for therapeutic communication between staff and young people to arise from everyday interactions in daily 'living alongside' each other (i.e. opportunity-led work) – see page 68;
7 in education, an emphasis on the value of child-centred learning in small groups, taking account of the connections between emotional and intellectual development;
8 in internal management structures, an emphasis on each person's role and potential contribution to the agreed task and philosophy rather than mainly on status, rank and formal titles;
9 in the overall management of the place, a commitment to the

value of an external and thus relatively independent structure
of management and to the use of consultancy for senior
managers as a means of personal and professional support;
10 in some places, but not all, there is also a commitment to the
use of the daily community meeting as a medium for both practical and therapeutic business between young people and staff
in each living unit.

A therapeutic community or therapy in a community?

It is the last of these elements – the daily community meeting –
which is often perceived from the outside as being the defining char-
acteristic of all therapeutic communities, although in fact it turns
out to be probably less common in the communities for children
and adolescents than in their equivalent for adults. It does appear
that some communities for young people have a daily meeting, while
others have such meetings at weekly or even less frequent intervals.
The 'pure model' of the adult therapeutic community is more
clearly premised upon the notion that all members of the community can give as well as take in therapeutic exchanges and indeed
that it is the community itself which is therapeutic, rather than (as is
perhaps more true in some of the children's settings) that it is
primarily only the staff who engage in therapeutic endeavour in a
'community' (i.e. in this case residential) setting. This difference in
emphasis can partly be accounted for by the fact that children and
adolescents obviously have greater needs for actual dependency
than do emotionally-troubled adults, in terms of their physical care
and their educational and health needs, for example. These young
people might also be assumed to be less able to contribute actively
to each other's therapeutic progress than adults, but there is probably a genuine and broad difference in assumptions revealed here
between the working methods of some of the communities for children and adolescents and of those for adults.

Comment

I have selected only the most evident and positive characteristics of
therapeutic communities and omitted certain other features which
have been noted elsewhere in relation to particular settings, such as
the relative under-emphasis in some settings upon the children's
family circumstances and possibilities for rehabilitation (Little

1995), problems associated with the comparatively remote location of some of the therapeutic communities (Millham *et al.* 1986) and the relative under-emphasis on policies for antidiscriminatory practice when compared even with the 'Guidance and Regulations for the Children Act', 1989. These gaps are real and serious ones, which mean that, however valuable the model is, it needs considerable adaptation if it is genuinely to address the needs of today's young people. We have attempted some of this adaptation by implication at various points in this book, although there is much more to do. Despite these remaining difficulties, however, our view has been that the therapeutic community offers the best start available in terms of a useful theory base for therapeutic work in the group care context.

One broad observation which can be made about the characteristics listed above is that many of them, especially the more general ones about styles of management and of practice, would also be claimed by many other residential homes and some boarding schools, which nevertheless would not profess to be therapeutic communities. Some of these elements of practice may first have been articulated in connection with the therapeutic communities, but they are certainly not their exclusive domain now. It is therefore perhaps more useful to think in terms of a 'therapeutic community approach', rather than seeking to devise an absolute blueprint.

There is an extensive literature on the theory and practice of the therapeutic community, which also draws heavily at times upon the related fields of 'systems thinking' and of group analysis (both of which we have drawn upon extensively in our training and therapeutic practice, although there has not been space here to consider them in any detail).

ENGAGING WITH YOUNG PEOPLE'S REAL NEEDS

Bearing in mind the discussion in Chapter 4 about the difficulties involved in working closely with young people, what is most significant about the therapeutic community approach is the strong emphasis which it places on the quality of communication between staff and young people and on the connections between the help provided to individuals and the overall task with the whole group. The success of the work is seen as ultimately depending on everyone in the place being willing and able to engage with each other in working at the real issues. This means being able to be genuine and reliable with each other and being able to sustain dialogue. Two ways in which such communication and dialogue can be planned are first in terms of the way everyday life is handled (through the use of opportunity-led work) and second in terms of regular planned occasions when people will meet to talk together (through the use of community meetings).

Opportunity-led work

Since much of the work with young people in group care settings happens in informal everyday encounters, it is important that staff have some way of planning for and thinking about this aspect of their work, rather than leaving it entirely to chance or to their own intuition. I have called this mode of work 'opportunity-led' work (Ward 1995a), in order to draw attention to the many opportunities for communication which can arise in this context, I have proposed a simple framework for thinking about this work. While it is clearly not a mode of working which is only found in the therapeutic community approach, it is a mode which is used extensively within that overall approach. The framework which I propose is based on an analysis of the process involved, from assessment and decision-making through to action and eventually to closure, tracing the skills required of the worker from the beginning to the end of a piece of work.

A typical example of opportunity-led work might occur when a worker notices a young person looking sad, confused or angry and turns this observation into an opportunity to help the young person express his or her feelings. Part of the skill required for this mode of work therefore lies in careful and reflective observation, coupled with the ability to assess people and situations. Thus, in the Assessment phase, the worker might notice the young person avoiding contact with his peers, and through a combination of observation and assessment the worker might judge that he may be feeling anxious about an impending visit home to the family, or on the other hand, that he may just be tired and not wanting to socialise.

This assessment will inform the Decision-making phase, in which the worker decides between a range of methods through which she might try to establish contact with the young person. In this case she might need to choose between a direct approach (e.g. asking him how he is feeling) and a more indirect one, e.g. just 'getting alongside' the young person and being willing to talk about

everyday trivia and waiting, in the hope that *he* will decide that he
has an opportunity to talk about his worries. She may need to have
a range of methods at her fingertips depending on the outcome of
the situation. This is sensitive work, requiring much tact and
tactical thinking on the part of the worker. There is therefore a
strong emphasis in this framework upon the decision-making phase.

It is in the Action phase that the worker actually tries out her
plan, in this case either asking the question or getting alongside. She
then watches for the young person's response before making
another judgement as to how to follow it up. This phase may
become quite prolonged through a sustained conversation or 'on-
the-spot counselling', or it may come to nothing and she may need
to withdraw and wait for another opportunity to arise. In the mean-
time of course, the group care context means that the worker is also
having to keep an eye on what is happening with all the other young
people and with her colleagues; this is demanding work. Finally, in
the Closure phase, the time comes when in any exchange of this sort
the piece of work has to be brought to an end so that people can get
on with everyday life and it is especially important that things are
left straight and clear and that as far as possible no loose ends
remain from whatever conversation has developed. If the exchange
has developed into a sustained piece of work it will need to be
reviewed and evaluated afterwards, and probably recorded in some
way so that it can be more formally incorporated into the rest of the
work with that young person.

Even this brief account of opportunity-led work reveals how
complicated it can be. Yet, these decisions and interventions often
have to be completed within the space of a few seconds if the
opportunity is to be seized. The opportunity-led framework is one
which can be applied to a wide range of situations, ranging from the
one-to-one exchanges as described above to the more complicated
patterns of interaction which arise between teams of staff and
groups of young people. It can also be adapted to a wide range of
settings, according to the communication and other skills of the
young people involved (see Ward 1996b). Several further examples
of opportunity-led work can be found among some of the practice
examples quoted elsewhere in this book.

Community meetings

The opportunity-led approach is a way of building upon events and comments which arise in everyday life and looking for opportunities for communication. On the other hand, it is also possible to plan for communication in a much fuller and more predictable way – by guaranteeing to the young people that they will have the regular opportunity to come together as a group to share their thoughts, feelings and concerns, and to be listened to and responded to by the staff. This opportunity can be provided through what are known variously as group meetings, young people's meetings, or 'community meetings'. There are various approaches to this mode of working and it will be important to adopt a model which is workable in the particular setting. What is usually involved is a regular time when all of the young people and the staff come together in a planned way to talk. Such meetings may be held on a fortnightly, weekly, or even in some places on a daily basis. The main aim will be for the voice of the young people to be heard, individually and sometimes collectively, and heard by each other as well as by the staff and perhaps others.

Getting such a system established can feel daunting for staff whether or not they are experienced in groupwork. A proposal to set up such a system may not always be received enthusiastically as some young people and some staff may be concerned about what may emerge, about whether what is said will actually be heard and taken seriously by others and whether any action will result. My own experience (Ward 1995b) in establishing regular community meetings in a children's home was that it was very difficult at first, for a number of reasons. People (both staff and children) were initially anxious at the prospect of sitting together in one room simply to talk to each other: some people find talking in a large group quite intimidating at first, and others find the idea of talking to anyone about their own thoughts and feelings fairly threatening. However, my experience was that, by starting with a simple format and developing slowly, it was eventually possible to achieve a great deal through these meetings. Children and staff gradually found the confidence both to express their own views and tolerate listening to others' views, which might be in conflict with their own. The message to those thinking of establishing such meetings in a residential setting can be summarised as follows: start small; be ready to adapt your methods according to need; be reliable and consistent and finally, work as a team and be sure of your support systems.

Both opportunity-led work and community meetings are examples of ways of promoting better and fuller communication between young people and the staff working with them. In both examples, what is called for on the part of the staff is some initiative, resilience and willingness to listen and to take young people's thoughts and feelings seriously. Both of these approaches can be implemented without huge amounts of planning and policy-making and in some settings some versions of these approaches happen largely through the informal and intuitive efforts of committed individuals.

CONCLUSION

Here we come to the end of Part 1. The aim of these chapters has been to introduce readers to some aspects of therapeutic child care as a backdrop to the focus in the rest of the book: a focus which is on a way of helping people to learn about this work, followed by some accounts of how some people have applied this learning in their own settings. It was never going to be possible to be comprehensive in these early chapters and some readers may have found many gaps left unfilled and many questions unanswered. Some of these gaps may be filled by the case examples provided in Part 3, while for those wanting to follow up in more detail on the theoretical background we have made some suggestions at the end of the book for further reading.

Part 2

Creating a model
The frameworks for learning

Chapter 6

The matching principle
Connections between training and practice

Adrian Ward

This chapter is intended to provide a bridge between Parts 1 and 2 of the book. In Part 1 our focus was upon what happens in practice and why, and what we need to think about (theory) while trying to help. In Part 2 we move on to talk about teaching and learning about this sort of practice. The bridge between the two will therefore consist of some thoughts about how theory and practice may be connected.

In particular, I will outline what we are calling the 'matching principle': the principle that in all professional training the mode of training should reflect the mode of practice. I will draw attention to the conscious and unconscious elements in both practice and training and suggest that the established concept of the 'reflection process' offers an especially useful framework through which the operation of the matching principle can be traced. I will then introduce the application of the matching principle in the overall design of the MA in Therapeutic Child Care, highlighting various elements of 'process' in training. The details of the application will then be explored in the rest of Part 2. I shall start, however, with a brief look at the general background to our work: what is the problem about providing training for therapeutic practice in child care settings?

THE PROBLEM OF TRAINING FOR THERAPEUTIC PRACTICE

The approach to thinking about therapeutic work with young people explored in Part 1 is based on a combination of psychodynamic thinking, systems theory and the concept of the therapeutic community, among others. Even though this was only intended as a general introduction to that approach, a lot of ground was covered and we aimed to convey something of the complexity of the challenge facing the workers. A significant problem which has faced those responsible for planning and managing such work has been that of staff training and development: how can people best be helped to learn about this approach? We have seen that the work demands a particular combination of personal, professional and academic understanding: what is required seems to be somewhere between the professional disciplines of psychotherapy, social work and group work. An abiding problem for those working in group care with children and young people (in the UK, at least) is that there has been no distinct body of professional knowledge identified and no discrete programmes of qualifying training. Those working in these settings may hold any of a broad range of qualifications from nursing to social work, or in many cases no qualification at all. What has been made available to such staff tends to have been focused on entry-level training (i.e. NVQ levels 2 and 3), while few senior staff hold anything more than a first (and usually non-specific) qualification. The level of academic and professional knowledge and understanding of this work has therefore often remained at a fairly basic level and people have largely been left to draw upon their own intuition as much as on trained expertise. While intuition, as we have seen, certainly has a role to play, it can never be enough on its own.

The work which we will be describing in Part 2 draws heavily on a different approach to the problem of training, exemplified in the work of the MA in Therapeutic Child Care at the University of Reading. Here we have worked with those senior or experienced staff who do hold a first qualification or degree, and aimed to help them achieve that mixture of personal, professional and academic development that we believe is required for practice in this field. The numbers able to attend any one course such as this are inevitably small and in that sense such a programme can only have a limited impact on the national problem. However, our aim from the start has also been to make as widely available as possible the approach and the material we have developed, so that others may be able to adapt it to use in their own settings, whether as trainers, managers or individual practitioners. This is why we have written this book: we are aware that there is not much literature available on this area of practice and still less which focuses on the problems involved in providing training for such practice and we want to contribute to filling these gaps.

In the rest of this chapter I shall introduce the work of the MA programme first by explaining the rationale for the approach taken and second by offering a brief overview of the work of the programme. The remaining chapters in Part 2 describe and reflect upon various aspects of the programme in greater detail.

THE MATCHING PRINCIPLE: DESIGN FOR PROCESS IN THE TRAINING CONTEXT

Our aim in the MA has been to create a programme that will fit closely with the learning needs people bring with them and to achieve this fit by attending carefully to the connections between practice and training. We have therefore based our work on what we have called the 'matching principle', by which we mean the proposal that in training for professional practice the mode of training should match the mode of practice. I now want to say more about this principle in general before illustrating its operation in relation to the specifics of training for therapeutic child care.

I was strongly influenced here some years ago by a former teaching colleague, Sara Stevens, who applied a similar principle to supervision and in particular to the supervision of residential workers. She argued that the model of supervision offered to these staff must include elements of group discussion, 'working alongside' and individual consultation in order to match the variety of modes of practice used in residential work. This is no longer such a novel idea, but it does suggest a principle echoed in other settings, such as groupwork, where it is well accepted that 'where possible the supervision context should reflect the therapeutic context which is being supervised' (Hawkins and Shohet 1989). However, apart from a general notion that there 'should' be a good fit between modes of supervision and practice (and I am extending this principle to apply to training and supervision), the question as to why this is desirable has been hardly explored.

My argument is that the basis for the matching principle (at least in training for therapeutic practice) lies in the important part played by 'process' in both practice and training. Psychoanalytically-based therapeutic work necessarily involves a strong focus on process issues – the ways in which individuals and groups affect each other over time consciously and unconsciously, and the developing awareness and understanding people can discover through these interactions. Training, on the other hand, necessarily concentrates more on the intellectual frameworks that will inform this under-standing and awareness and has traditionally focused less on process: thus, there is a risk of dislocation between practice and training.

There must be *some* gap between practice and training, otherwise trainers might aspire or revert to being therapists to their students. Even the best therapeutic training should not aspire to become, and indeed cannot itself become, good psychotherapeutic practice, because it has a different task: that of facilitating learning rather than facilitating healing (the exception is probably the case of the 'training analysis' in psychoanalytic practice). On the other hand, some element of healing is inherent in the process of training for therapeutic work because of the necessary understanding of self identified earlier. It can be argued that many people apply for training in therapeutic practice partly out of a need for a thera-peutic experience themselves: trainers can accept this need and work with it, but only up to a certain extent. If people's primary need is for therapy, then that is what they should seek rather than coming for training at this point; if on the other hand their need for therapy is in various ways secondary to or a manageable component within their need for professional training, then this can usually be worked with in the training context.

The aim of using the 'matching principle' is to address this gap between training and practice, by importing some elements of the process of practice into the process of training. The aim is not to deny or obscure the gap completely (otherwise training would risk becoming practice), but to reduce it sufficiently to allow for some of the conditions of practice to be recreated in the training context. The effect of using this principle can be seen in both conscious and unconscious terms, just as we have identified conscious and uncon-scious elements in the 'holding environment'.

At the conscious level, it might feel appropriate to the manager of a family centre, for instance, that the welcome which she receives at the start of a day's training should have some equivalence with the welcome she and her team offer to the parents attending the family centre at the start of a day. She can certainly expect things to be properly organised and prepared for the day and may feel espe-cially welcome if, for example, facilities for tea and coffee are ready. On the other hand, she may not want or need the type of individual welcome some of the parents in attendance might need, including for example, concerned questions as to how she may have managed her own household and family since her last attendance. The balance between the various elements of the welcome and the extent to which they are emphasised will need to be thought about by the staff of the training programme and she herself will doubtless have views on the matter. Similar things will apply to other aspects of the student's conscious experience of the training programme, including some aspects of teaching styles and curriculum planning, as well as to the apparently more mundane aspects such as the coffee facilities, and these can mostly be planned drawing upon traditional models of adult learning, e.g. valuing the student's current practice and history of personal development, capitalising on the student's own motivations, etc.

At the unconscious level, meanwhile, there may be other messages conveyed through the medium of the training process. If, for example, a cup of coffee is provided at the start of the day, the student may experience this provision in a number of ways. She may be simply cold and thirsty and glad of a cup of coffee. On the other hand, she may also read it as an indication that she is being treated as an adult rather than as a child at school, or she *may* read it unconsciously as if she were a child being provided with some 'primary experience'; equally, she may judge the quality of the experience according to whether the coffee is fresh-ground or instant, hot enough or otherwise, etc. In any of these scenarios her personal history and/or current experiences in the work setting may predispose her to experience a range of feelings in response, such as a sense of validation and perhaps gratitude, or feelings of resentment and confusion if she feels she is not really entitled to being treated well, or of suspicion if she feels she is being 'softened up' for some aspect of the training which will be less pleasant. She may thus interpret the experience to fit in with her previous models, some of which may be constructive while others may be quite destructive and counter-productive for her. She may be more or less aware of the nature of this response and its origins and may then communicate this response both to other students and to the trainers through a variety of ways. The others will in turn react according to their own predispositions as well as to implicit and explicit group pressures. Much of this process will take place at a less than conscious level and may appear to be purely incidental to the content of the training programme, and yet it may actually have a large effect upon the way in which the content itself is experienced and incorporated by the participants. (For further discussion of this theme, see Hughes and Pengelly 1995.)

I have deliberately selected an apparently trivial example of a 'process' – the provision of a cup of coffee – in order to keep the argument straightforward. Many other and more involved aspects of process arise in training, especially in relation to the patterns of interactions between those involved and to the formal and informal arrangements for these interactions – seminars, groups, meetings, tutorials and so on. Some version of these 'process' experiences will arise for anyone on any training course and in most circumstances they will probably (and perhaps rightly) be seen by all parties as having little direct relevance to the content of the training. However, it can be argued that in the context of training for therapeutic practice there is potential value in making these experiences more evident and more available for discussion and reflection, because in this respect the process of training has such close parallels with the process of practice. For example, if the family centre manager is to enhance her understanding of the concept of the holding environment as it may apply in her practice, it may be useful for her to be encouraged to reflect upon her own experience of other versions of the holding environment. The way in which the training programme is organised and provided and the quality of the involvement on the part of the staff of the programme, offer one version of a holding environment (admittedly an environment primarily for learning rather than for therapy) and her experience of this environment may, as we have seen, trigger thoughts and feelings in relation to her previous holding experiences. If she can be encouraged to become more conscious of these parallels and of the learning which can be derived from exploring their meaning, then the process of her learning will have become helpfully 'matched' both to the content of her learning and thereby also to the process of her practice. This is the outcome which we are aiming for in applying the matching principle.

However, there is a further element to the matching principle. If training is really to affect the quality of people's therapeutic practice, it needs to reach the unconscious as well as the conscious elements of this practice. A further aim of using the matching principle in this context therefore is to facilitate this connection between the experience of training and the unconscious element of process in practice. One significant means by which this connection can be traced is through the operation of the 'reflection process' (Mattinson 1975).

It will be recalled that the reflection process is defined as the phenomenon by which workers bring into supervision unconscious material that relates to their own reaction to the transference which they are experiencing from their clients. Thus, in the most simple example, the worker tends to treat her supervisor in much the same way as her client treats her. Variations on this phenomenon include the situation in which the client makes the worker feel what it is like to be her (e.g. by re-enacting the behaviour of a hated parent or partner) and subsequently the worker unconsciously re-enacts a similar pattern in supervision to let the supervisor know what it felt like. Mattinson and others have described this process as it operates in the supervision of casework and individual psychotherapy and in particular have shown how an understanding of this process can not only help to maximise the learning from supervision, but can also facilitate the resolution in a casework situation of the anxiety or difficulty originally being expressed.

My argument here is that if this phenomenon operates in relation to one-to-one work, it will also arise in relation to group care work – but in more complex manifestations, since, as we have seen, the context of group care is potentially so much more complex than that of one-to-one work. Simple examples would include the staff team which begins (unconsciously) to act out the difficulties of individuals or groups of children and/or of their families, or the alternative version in which the group of children give voice or action to, for example, unresolved conflicts or undisclosed intimacy in the staff team. For this reason, effective supervision in therapeutic child care will require an understanding of the ways in which such phenomena may affect the operation of supervision groups, staff meetings, or staff consultancy sessions. Further, I am arguing that if this process operates in relation to supervision and supervisors, it will also operate in relation to training and trainers and that training for therapeutic child care work therefore will necessarily give rise to many versions of the reflection process. Mattinson also argues that the reflection process is an integral and inevitable part of both supervision and practice and that, although this phenomenon can lead to some confusion and difficulty in the supervisory process, it can actually be harnessed to the tasks of supervision and ultimately of practice, if it is understood and worked with. Again, if this is true of supervision it is also true of training.

To summarise, the matching principle provides a simple framework for starting to tackle a complex problem: the problem of finding ways of establishing connections between practice and training and practice and theory. I have outlined the need to consider both conscious and unconscious elements in the operation of the matching principle and have suggested in particular that the concept of the reflection process offers some useful clues about how the unconscious elements operate. The proposition which I have been working towards is that, if there is sufficient matching between the processes of practice and training, there will be more opportunities for the reflection process to operate and therefore more opportunities for potential learning about the unconscious elements in practice. It just remains now to begin exploring how this principle operates in a particular example.

THERAPEUTIC CHILD CARE: APPLYING THE MATCHING PRINCIPLE IN PROGRAMME DESIGN

In this final section I want to introduce the application of the matching principle to the therapeutic child care context, using some examples from the MA in Therapeutic Child Care. As stated above, this is a post-qualifying programme, intended for experienced and qualified staff working with children in a range of therapeutic settings predominantly in the group care sector, such as therapeutic communities, children's homes, family centres, special education and adolescent psychiatric units. It is a part-time programme, involving one day's attendance in college per week over two years. It is a small programme, with an average of between ten and sixteen students in each year group. On this course we have attempted to create a learning environment for this group of students which will provide an appropriate and facilitative 'match' with significant elements of their practice. In addition to a substantial focus on the skills of therapeutic communication (see Chapter 8) and on broader themes such as the philosophical base which underpins practice (see Chapter 10), the content of this programme includes much material from the therapeutic community literature, as well as from a 'systems' approach to practice, including discussion both of the holding environment and of the reflection process. Linked with this content and building upon what we know about the students' work settings, we have planned for the process elements in the design of this course on the basis of the matching principle.

In most training programmes (even those in relatively uncharted waters such as therapeutic child care), deciding on the content is comparatively straightforward: it is interesting work and allows for some creativity, but it is fairly predictable since the material exists somewhere out there in the literature and it can be assembled in a number of possible combinations and sequences, then delivered and evaluated, with suitable revisions and adjustments in future years. Design for *process* in training is more complex and unpredictable: there is again a wide range of possible issues and methods, from the experiential to the prescriptive, but it is much harder to anticipate what will happen. It is especially difficult, of course, to make predictions in relation to the particular combinations of students and staff and the dynamics which will arise within and between groups.

OUTLINE OF A TYPICAL WORKING DAY ON MA IN THERAPEUTIC CHILD CARE

10.15–10.40	**Opening Meeting**
10.45	**Seminar**: 'The Therapeutic Community for Children and Adolescents'
12.15	Lunch
1.30	**Seminar**: 'Philosophical Issues in Therapeutic Child Care'
2.30	Library Time, Tutorials, etc.
3.30–4.30	**Professional Workshop**, using the 'seminar format'
4.35–4.45	*Staff Team Meeting*
4.45–6.00	**Experiential Group**
6.10	**Closing Meeting**
6.30	Depart
6.40–7.30	*Staff Team Meeting*

In designing the process element of the Therapeutic Child Care programme, we identified a number of components of practice which it seemed appropriate to re-create in the training context. Principally, these were those more formal elements which contribute to the emotional holding environment in practice – the community meeting, the use of Experiential Group work and the use of staff meetings for the holding of the staff team – plus some aspects of the informal 'work of the day' and some aspects of the academic work which aim to make the 'reflection process' more evident and available for study within the group. I will say something briefly about each of these in the examples which follow. As a guide to help readers envisage how these elements fit together, the outline of a typical working day on the MA programme is as shown in the box on page 83.

The Opening and Closing Meetings

On this programme the whole group of staff and students meets together at the start of the day's work for twenty-five minutes and again at the end of the day for twenty minutes. These meetings serve several purposes, each of which has some parallels with the use of community meetings in the therapeutic community. The opening meeting is intended to enable students to 'tune in' again to working in college and with the other group members, to share information and feelings about the intervening week's work and to anticipate the process and content of the day's work. The closing meeting is intended to bring the day's work together and finish it appropriately, and to encourage analysis of and reflection upon the whole day's work. These meetings are used for discussing feelings and facts and just like a community meeting, they need to be firmly managed in respect of time-boundaries, keeping on task and other boundaries.

At one level, the meetings offer the students the chance to rehearse their skills of group membership and leadership; beyond this, however, the whole process of the meetings is intended to 'match' the process of practice in the therapeutic community. In terms of the reflection process, the dynamics of these meetings are probably influenced at least as much by the members' unconscious reflection of what is happening to them in their place of work as they are by their conscious analysis of the information which they bring. Our hypothesis is that this version of the reflection process and the learning which can be gained from thinking about it, is facilitated by the fact that the style and structure of these meetings bear considerable similarity to the way in which community meetings operate in the therapeutic communities. Chapter 7 provides a more detailed analysis of the functions of these meetings both for the students and for the work of the programme as a whole.

Experiential Groups

The group of students meets weekly for an 'Experiential Group' led by a group facilitator, the task of these groups being to enable students to learn from personal and shared experience about the dynamics of groups and to increase their personal awareness by participating in an analytic group. This element is to some extent modelled upon the use of staff sensitivity groups in the workplace, except that whereas in sensitivity groups the task must be related to the overall aim of contributing to the therapeutic task with the young people, in the training context there can be more of a focus upon the individual and collective learning needs of the students, albeit within an understanding that the task of the course overall is to provide training rather than therapy. These groups are in one sense the 'heart of the work' of the course, the point at which people work most closely and intensively together to integrate their personal and professional learning. In another sense, they simply provide a central focus, a planned opportunity for people to actively work together as a group at the issues which arise. In Chapter 10, Teresa Howard describes her work both with these groups and with equivalent groups in other programmes. In particular she highlights the ways in which such groups can help people to focus and develop their personal learning about issues of power and culture.

The seminar format

Most training programmes have formats through which students can bring examples of their own practice for discussion and analysis within the group. On this programme, among the most fruitful of the formats which we have used (under the heading of 'professional workshop') has been the 'seminar format' devised by David Wallbridge and written up in a paper by Danbury and Wallbridge (1989). Linnet McMahon illustrates the use of this format when she describes her work on training for therapeutic communication in Chapter 8.

The staff meeting

At the end of the day's work, the staff team meets to review and process what has happened, both for individuals, small groups and the large group as a whole. This meeting is a forum in which some of the overall 'holding' function can be exercised, in that staff can pool their collective experiences of the whole group and of the whole day's work and work together at understanding the details of what is happening for individuals. Sometimes decisions need to be taken at this meeting about future action, but more frequently the outcome is simply further understanding of our training task, understanding which will hopefully inform our practice in future sessions.

As a team, we have often needed to consider how the reflection process may be affecting our work together, in that unconscious material from the student group may evoke particular reactions in individual staff or in the team as a whole. All of the effects the reflection process can highlight in a team in practice can similarly arise in a training team. Therefore, we have needed to pay particular attention to our own needs for mutual support and sometimes for external consultancy. We say more about the process and functions of these meetings in Chapter 11.

The work of the day

In addition to these planned and formal elements of 'matching for process', there is also an emphasis throughout the programme on matching the less formal aspects of training with their equivalents in practice, including, for example, thinking about the extent and limits of staff availability to students and to each other for informal consultations during the 'in-between times' of a day's work. The concept of 'opportunity-led work' applies here just as in practice, in that staff have needed to cultivate the art of reading the messages conveyed through informal interactions and spotting opportunities for particular kinds of communication. Given the earlier discussion on the cups of coffee, it also seems relevant to note that some of these opportunities arise from the informal discussions that evolve during coffee-breaks and we have tried to pay attention to the physical needs of the group in terms of decently equipped and prepared rooms, appropriate facilities for tea and coffee, etc. The staff team as a whole tries to hold the day's work together by concentrating on what is happening in the whole group as well as with individuals and through encouraging communication of what is happening within the group. This less formal and sometimes more intuitive element in the holding environment has its equivalent in what has been called the team's focus upon the 'work of the day' in therapeutic settings (Kennedy 1987).

CONCLUSION

In this chapter I have begun to address the problem of how to help people learn about therapeutic practice, by outlining the concept of the 'matching principle' and I have used the Therapeutic Child Care programme as a case study in the application of that principle. My aim at this stage has been to describe and explain this principle rather than to evaluate its usefulness. Some degree of evaluation at least will be implied in the later chapters, when people who have attended the programme reflect upon their experience both of taking part in the learning (e.g. Chapter 12 on the use of a reflective journal) and of applying the learning back in their workplace (e.g. Chapters 13–18 in Part 3). We will return to the matching principle at the end of the book and comment further both on its connection with other forms of 'reflection' and on its potential application in other forms of professional training.

Chapter 7

Meeting to learn and learning to meet

Adrian Ward

As trainers, how can we help people to engage in their learning? We know that people learn most effectively if they are fully engaged in the process, if they 'own' their learning needs and take responsibility for achieving the best learning, but how can we encourage these processes? The starting-point for my interest in this subject was a problem which is faced by all those engaged in training for professionals (and especially in part-time training): how can we deal with the fact that people arriving for training may be pre-occupied with other personal and professional problems? I had encountered this problem in my own experience both as a trainer and previously as a student. In both roles I found sometimes that much potentially valuable learning had been lost because people were not sufficiently 'psychologically present' to attend to it. I had also been struck by the fact that the things which were pre-occupying people often turned out to have significant (although not always immediately clear) relevance to the themes of the learning.

In this chapter I shall be outlining one approach to this problem, describing what happens when a training programme is designed specifically to allow participants to share their pre-occupations and anxieties at the start and finish of each day's work. This approach is based on the assumption that we can best engage people in their learning if we engage directly with them as people and since it involves the use of daily meetings between staff and students, it is a method which has a strong element of 'matching' (see Chapter 6) with one aspect of therapeutic community practice. I shall outline the problem, then describe the meetings and analyse their task and format, suggesting some typical anxieties which arise and discussing the respective roles of staff and students in the meetings. It will be seen that the simple starting-point I have identified can open the door into deeper concerns central to all professional training. Readers will have to make allowance for the fact that as leader of this programme I may be presenting a one-sided view of the experience. However, while I shall necessarily focus on the detail of this particular experience, my aim is to draw out more general points of learning which can be applied to other settings.

THE NATURE OF THE LEARNING ENTERPRISE

When people assemble to learn they bring with them a wide range of thoughts and feelings, pre-occupations and anxieties, often regarded by all parties as peripheral or tangential to their training. Some of these issues belong to the students' work-life, some to their educational concerns, some to their personal life and some to the overlaps and tensions between all three areas. Such issues arise on any training experience, but where the nature of the students' professional work is as demanding as that of those engaged in therapeutic help for deeply troubled people and where the time for training has had to be squeezed into perhaps one day per week out of a busy professional schedule, the extent of the students' pre-occupations with such concerns may be very great at times and there is indeed a risk that they may become totally distracting and antithetical to the task of training.

The question facing the trainers is whether to address such pre-occupations directly (and if so, how), or whether to focus primarily on the task in hand – the content of the planned programme. It might be argued, after all, that it is purely a matter of individual responsibility for each student to arrive ready to do the day's work and that any tensions between the day's work and students' other pre-occupations are primarily for individuals to resolve as best they can, perhaps over coffee during breaks from the formal programme. I have proposed elsewhere (Ward 1993a: 91) that at the start of a day's shift in professional care practice we each have a responsibility to arrive ready to engage with the task and not excessively pre-occupied with our own issues. In the training context, however, I would argue that the situation is somewhat different and for several reasons. *First*, there is a real risk that scarce training time will be under-utilised if teaching does not actually 'reach' the students because they are pre-occupied with other concerns. *Second*, the nature of the transition involved in arriving on a training programme is often more complex than that involved in simply arriving at one's familiar place of work, because it involves the three-way juggling of personal, professional and academic concerns; this complex transition may therefore be more difficult to achieve successfully. *Third*, the task of training includes learning about how to arrive and depart, as well as about how to 'meet'. The training context creates opportunities for people to gain knowledge about how they manage such transitions – an opportunity that deserves to be exploited rather than overlooked. If the overlap and tensions between the personal, the professional and the academic are relegated to informal discussions over coffee, there is little chance that people will achieve any more than the week-by-week relief from a proportion of their burdens, and they will learn from experience that personal and professional boundaries should be kept watertight – hardly a realistic model in such personal work. If, on the other hand, some version of these discussions can be fully incorporated into the day's work on the training programme, there is a good chance that people will be able not only to achieve this relief but also to learn something about how the stress may have built up in the first place, why certain events or themes have such particular resonance and impact for certain individuals and how things might be handled more productively in the future. In the process, they may additionally be learning about the general principles underlying the overlap between the personal and the professional; learning about how to achieve a real 'meeting of minds' with fellow students and perhaps also learning about the 'meeting-place' within their own mind between the different areas of concern and pre-occupation. *Fourth*, the training context can provide opportunities for students to develop the skills required for managing such transitions and overlaps better within their own workplace. If the right opportunities are provided, they can develop these skills partly by exploring their own and each others' thoughts and feelings about these issues, but also by observing how programme staff themselves handle them.

Indeed, if there is a way for these discussions to be incorporated into the day's training, what might it look like? The model which is offered for consideration in this chapter involves a simple format whereby each day's work on a part-time training programme begins and ends with a meeting between students and staff. The format is simple but its implications are great and my aim now is to explain the format and explore the implications.

EXAMPLE: THE MA IN THERAPEUTIC CHILD CARE

On the Therapeutic Child Care course students come to college once a week for a full day of seminars, groups, meetings and tutorials. There are a dozen or more students in each cohort, all of whom are mature with either a degree or a professional qualification before commencing the course; most of them hold a middle-management role in a care setting, or the equivalent. People come a considerable distance (up to 150 miles each way) and from a wide range of settings: some from therapeutic communities, some from schools, adolescent units, children's homes, family centres and so on. There is an ethos of participative and reflective learning throughout the course, and the content includes a wide range of seminar work on therapeutic practice, management issues, philosophical and ethical issues and on research methods, as well as more personal learning in an Experiential Group.

The Opening and Closing Meetings I will be discussing have an agreed task but an open agenda within that task. They are attended by all students and staff, apart from the facilitator of the Experiential Group, who attends the closing but not the opening meeting. The overall purpose of the meetings is to provide a structure, separate from the other structures of the day, within which the day's work together can start and finish. The meetings provide opportunities for students and staff to share thoughts and feelings about the intervening week's work and any other issues which they feel are relevant, including any aspect of the group's work together on the training programme. The assumptions behind this approach are that, far from being peripheral, the personal and professional concerns of the students may turn out to be of direct relevance to the day's work and that in some senses they can be used as the essential raw data out of which some of the most useful real learning may be developed. In particular, the meetings provide opportunities for course members to work at understanding and learning about the overlaps and tensions between personal and professional concerns.

The opening meeting

In respect of both the Opening and Closing Meetings, considerable work has been invested by staff and students in clarifying the precise task of each meeting. Clarity about task is an essential component of therapeutic community practice (Miller 1993a) and a readiness to work continually at re-defining the task is often necessary. The primary task of the opening meeting, as currently defined, is to *enable people to make a successful transition back into the learning group so that they can have a productive day's work.*

For each member of the course, then, the question is: 'what do I need to say or know in order to have the most productive day's work?'. In some respects, the opening meeting should function like a handover meeting in a shiftwork setting: that is, for the communication between team members of thoughts and feelings in preparation for a day's work – except that in shift work there is usually one outgoing shift and one incoming shift, with a focus on the transfer of knowledge and understanding between the two teams. In the situation of this training programme there is just one 'team' which assembles for the day and has to make a collective transition from being apart to being together again, from being 'out' at their respective workplaces to being 'in' at the training event. In the traditional handover meeting, the outgoing team has to decide what needs to be handed forward and the incoming team has to decide what it needs to know (for a useful discussion of the dynamics of handover meetings, see Mason 1989). At the opening meeting, by contrast, each individual member of the training group has to decide what she needs to bring with her to the day's work and what she should leave behind at the door, while the group as a whole has to decide what it can deal with productively in these meetings. Even of those things which are brought in, there will be some which can be satisfactorily dealt with by simply mentioning them in the meeting, while others will need fuller discussion and some may need to be brought up again at a later point in the day's work. For example, since on this course there is a guaranteed time of the day when there will be opportunity for deeper personal reflection together – the Experiential Group – the individual may feel it is appropriate to save her more personal concerns for then. Equally, an individual's practical concerns over a detail of her training may be best dealt with in an individual tutorial. On the other hand, the feelings associated with personal concerns may be so strong that at least she needs to let her colleagues know that she has these concerns, even though the appropriate time to pursue them in more detail will not come until later in the day.

For example: one student reported in the opening meeting one week that she had had to decide whether or not to attend the funeral on that day of a distant but significant relative and that on reflection she had decided that she wanted to spend the day with the student group. It was clear as she talked that this had been a difficult decision, but that she did not want to say more about it at this point. Later in the day, she used the opportunity in the Experiential Group to speak movingly and in much greater detail about why the deceased had been of such great personal importance to her. She also said more about why she had nevertheless felt it more appropriate to come to the day's training rather than attending the funeral. The theme then took on a more general meaning for others in the group as they were enabled to reflect on how they handled their own ambivalence about their training experience and about other aspects of their work.

Functions of the opening meeting

The analogy with the handover meeting does not, however, do justice to the full range of functions of the opening meeting, and within the task of the meeting there are certainly more functions than merely the business of exploring personal pre-occupations in order to learn about their relevance or otherwise to the professional task. Some of these functions are outlined below – these are not presented in order of priority: indeed at different times different functions will need to take priority.

Reporting in

There is usually an expectation in the group that each person will at least make a brief statement either about their week's work, or whatever personal business may be pre-occupying them, or about their state of mind on that particular day – something which will help the individual to locate him or herself back into the group. At times this 'reporting-in' has been achieved through a formal 'round', while at other times it has been managed more informally.

Learning to make connections

The meeting also facilitates the linking of one week's work and themes to the next. Within a holistic approach to training there is always potential for the learning to extend well beyond the subject-matter of individual seminars and the staff of this course encourage the recognition of themes which develop from one week to the next. Thus the opening meeting will often include further reflection and debate on an issue which had arisen in the previous week.

Learning from absence and ambivalence

Time is often taken hearing news about any absences and about anyone who is going to be late and the reasons for these. In most higher education programmes, there is an implicit assumption that people's level and quality of attendance is either their own business or a formal matter of apologies and explanations between student and staff. In the opening meeting, however, fuller attention is given to these areas as they really do matter, not only to the staff, but also to other members of the group as to whether somebody has had an emergency during the week or some other cause for lateness or absence. Beyond these real practical difficulties, it also matters that people learn from each other about how each of them is managing their ambivalence: in any experience as powerful as a professional training programme, it is to be expected that all participants will experience some degree of ambivalence about the experience. There may be a wide range of factors in this ambivalence – the theoretical material may feel too hard or confusing to struggle with, for example, or the personal issues thrown up by exploring the material may feel too painful to manage or to face acknowledging to oneself or to others. Other people feel very torn between the demands of their workplace, or family, and the demands of the course. Many people find it hard to manage such ambivalence and find it especially hard to believe that it will be acceptable and even productive to talk about such ambivalence within the training setting itself. The ambivalence therefore tends to find other means of expression, such as, arriving late or missing sessions altogether, for example, or taking refuge in minor illness. Furthermore, for many people these symptoms of ambivalence match closely with the equivalent struggles they may have in relation to the more painful aspects of their practice. Such issues can easily come to dominate the practice setting. On the MA programme, therefore, we hope to encourage the recognition and exploration of such ambivalence and to provide opportunities for the expression of the feelings through the combination of the Opening and Closing Meetings and the Experiential Group.

Learning to interpret external influences

Time is sometimes spent discussing current political and social events and relating these to the personal and professional concerns of group members. Some such events have clear and immediate relevance to the group, where they touch on issues of professional concern, but other events may initially appear to have little direct relevance – and yet some connection usually emerges, as there is usually a good reason why someone has chosen to raise an issue. Naturally, the traditional UK obsession with the weather means that it is a frequent topic of conversation. As the group develops its collective ability and confidence in appreciating the different levels at which any given subject may have meanings, so the significance of these discussions becomes clearer. Thus the political climate may impinge directly on people's morale in daily practice, while responses to varying weather conditions may also say something about people's emotional state: examples have been feelings expressed about the effect of stormy conditions and of the parallel between being 'snowed in' and feeling 'snowed under'.

Learning to plan and negotiate

Returning to the practical functions of the meeting, it is a forum in which the group can anticipate particular aspects of the coming day's work and plan together accordingly. Even small changes in the usual routine (such as the postponement of a planned visiting speaker) can be experienced as quite disruptive and confusing and such effects can be ameliorated by a collective approach to planning – and of course there is useful learning for practice inherent in such discussions, as students learn the importance of an open and reflective approach to the negotiation of arrangements. As a staff team, too, we have had to learn to negotiate rather than impose and to restrain our own defensiveness when under pressure in such discussions.

The closing meeting

The primary task of the closing meeting is currently formulated as: *to end the day's work together appropriately and to enable people to make a successful transition from the learning group back into the rest of their week*. The meeting is chaired by the person who has chaired the opening meeting for that day, and there have been considerable debates as to the style and format of the meeting, though what has generally happened is that, rather than using a 'round' or other structure, it is left for individuals, working collectively, to find their own way to close their day's work. The functions of the closing meeting include the following:

Reviewing the day's work together

Reviewing what has happened both in terms of process and of content and picking out themes which emerge. Sometimes these themes will relate to the content of the seminars and workshops, at other times organisational or 'boundary' aspects will emerge as important – e.g. on one occasion every seminar in the day seemed to have run over time, with students and staff equally incapable of working within time-boundaries. When space is allowed at this stage for mutual reflection on a phenomenon such as this, there often turns out to be an underlying reason, such as (in one case of over-running) collective anxiety about a forthcoming break at the end of term. On further reflection, participants will then often discover that similar phenomena happen in their workplaces and perhaps for similar reasons. Equally, there have been many occasions when the closing meeting has been used to reflect on the way that a theme which started as 'content' in a seminar on, e.g. therapeutic communication with abused children, has been taken up as personal 'process' by individuals because of special meaning for them and has subsequently evolved into group process during the work of the Experiential Group. The closing meeting then offers the opportunity to tie in all of these meanings for the group as a whole by promoting collective group reflection.

Closing down the business of the day

In addition to simply reviewing and reflecting upon the day's work, there will sometimes be unfinished business between members of the student group, or between different sub-groupings, or between students and staff, which needs to be attended to in order that not too many 'loose ends' are left. There is a strong element of modelling good practice here in that the 'ending' phase of any piece of therapeutic work involves similar attention to rounding off communication.

It will be evident that the closing meeting is not normally the time to open up new themes for discussion, or for staff to make significant announcements about changes in the programme etc. Most of the business should have the status of 'reminders' at this stage. There are a few occasions when new events do need to be reported from the staff or student group – sudden unexpected departures or arrivals during the day, for instance – events which may be known about by some members of the group, but not by all, or events whose significance may not yet be fully understood.

Clarifying any arrangements for the following week

There is first a practical level at which arrangements about the work of the intervening week and for the next day's work in college need to be confirmed in the closing meeting. Second, people sometimes wish to register their view of a theme, perhaps about a development in the life of the group, or about a connection between the personal and the professional, which may have developed during the day and to which they wish to return on the next occasion.

Further functions

Beyond these specific tasks of the Opening and Closing Meetings, there are other functions to which both types of meeting contribute, including the following:

Facilitating personal learning

While these meetings are not usually the place for in-depth discussion of personal business, there may well be times when this takes priority. For example, a student who had used the Experiential Group to explore the connection between a personal issue and the content of one of the seminars might then wish to reflect further on this learning in the larger meeting at which all staff and students are present, or might want to challenge a staff member over the way a subject had been handled in the academic discussion.

Modelling good practice: facilitating 'learning to meet'

One benefit of matching the format for the day to the mode of students' professional practice is that this encourages direct learning about ways of working that can then be imported back into the workplace. Thus, students will be learning from experience in these meetings about the use of community meetings and more generally about how groups operate and how meetings can be made to work. The outcome of this learning has sometimes been that students have subsequently developed equivalent meetings in their work setting – thus the manager of a family centre instigated the use of a daily 'morning meeting' at which parents and staff would reflect together on their thoughts and plans for each day's time together (see Chapter 15). Again this aspect of the meetings will not often be focused on as a high priority, but there is always potential in these meetings for important learning about how meetings may be constructively used.

Cultivating a 'reflective' ability in group members

Part of 'learning to meet' will involve learning to reflect – cultivating the ability to make connections between different aspects of one's experience and to think more deeply about these connections. This ability is itself closely connected to the quality of 'reverie' in therapeutic practice and the meetings offer many opportunities for people to learn about this quality – by learning to attend to silence as much as to noise, for example and to attend to another's needs as much as to one's own.

Developing awareness of unconscious communication

As a staff team we assume (following the therapeutic community model) that where personal distress or strong concern is being withheld from the group at a conscious level, it is usually being communicated at an unconscious level anyway – perhaps through such 'minimal cues' as small changes in body language or facial expression, or through the use or avoidance of emotionally 'loaded' terms. Such unconscious and indirect communications nevertheless can be very real and can have a powerful effect on the recipients, but they can be much harder for others to detect and understand and people will therefore often *react* at an unconscious level, too, bringing the risk of cycles of unconscious reactivity. In a therapeutic community this is how you end up with verbal or physical 'acting out' (the unprocessed externalisation of inner distress) and in the training setting just the same sort of thing can happen. This is how you end up with people suddenly and mysteriously leaving a unit, or a course, without anyone knowing why, but leaving every-body feeling guilty. Building on the learning about unconscious communication which evolves in the Experiential Group, we there-fore use the meetings to help people learn about unconscious communication as it happens. This also means that, while the anxiety about disclosure in the group is something which we need to respect, we also need to encourage people to address it and eventu-ally overcome it.

Managing the process

It is not enough simply to be clear about the tasks of the meetings: we need also to be clear about their format and structures, how they should be chaired and by whom. The primary task of the chair-person, as currently agreed, is *to ensure that people are clear about the task of the meeting and are enabled to work appropriately on that task*. The enabling function includes making opening remarks of welcome, drawing any appropriate connections with the previous week's work, etc. Included within the task must be a readiness to re-examine the task of the meeting from time to time and to review the working methods, but the usual priority on any given day is the achievement of the agreed task.

There has at times been considerable debate in the meetings as to the appropriate working method for the meeting: how can we ensure that everyone who wants to speak has the opportunity to do so and what about people who appear not to want to speak? Should there be a formal 'round', or should it be left to individuals to choose whether and when to speak? The practice which has evolved has been an informal 'round' in the opening meeting, with people speaking as they feel ready to, rather than literally in turn around the room and a more open agenda at the closing meeting as was seen above.

In terms of chairing the meetings, in the first year of the course there was a need to establish a model of a way of doing things. As the course leader I chaired the meetings myself for the first two terms before the students themselves felt ready to take turns in chairing them. Since then (i.e. for the last seven years), the meetings have usually been chaired by students. This feature of the meetings has brought further learning opportunities as well as challenges. While some people take on the task of chairing with appropriate confidence and skill, there have been times when people have not felt sufficiently confident or have not yet developed the relevant skills. Although this model may offer good opportunities for students to develop skills and confidence in chairing meetings, it may create problems on the day (problems which will again be familiar to those working in therapeutic communities). Thus, if a student needs to bring a particularly stressful experience or set of feelings to the meeting, he or she needs to feel 'held' by the meeting and in some respects by the chairperson. If that week's chairperson has not developed the relevant skills of, for example, facilitating expression, encouraging appropriate responses from group members, or knowing how to move sensitively from one person's contribution to another's, there is a risk that people will feel unheard and that they will be left pre-occupied with their difficulties and perhaps hurt or confused as well, and the task of the meeting will not have been achieved. Preventing such a scenario may require an intervention from another student who has greater skill or confidence or perhaps from a staff member, in ensuring that the proper containment is achieved – and this intervention itself will have to be effected without undermining the learning opportunities of the chairperson. On most occasions, it may be better in the long run for the chairperson to do their best and for others to trust in the longer-term learning process. This is a test of the sensitivity and effectiveness of the group as a whole as much as it is of the chair or of any other individual.

A recent variation on the theme has been that group members have decided that the time to volunteer to chair the following week's meetings is at the start of the current week's opening meeting. The rationale for this practice is that it encourages greater continuity from one week to the next, in that the 'chair-to-be' is likely to pay extra attention to process issues and to the connections between the weeks' work.

The role of the staff

It will be evident that the format for these meetings makes demands upon (and creates opportunities for) the staff of this programme which are somewhat different from those of the traditional academic role. Thus staff, too, work at the overlaps between their personal, professional and academic concerns and contribute to the meetings accordingly. Staff therefore usually contribute to the 'round' in the opening meeting in whatever way seems appropriate, which may mean disclosing personal business or professional concerns that on most academic programmes would be kept strictly separate from students. Examples have included times when staff members have been pre-occupied with family concerns – or occasionally with departmental wrangles – which might otherwise inhibit their contribution to the day's work. Such contributions can be viewed as involving some 'modelling' of the ability to make appropriate disclosures in such meetings, although this might not be the main rationale staff would use in deciding whether or not to disclose in this way. The key factor is often that, where a staff member is pre-occupied with such matters, this would probably convey itself to the group at an unconscious level anyway, so it is often better that things are made explicit and thus more accessible for understanding and learning. Such decisions also need to take into account the risk that staff anxieties might overwhelm or inhibit the student group, since excessive vulnerability in this context can be just as counter-productive as excessive apparent *in*vulnerability. The dilemmas facing staff when using this approach therefore are not identical to those facing students, although they do have parallels with the dilemmas the students may face when in the 'staff' role back at their own workplace.

Similarly, staff face a set of decisions about when and how to make interventions or interpretations in connection with the process of the meetings. A judgement has to be made between, on the one hand, offering comment and interpretation where this might be helpful and on the other hand trusting in the inherent ability of the group to arrive at its own learning in such areas. My own inclination is usually to adopt the latter approach, since, as Winnicott says, 'it is not the moment of my own clever interpretation' which will make the difference, but the group's collective realisations of its own interpretations. Thus even if an opportunity to intervene is passed by at one particular moment, it may be returned to by a member of the group later in the day or on a future day. However, there are definitely some occasions when a clear and direct interpretation *is* required: on one occasion, for example, the chairperson for the day appeared to be losing the focus upon the task of the opening meeting, to the real detriment of a troubled individual who was simply not being noticed at all: in this case, the best intervention seemed to be to draw the attention of the group to that individual rather than to make an explicit criticism of the work of the chairperson.

On a personal level, as leader of this programme, I have certainly found some parallels between my role in these meetings and my previous role as leader of a small therapeutic community for children. As a leader I have to be quite clear about the responsibilities of management, e.g. establishing and confirming clear boundaries, but I must also not pretend to have all the answers to every situation which may arise. Sometimes it is better that we should flounder together in a state of temporary confusion than trying to impose a parental or even 'paternal' certainty where there can be no real certainty. All the familiar scenarios of projection arise and my awareness of the counter-transference issues has been strongly tested at times.

Managing anxiety

It is well established that some degree of anxiety is always present in therapeutic work and indeed in most forms of human endeavour and that it is anxiety which tends to impinge upon the achievement of task, although, when harnessed and understood, anxiety can also drive the process onwards (Menzies Lyth 1988). For this reason it is useful to be clear about the types of anxieties which typically may be associated with any activity, in order to anticipate how the enterprise may be kept on task. In the case of the Opening and Closing Meetings, typical anxieties have included the following:

(a) Anxiety that strong emotion will take over the session, or that one individual or group will dominate in such a way that others will not be able to use the meeting effectively. In reality, such events have happened only very rarely, when somebody has had an intolerable piece of personal news, or has made an unexpected attack upon the group or upon an individual. On occasions, an implicit bid to take over the meeting with personal business might be interpreted in relation to its possible effect on the task: thus if an opening meeting were to be 'taken over', the day's work together could not begin and if a closing meeting were to be taken over, the day's work could not be brought to an end – individuals or groups might have an unconscious investment in either scenario and there will be something to be learned from the group's recognition of such phenomena.

(b) Anxiety that 'I will feel worse rather than better if I disclose something', or that 'I will be compelled to disclose something against my will'. These anxieties, although not often expressed directly, are probably often present especially in the early stages of the development of the group and they present a test of the effectiveness of the meeting and of the chairing in particular. They are also themes which will be familiar from other group settings, of course.

(c) In relation to the closing meeting, anxiety that 'I will be abandoned, that you will all forget about me, that I (or you) will die or disappear', etc. Here the mutuality of the therapeutic community can be the means through which the group provides containment for all its members – 'we will not forget or abandon each other'. Sometimes these concerns may find direct verbal expression, as when after a particularly emotionally draining day's work group members encouraged each other to drive safely on their way home.

I would suggest that all of these anxieties, although I have identified them in connection with the meetings themselves, actually relate more broadly to people's feelings about the whole experience of engaging in a programme of training over a period of time together with a group of other people. One effect of having the meetings is to provide a regular time and place in which such anxieties can be acknowledged and explored.

There have also been periods when the meeting has drifted 'off-task' into small talk, or argument about detail, or other trivia, as if the meeting were simply the equivalent of a coffee-break, where the purpose (if any) is simply to relax together in whatever way seems to fit at the time. The task of the meeting is not to relax together but to prepare for – or disengage from – working together. Where this 'drift' has begun to happen, the phenomenon will usually be recognised by group members after a short time and the group will work together to bring the meeting back on task: if the group as a whole does not make this happen, it is the responsibility of the chairperson to bring the problem to the group's attention. There are often reasons why the group may have felt it safer to keep off task, of course, if working to task might involve saying or feeling uncomfortable things and the work of moving back 'on-task' and acknowledging the difficulties again provides important learning opportunities for participants. As we saw above, if the group itself does not manage to recognise the problem or to get itself back on task, the staff will occasionally intervene to encourage such a move.

Finally, a similar problem sometimes arises over the clarity and rigidity of the boundaries between the different types of meeting. This question has sometimes been raised in the form: 'Are the Opening and Closing Meetings supposed to be Experiential Groups or are they "business meetings"?' The reality seems to be that they are not wholly either of these, but they are meetings about the overlap and tensions between the two. Thus a meeting which was wholly 'factual' and devoid of personal investment would be unhelpful if it still left group members unclear about what each other was feeling. On the other hand, a meeting wholly focused on the deep and personal feelings of one or more individuals would be equally dysfunctional if the outcome was such that the practical business of the meeting had not been done. In this case anxiety would have taken over: thus the broader task of the meetings might be expressed as to *manage collective anxiety appropriately, so that the maximum learning can be achieved.*

CONCLUSION

In this chapter I have attempted to analyse the rationale and functions of a system of using Opening and Closing Meetings on a part-time professional training course. I began with the relatively simple theme of how to help people to engage fully with the task of their learning and have moved on, through exploring the various tasks and functions of the meetings, to show how this system allows a broad range of personal and professional learning to be achieved. I have not explicitly discussed the wider application of this model into other educational settings, although I would hope that some aspects of such application will have been at least implicit. Since, as we saw earlier, the closing event is not the time to introduce new material, I will not open that debate now, but we will return to it later in the book.

Chapter 8

Working at understanding and helping troubled children[1]

Linnet McMahon

Recent years have seen much social concern about children's behaviour, often accompanied by an injunction 'to condemn more and understand less'. Yet seeking to understand does not mean condoning. It is possible, as even some politicians have realised, to be 'tough on crime and tough on the causes of crime'. But without understanding we risk perpetuating the cycle of deprivation and damage, since for us, as for the children, 'that which we fail to comprehend we in some manner enact' (Danbury and Wallbridge 1989: 56). We need to see a child's behaviour not simply as something to be modified, but as a communication, however unwitting or unconscious, about their inner world (see Chapter 1), to which we can make a helpful response.

Although woven into the whole fabric of the Therapeutic Child Care programme, the development of skills in therapeutic work are specifically addressed in two main sequences, the professional workshop in which members can bring examples of their own practice for discussion and analysis within the group and therapeutic communication with children and young people. In this chapter we examine working methods in training and propose a match between emotional development and therapeutic process as a basis for course design in therapeutic communication.

METHODS OF TEACHING AND LEARNING

The seminar technique

One of the challenges facing trainers in this field is how to facilitate people's learning about unconscious elements in practice. By defini-

1   Practice examples supplied by: John Tuberville and Simon Peacock.

tion it is difficult to teach in the conscious domain that which emerges from the unconscious; these are things which people need to be helped to realise, rather than being instructed on. One way to approach this challenge is to create situations in which such realisations can take place. One particularly effective way of doing so has been to use the seminar technique devised by David Wallbridge (Danbury and Wallbridge 1989).

In this the member presenting speaks without notes for no more than five minutes, then for twenty minutes observes the group discussing both the content and the process of the presentation, before rejoining the group to reflect with them for a further twenty minutes on the connections between process and content. A final five minutes of review and recapitulation rounds off an intense fifty minutes of analysis and reflection.

> The aim of this tightly-structured format is to highlight the operation of the reflection process (Mattinson 1975) when case material is being discussed and so facilitate not only the discussion of whatever conscious content the member wished to bring in presenting an example, but also the learning within the whole group about the connections between content and process – connections which can then be generalised well beyond the constraints of these seminars. This format has consistently produced impressive results in bringing the reflection process to life for many members who perhaps might otherwise remain unclear or sceptical about its existence.
>
> (Ward 1995a: 196)

Some examples may serve to illustrate how the workshop group may re-enact the unconscious feelings involved in a work situation. The group's work at understanding the process can reveal some helpful insights into what may have been going on in the original situation and so open up ideas about how to address it.

A family centre worker presented a situation in which she wanted to know whether the centre was 'managing correctly' the phasing out of contact between a child and her mother, who was herself adopted and who suffered from severe depression and was unable to care appropriately for her child. When the worker had presented the situation to the workshop members, describing the delays in decision-making and the conflicts between the professionals involved, these emotional dynamics of the case became mirrored in the discussion by the group's initial depressed mood, which was then followed by anguished argument. The underlying themes in the case – for the mother, child and family centre workers – seemed to be about the anger and emptiness in separation, losing and being lost and equivalent themes emerged in the workshop discussion. By experiencing these feelings and subsequently realising their power and their origin, the group became aware of the importance of acknowledging rather than denying such painful feelings.

A similar polarisation of feelings, reflecting those in the care setting, occurred in discussing the dilemma of a white residential worker caring for an Asian girl who had run away from her Muslim foster family, but who wanted to return to her own abusing family. Anxiety at ignorance of cultural issues led to members feeling stuck with an 'impossible' decision just as the original worker had been; a cultural bridge was needed to enable thought.

A play therapist's presentation about a child client's sense of isolation led to thoughts about her own feelings of isolation in the group. This in turn was seen as a reflection of her isolation as an independent worker within the care system, identifying the risk of being treated by others involved in the case as if she were in the same position as the child and equally powerless. Although this put her in a good position to understand the child's feelings it also could push her towards an unhelpful 'merger' or collusion with the child.

A related theme of resisting unconscious collusion emerged from discussion of a mother's demands that a residential setting should follow her rules for her child's diet and medication or she would withdraw him. The whole organization, like the workshop group, risked being drawn into splitting and a collusive response. In each case the need to set boundaries became evident.

Sometimes a presentation may take the form of role play or sculpting, providing another mirror of process. For example, role play of a smelly adolescent who sat for hours in his filthy room, ignoring all overtures, revealed both the young man's own self-disgust as well as how hard it was for his care worker literally to get alongside him.

The seminar technique can provide a series of mirrors in which it becomes possible to become aware of some of the unconscious processes involved in practice. It can be both surprising and illuminating to realise that what is happening in child and family relationships can become so readily mirrored by workers in their professional setting. The unconscious feelings involved in a family or a work situation may similarly be reflected in a group discussion. There is one further mirror which I have not described: the theme arising out of someone's presentation sometimes has a particular personal meaning for that person and reflects an issue of some significance in their lives (see the concluding chapters of this book for a further discussion of aspects of reflection). To realise how unconscious elements enter a situation is to be better able to think about their meaning and to be able to make a more informed response.

Teaching and learning about therapeutic communication

While it is most valuable for people to learn about the unconscious dynamics in therapeutic work, this is elusive learning, which emerges gradually and sometimes unpredictably from the regular use of methods such as the seminar technique. There is much else about method and process in therapeutic communication which can be taught more directly. For the rest of this chapter I will concentrate on the range of methods of teaching and learning which we have found effective for this task. These include experiential exercises as well as practical exercises in communication, and since it is important to keep a clear focus on the connections between theory and practice, we have found it helpful to complement these exercises by seminar discussion of prior reading (of a journal article or book chapter). These discussions are further enhanced, of course, by detailed consideration of examples of people's own therapeutic work with children and young people.

The quality of therapeutic communication with children depends ultimately on the worker's use of self, a blend of the personal and the professional. Part of training involves working at this, developing and deepening self-knowledge and getting in touch with the child within the worker (see Chapter 10). The use of experiential exercises gives some prior warning of the feelings which may be aroused in work with a child, as well as giving some indication of the power of that experience to a child. Experiential work helps people to understand their counter-transference feelings, distinguishing those which arise out of their own previous experience from those which are a more direct response to transference from the child. There is not always sufficient opportunity within a particular session for individual painful feelings to be worked with and here the 'holding environment' of the whole programme becomes crucial. The containment offered by the separate Experiential Group led by a facilitator later in the day and the closing meeting with the whole staff team present, make it more possible to think about some initially unmanageable feelings. The importance of integrating the teaching on therapeutic communication into the structure of the programme as a whole is illustrated by the following example.

In a 'good memories' relaxation exercise (derived from Oaklander 1978) students were asked to imagine feeling warmed by the sun. Far from finding it relaxing, one European student recalled horrendous memories of the sun burning her as a refugee child in flight and an African student also had memories of being burned. For some others even the recall of good memories unleashed strong feelings. The Experiential Group and later the closing meeting, gave space for these feelings to be further expressed and explored. The staff meeting at the end of the day enabled the whole staff team to deepen their understanding of the different feelings involved. While it may be the case that the choice of this specific exercise was inappropriately ethnocentric, it will always happen that people experience things differently and we need to work with those feelings. The holding environment of the whole programme can enable such reflection.

THE MATCH BETWEN EMOTIONAL DEVELOPMENT AND THERAPEUTIC PROCESS

A basis for course design

In planning teaching about therapeutic communication we have found it helpful for the sequence design to reflect both the stages of a child's emotional development and the related process of therapeutic work.

Exciting recent developments in research based on Bowlby's (1969, 1973, 1980) attachment theory, are clarifying the connections between impaired attachments in infancy and later disturbance (Greenberg *et al.* 1990, Fonagy 1996, Main 1996). Winnicott (1965a) earlier described both the evolution of the gradual maturation processes of emotional separating out of mother and baby by which the child would achieve integration, and the need to understand these processes and the point at which they were interrupted since they determine the child's current survival mechanism and suggest the appropriate therapeutic intervention. Dockar-Drysdale (1968a, 1968b, 1990), who applied Winnicott's ideas in residential therapeutic work with children, usefully summarises:

> We are thinking in terms of a series of processes which must be gone through in order to reach integration. These are experience, realization, symbolization and conceptualization. By this I mean that a child may have a good experience provided by his therapist, but that this will be of no value to him until he is able, eventually, to realise it; that is to say, to feel that this good thing has really happened to him. Then he must find a way of storing the good thing inside him, which he does by means of symbolizing the experience. Last in the series of processes comes conceptualization, which is understanding intellectually what has happened to him in the course of the experience and being able to think this in words . . . . It is not enough to give emotionally deprived children good experience, we must also help them to keep the good things inside them, or they will lose them once more.
>
> (Dockar-Drysdale 1990: 98–9)

This account of the sequence of processes involved in therapeutic work provides a useful model which a therapeutic communication course may broadly match.

EXPERIENCE AND REALISATION: THE UNINTEGRATED CHILD'S NEED FOR PRIMARY EXPERIENCE

> First, as Anna Freud says, build the house; first, as Klein says, introject the good breast; first, as Bion says, you have to have an adequate container; first, as Bowlby says, have a secure base.
>
> (Alvarez 1992: 117)

The first part of learning for therapeutic communication is about how to enable children to have and hold on to that crucial good primary experience. This is the starting-point for many emotionally damaged children, certainly for those children whose deprivation may have started in infancy and whom Winnicott terms 'unintegrated' (see Chapter 1). Any previous training experience which our students bring has rarely addressed the provision of primary experience and we have found it important for the sequence to make it not only the first but also the main focus.

To understand what unintegrated children have lacked and still need, it helps to consider the experiences of children in the course of normal development. Winnicott's notion of the holding environment and maternal pre-occupation has echoes in Bion's reverie or containment (Copley and Forryan 1987). Recent research into infancy has elaborated our thinking about 'motherese' (Bruner 1983) and the mother's attunement to her baby (Brazelton, Cramer 1991, Stern 1985). (I use the word mother while recognizing that mothering does not necessarily come from the biological mother, or even from women; mothering can also be done by men.) The common thread is the notion of the mother's attentiveness to her child's communication and her ability to bear and to think about this, holding on to all the baby's feelings without feeling overwhelmed and giving them back to her infant in a more manageable form. This enables the infant to take in more good feelings than bad ones, holding on to them and in time becoming a container in turn.

A further aspect of mothering involves the ability to notice and respond not only when the child is vociferously angry or distressed but when he or she is depressed or mentally distanced. Such a mother is able to reach out to the infant, carefully managing the timing and intensity of her approach, to bring the child back into contact with her and through her to the world. Alvarez (1992) applies this notion of reaching out in psychotherapy with 'borderline' (unintegrated and fragilely integrated) children. It is also applicable to therapeutic communication in daily living with damaged and abused children.

We can use understanding of the 'normal' processes of parenting when thinking about therapeutic communication with unintegrated children. Fundamental is the provision of the 'holding environment', a safe space physically and emotionally within which the child can start to grow. Alvarez describes it as the child needing to forget before being able to start to remember; 'while this non-abusing world is built up, the therapist may have to respect the child's need to keep out both abuse and the past' (Alvarez 1992: 162). Sometimes there is an added dimension to the holding environment; e.g. in family centre work, the child may also be supported indirectly through the holding environment provided for the parent.

As the mother meets her infant's physical and sensory needs, for warmth, comfort, sensual contact and food, through this first relationship, so we can make appropriate parallels in primary provision in child care. A child needs sensitive and responsive care, with attention to reliability and continuity in managing the events of daily life, from waking and dressing, to play and school or work, food and mealtimes, travel and other in-between times, bath and bedtimes. Provision of good sensual experiences restore a child's blunted senses. An important part of this work involves providing complete experiences with attention to the child's experience of their beginnings and endings.

Working at containment and surviving annihilation

The whole task is too great for a single worker, although her contribution may be significant; provision for an individual child must be managed by the staff team as a whole. Some workers intuitively provide some aspects of primary experience but always need to work within a framework of support from their workplace if they are to get very far. As we saw in Chapters 2 and 3, intuition is not enough and even a productive individual relationship needs to be firmly located within the context of an overall 'holding environment'. Unless they already work within a therapeutic community people are often unfamiliar with the idea of primary provision and can, for instance, be anxious about managing children's regressive behaviour.

Learning through experiential exercises in training can enable reflection on the powerful feelings of primary experience. Practical exercises and specific exercises in communication may help in working at an appropriate therapeutic response. Because of the power of some exercises a 'health warning' may allow members to decide to opt out or modify the exercise if it is too much too bear on that occasion. Of course one cannot always predict how one will be affected by an experience; hence the 'holding' offered by the structure of the whole programme becomes vital.

Some examples of exercises illustrate some aspects of working at providing containment for powerful feelings. One course began with everyone asked to work together to draw a house. As well as the direct engagement in the task of working together, strong feelings about 'a good home' began to be shared and similarities and also differences between people recognised. Winnicott's squiggle game, played in pairs (one person draws a squiggle which their partner has to turn into something; they talk and then change roles) often helps people start to become aware of one another's inner worlds and provides some insight into the meaning of 'containment'. There is a need to make the connection between the wider 'holding environment' and the containment offered by the inner mental space of the worker.

Another paired exercise has one person as a 'child' playing but with the instruction to ignore overtures from their 'adult' partner, an experience in the feelings of annihilation, shared also by the tutor on one occasion when one pair refused to do the exercise. The exercise led to workers' accounts of how they felt 'wiped out' by children: by contemptuous indifference, anger and violence, soiling and mess – shit in the bath, a black worker called 'shit colour'. One worker described how he had had increasing numbers of 'cannonballs' fired at him by a child who demanded he catch them (a real test of containment!) and then wanted them fired back; he described his urge to retaliate and the effort needed to resist this and think instead about the meaning of the communication. Since the worker's task is not to defend against the feelings of annihilation but to experience them and yet survive, with undiminished concern for the child, the emotional demands are enormous.

The child's game (Forehand and McMahon 1981), a paired exercise in which the 'child' plays and the 'adult' follows the play, providing a reflective commentary and avoiding asking questions, joining in only as the child directs, provides a useful training in reflective attention without intrusion. Workers can develop attentiveness to the child's feelings and ways of reflecting them back to the child. The child's game is widely used elsewhere to help parents become attentive to their child's play. However, those working with young parents often remind us that parents who have not experienced play themselves first need their own version of primary play experience if they are not to compete destructively in play with their children.

Providing sensory experience

Sensory work in training always feels important and raises strong feelings. People may be asked to bring something which holds some sensory significance (past or present) for them or may be offered materials to explore. The enormous significance of family and culture becomes apparent; unfamiliar materials are alienating. The connection is readily made with appropriate cultural provision in practice, drawing on sensory memories and meanings of food and cooking, music, clothes, play materials, or aspects of the wider physical environment.

Sensory work may also enable feelings about mess and messy play to be explored and understood. For example, a residential worker described an outing on which children were bought expensive ice-creams with flakes which they then proceeded to smear all round their faces and how his initial anger at the waste was modified by his understanding of the need for primary sensory experience. Another described children who got great satisfaction from getting into a wet muddy mess all over; these 'messy babies' could then go on to grow up a little. A family centre worker's account of infants playing with their food and of young children who sucked paintbrushes and played with dough clarified the role of sensory exploration in normal development. Age-appropriate ways of providing sensory play experiences need working at. An autistic young man's cry of 'oh fuck' as a big wave broke over him while playing by the sea indicated a rare and important encounter with the real world.

Looking after Tom's feet

Good primary sensory experiences help an abused child to 'forget', which goes alongside and sometimes precedes their need to 'remember'. Describing this process Alvarez says that 'in order to remember usefully, it is necessary . . . to put at least two thoughts and two feelings together . . . the child may need to remember from a safe and protected and hopeful perspective' (Alvarez 1992: 161). The following account shows a training group working at how to facilitate this process in relation to perhaps the most powerful and correspondingly the most difficult to manage sensory experience – touch (Ward 1990).

A residential worker described how Tom found bedtimes very difficult, often provoking staff and taking two or three hours before he would settle down. One bedtime he asked his worker to hold his feet while he went to sleep. Initially uneasy, he agreed, wrapping Tom's feet gently in a duvet and looking after them on his lap. Tom confided how his dad would grab him by the ankles and drag him off the foot of the bed; he remembered that the bed had been small and he had curled up but he was still grabbed (this second memory confirming Alvarez's notion of putting two things together). His worker realised that this had been the prelude to the severe abuse he knew the child had experienced. He felt that Tom was trying to find out whether things could be different, whether he could feel safe. Tom went on to ask his worker to tickle him, which he refused, feeling that this was inappropriate. He asked the group for their views.

In careful discussion the student group explored how Tom's feet could be held in a safe way. Someone suggested putting a shield round the bottom of the bed, which Tom's worker said he had in fact made later, using chairs and he was going to help the child build a proper shield around. They considered whether Tom's feet could be held on the worker's lap without it feeling abusive; most thought with care they could – the soft wrapping in a non-constrictive duvet was entirely right. There was agreement that tickling would be wrong and collusive, perhaps connected with sensual, sexual and exciting feelings in past abuse. The worker told how he had stayed by Tom's bed for a further hour while he peacefully went to sleep. Someone suggested a nightlight but was told that Tom preferred total dark so that there were no shadows. Another was thinking about finding a more symbolic form of holding and suggested a next step of connecting his feet with the rest of his body, perhaps through the song about 'the hip bone connected to the thigh bone'. So the group recognised that the worker was at the cusp – of good and bad feelings – and worked at developing a therapeutic response.

Hope and anxiety

Getting better involves change and risk. For both child and worker alike the stirring of hope that growth is possible – that there is a future – can produce anxiety and fear, acted out in behaviour and an awareness of all the countervailing forces in the outside world. Powerlessness is often a key theme in course discussions, for example where a family centre was reporting abuse that others did not want to hear. There is anger and despair at the failure of the outside world (including some owner-managers of residential homes) to share workers' understanding that getting better can make children's behaviour temporarily worse (Kegerreis 1995). For instance, a worker reported that an angry young person in residential care who used to talk 'repetitive drivel' was at last making sense, but his worsening behaviour led to other agencies seeing him as a schizophrenic breaking down rather than an unintegrated child getting better.

Further examples of the provision of primary experience based on course members' practice are found in Part 3.

SYMBOLISATION

Continuing our theme of a match between the pattern of training in therapeutic communication, the process of emotional development and the associated therapeutic response, the next part of the teaching and learning sequence concerns symbolisation. Symbolisation in Dockar-Drysdale's sequence follows the child's good primary experience and his or her realisation that this good thing has really happened. The child uses symbolisation as a way of storing the good experience inside. Early forms are 'symbolic equations' (Segal 1988), in which the symbol is also the experience, illustrated in the following example from a course member working in a therapeutic community:

> Robert had been found concealing in his bedroom six yoghurts which he had taken from the fridge. Although taking food without asking was not met with approval by the rest of the people living in the house, it was decided to make it possible for Robert to have something which he appeared to need, but in a way defined in terms of appropriate time and place. Robert received a pot of black cherry yoghurt as his special provision five times a week for over a year. He saved all his yoghurt pots and soon had a stack several feet high, a physical statement of what he had now stored up inside him in emotional as well as nutritional provision.

Robert had been helped not only to have but also to hold on to that crucial primary experience, by means of a permitted regression localised to a particular time and place, which met his infant need to be fed. Another child received a daily pink grapefruit, his worker planning the length of the individual provision knowing they would go out of season in nine months. Some kinds of play may also provide a symbolic primary experience; for example the child who played at being a lone eagle who nearly died – his worker put on lots of healing 'ointment'.

Symbolic communication, in which a child uses symbols to represent something *else*, is a developmentally later stage, although even some profoundly unintegrated children have pockets of integration and can make use of symbolisation earlier in the therapeutic process (M. Lucas 1992, 1993). As the child's integration increases and a sense of a separate self develops (whether the child has arrived at this point through a therapeutic primary experience or because the interruption to their good enough experience only occurred here) painful feelings about neglect and abuse, separation and loss, often surface. Play in Winnicott's (1971) 'transitional space' between child and parent/worker, another version of the holding environment, becomes a way of dealing with these feelings. The use in play of symbolisation which is not initially interpreted back to the child but worked with within the metaphor helps give the child enough distance to think about some painful experiences.

Developing skills in symbolic communication

There is much interest among child care workers in developing skills in play therapy, in which play becomes the medium for symbolic communication. The second part of the therapeutic communication course explores therapeutic play and play therapy and considers related forms of symbolic communication, sometimes more accept-able to adolescents, such as art and drama therapies, books and story-telling. Methods of learning include exercises in symbolic communication, some directly drawing on personal memories and feelings, some a practical application of techniques. These have proved productive, although sometimes painful, and have included some of Oaklander's (1978) drawing and painting exercises about feelings, 'make a world' sand play, story (or poem) making and telling.

The use of play and other materials – dough and plasticene, clay, toys, stones, shells and buttons – to represent the child and their family and care relationships, including the place of the worker, can offer useful insights, as can using the group to sculpt a situation. For example, to explore where a young person in care could best move on to, a group sculpted the child's family and social network, moving him and others around and reflecting on the feelings aroused in each move.

In another example, each member of one group used junk mate-rials to create a symbolic representation of their work situations where they were undertaking a project in managing change. This enabled more understanding of what it was they were dealing with and their own feelings about what was happening, but also enabled other members of the group to think about each project, with the resulting reflective discussion deepening understanding. For example, one senior worker's struggle to contain a difficult group of young people and his feeling of isolation and lack of support was reflected in his creation of a boat which could be split in two. The manager in his bed of prickly leaves plus a huge prow of management committees and consultants could be cast adrift, leaving himself and other workers on the bridge trying to haul in a netful of young people drowning in the sea!

Symbolisation offers a way of identifying and clarifying feelings, often in relation to issues of separation and loss, power and powerlessness, difference and identity. In the child these are related to experiences of abuse or deprivation, or to feelings about disabilty, race, gender and sexuality. There are personal versions of these feelings for workers. Training works at bringing these together to deepen understanding and make for thoughtful practice. At the end of the course one group, asked to find a symbolic way of representing their feelings about ending, realised that each of them had used a different medium. They expressed with pleasure their recognition of the differences between them and the confidence each now had in using a method that felt right for them.

CONCEPTUALISATION

> These other processes, realization and symbolization, provide the essential stepping stones to what, after all, conceptualization really is, an economic method of storing experience and at the same time establishing the means of communicating experience . . . . Conceptualization is only of value if it is retrospective – ideas must be the sequel to experience.
> (Dockar-Drysdale 1990: 99)

The final stage of conceptualisation of experience can be given expression in training through the exploration of more focused and sometimes more directive approaches, in which the child or young person is helped to think in a concrete way about past and present experiences and to consider the future. The child needs to be able to understand intellectually what has happened and to be able to put this into words. Since part of this means thinking about painful experience as well as good experience, it can only happen usefully after a child has had enough good primary experience to sustain him or her, then symbolisation of this good experience, followed by working through painful experience in symbolic ways. Conceptualisation can begin to develop as symbolic communication is increasingly interpreted to the child rather than remaining within the metaphor.

Play-based work (using C. Winnicott's (1968) notion of a 'third thing' to facilitate communication between child and worker) remains helpful to young children and some older ones too. A counselling approach may be more suitable for some adolescents. Many social workers have skills in 'direct work with children' but need understanding of the *process* of development which could guide their use. Consideration of work with the child and their family, while never unimportant, becomes crucial at this stage, whether or not the child is actually returning to live with family (including adoptive or foster family) or is a young person preparing for independent living or themself has become a parent. Family therapy offers some helpful techniques. Tools for conceptualisation include genograms, ecomaps, life story work, play materials, card and board games such as The Bridge 'Needs Game' or Barnados' 'All About Me' (and there is abundant literature, e.g. Redgrave (1987), Owen and Curtis (1988), Ryan (1993), Jewett (1994)). Using these tools in training to explore aspects of their own lives, perhaps past experiences of separation and loss, even experienced workers continue to be surprised at the power of these exercises.

Endings are often painful, leading to defences against experiencing the pain which then deny the reality of the loss. Workers are often aware of the awfulness of abrupt endings, both when a child arrives suddenly in a setting (an unfinished ending somewhere else) and when a child leaves, as when a placement is suddenly terminated. As the end of a course approaches personal feelings about endings re-emerge. Reflection about these feelings helps a worker develop therapeutic practice in managing endings.

CONCLUSION

In this chapter we have looked at ways in which workers can develop a growing understanding of both the unconscious and conscious processes underlying children's disturbance and use this understanding to develop their ability to provide a therapeutic response. We have considered a match between normal emotional development and the process of therapeutic work and the further match of this process – from primary experience, to symbolisation and conceptualisation, as the child struggles towards some degree of integration – in the structure of a training sequence on therapeutic communication. Developing skills demands a very personal engagement from the worker, which can be supported by the location of such a sequence within the holding environment of a whole training programme.

Many end their training aware and concerned that others will now see them as 'experts'. They wonder how to take back to the workplace what they have learned, which is often an awareness of what they do not know, 'modest qualities', as one put it, of humanity and equality; they have learned that each situation requires a desire and effort to understand. There are no short cuts to the informed reflection which enables workers to engage with the exciting and exacting task of helping children find themselves and live with what they find.

Chapter 9

Learning through philosophy

Paul Cain

The decision that philosophy should be an integral part of the MA in Therapeutic Child Care was, in some sense, intuitive. It was not clear, at the outset, quite how it might contribute to the students' training; it was even less clear in what way it might exemplify the matching principle. It may be felt, even, to have been a surprising decision. After all, a common view of philosophy is that it is the most abstract of subjects, at one remove at least from the realities of practical concerns. Warren (1992), for example, refers to the dominant idea that, for the most part, philosophy is a relatively specialised exercise that is quite properly removed from 'real life'.

The intuitive conviction of its importance had, however, some basis in current training programmes. Ethics, a branch of philosophy, was established as a component of many social work qualifying courses, both at Reading and elsewhere; and Donald Evans, at the University College of Swansea, had pioneered an MA in Philosophy and Health Care, the aim of which was to enable practitioners to work effectively on the ethical dilemmas arising in health care. This in turn reflected a move within philosophy away from highly specialised issues towards concern with practical problems.

We were not aware, however, of any moves to introduce therapeutic child care workers to philosophy that might provide us with guidance; there was not, to our knowledge, any body of specifically philosophical literature relating to this area of practice; and unlike, say, the Swansea MA, there was little time available – in a two-year, part-time degree, there was just one session a week in the first year. This lack of time was, and is, further compounded by the nature of therapeutic child care: the demands of their work on practitioners leave little time for reading and study.

Within these limitations, the course has developed in ways that appear to justify the decision that philosophy should be an integral part of the training programme; also, it can now be seen to exemplify, in various ways, the principle that there should be a match between training and practice. In what follows, I will indicate the conception of philosophy with which we have worked and describe, in terms of content and process, how this has worked out in practice. From this, the ways in which, and the extent to which, there is a match between training and practice will be displayed.

Philosophy as critical enquiry

Philosophy is seen on this programme as a process of critical enquiry, the aim of which is to develop students' ability and disposition to reflect on and analyse aspects of their practice. The term 'develop' indicates a respect for the likelihood that students already possess, in some measure, this 'ability' and 'disposition'. The aim indicates that what is envisaged is not just an intellectual skill ('ability') but also an orientation or cast of mind ('disposition'). Associated with this is the further aim of developing qualities intrinsic to such enquiry, for example the capacity and willingness to consider points of view different from one's own, to suspend judgement, to stay with complex issues where what is right is intrinsically contentious, and so on.

However, the designation 'critical enquiry' is, so far, bland and the reader may be wondering 'enquiry into what?'. Some indication is needed, therefore, of the particular concerns that specifically philosophical enquiry might have; in what follows I outline three of these: conceptual clarification, reflection on moral and ethical issues, and the identification, clarification and consideration of fundamental assumptions.

Clarifying concepts

One form of philosophical enquiry involves attempting to get clear about the meaning and range of application of particular concepts. This may involve considering the language through which they are expressed, what must be the case if they are to apply (their 'necessary' and 'sufficient' conditions) and their logical relationships with other associated concepts. What, for example, is it to 'know'? How is this distinct from 'believing'? Is 'intuition' a form of knowing? Again, how do you tell a 'therapeutic' relationship when you see one? Is it marked by a certain outcome, by one or more qualities, by the intention of the worker – or by some combination of these? How is it to be distinguished, conceptually, from an 'educational' relationship? Again, what is a morally 'right' action? Is it an action that promotes a good outcome (and if so, how is this identifiable?), or is it one that conforms to some moral rule or principle?

Thus, this form of enquiry involves standing back from everyday discourse. In this sense it is indeed at one remove from real life; however, in the view of the course team, it feeds back into the realities of practice, by giving the practitioner a better, because more critical, grasp of the concepts and language of practice.

Moral and ethical issues

Another form of enquiry relates to substantive, that is, not merely conceptual, questions of right and wrong. The starting-point might be general (for example, the question 'is paternalism ever justified?'), or particular (what are the rights and wrongs of a specific action or decision?). Such questions can't be settled by appeal to the facts alone, since the facts tell us what 'is' the case, whereas what is wanted is a view of what 'ought to be'. There is therefore no alternative to careful, reasoned argument. It might be felt that, although such enquiry is relevant to, and unavoidably part of, professional practice, there is nothing philosophical about it. However, the basic assumption that reasoned argument can be productive is clearly true to the philosophical tradition, as is the way in which such enquiry is carried out (seeking consistency, clarifying assumptions, checking out grounds for particular claims).

Underlying assumptions

A third form, or perhaps one should say area, of enquiry relates to the assumptions underpinning the kind of discussion referred to. One assumption is this: in claiming, say, that 'X is wrong' we appear to be saying something objective. Can we escape the charge that this is simply a statement of personal preference, lacking objectivity? Another, related, assumption might be that particular principles have universal validity; but how can the charge be met that these are merely relative to culture? In discussing such questions, the personal and professional values of the practitioner come into focus.

It may be useful to point up the fact these three kinds of enquiry are interrelated. For example, discussion of a case where the question is 'would it be right, in this situation, to break confidentiality?' raises, first, the conceptual question 'what is it to break confidentiality?' (telling anyone else?, telling someone who has no right or need to know?, telling someone who is not part of the team?, etc.); second, it requires careful reasoning, of the kind sketched out above; and third, it presupposes certain assumptions, two of which have been noted (that our judgements of value are not merely subjective or relativistic).

DOING PHILOSOPHY: THE PROCESS

If philosophy is thought of as a process of critical enquiry, then a purely didactic method of teaching is inappropriate. Just as learning to ride a bicycle entails riding it, so learning philosophy implies doing it, that is, engaging in critical enquiry. So learning philosophy implies questioning and reasoning and learning in a group implies discussing and debating and allowing your own claims and reasoning to be open to question.

Such a process presupposes certain values. Clearly, a basic value is rationality, in the assumption that understanding can develop through reasoned argument. The process is democratic, in that truth is not a function of eloquence or status or personality. And it implies, and therefore has the potential to foster, particular virtues, such as respect, seen in the requirement to give attention to others' claims, views and arguments.

This kind of group process is akin to what Gadamer has termed a 'conversation'. He describes this as follows:

> To conduct a conversation requires first of all that the partners to it do not talk at cross-purposes. Hence its necessary structure is that of question and answer . . . . To conduct a conversation means to allow oneself to be conducted by the object to which the partners in the conversation are directed. It requires that one does not try to out-argue the other person, but that one really considers the weight of the other's opinion. Hence it is the art of testing. But the art of testing is the art of questioning.
>
> (1981: 330–1)

The teacher's role, apart from setting up the process in the first place, is therefore primarily that of facilitator, managing the group, drawing in contributions, posing questions, playing (perhaps) devil's advocate, proposing clarifications as necessary, picking up threads and suggesting possible ways in which the discussion might develop.

So far, an outline impression of the process has been given. To fill out the picture, and to illustrate how it might be claimed to match aspects of practice, a more detailed description is needed.

Some aspects of the process

The powerlessness of the teacher

In certain respects, the teacher is undoubtedly powerful. He or she can determine the syllabus, decide what is to be discussed in any session, set essay titles and assess the student's work. In other respects, and especially if the enquiry is to be meaningful and a source of learning, there are strict limits to the teacher's power. Learning cannot be imposed, but arises, if at all, out of the interaction and exchange within the group, of which, of course the teacher is a part. What is to be learnt can't be imposed either, for 'content' must not only be relevant but felt to be relevant: if philosophy is conceived as enquiry, and if the students are to be wholeheartedly involved in this, the point of the enquiry must be evident. Hence, decisions regarding course content may have to be checked out with the group, explained to the group and indeed taken by the group. This relates both to what is discussed and also to how much time is devoted to individual topics. (In this respect, the teacher is also in the role of learner, learning from the group what counts for them.)

This perspective (the teacher as learner) calls into question an image of the link between philosophy and practice discussed by Jonsen (1991). Here the philosopher is pictured as floating aloft in a balloon, calling down guidance, in virtue of his panoramic perspective, on a cyclist (the practitioner). However, up in his balloon, the philosopher is cut off from the practical concerns and intentions of the cyclist: what, for example, for him may be a blind alley may be precisely where the cyclist wishes to explore. The lesson from this is that the philosopher, in the capacity of teacher, must listen to the concerns of, and learn about the complexities of practice from, the practitioner. Even if the teacher, in addition to having a background in philosophy, has practical experience of therapeutic child care, it will still be necessary to learn from students about their particular concerns, in order to draw these into a curriculum felt to be relevant.

However, even where the curriculum has felt significance, the course of the enquiry (the discussion) is not by any means entirely within the control of the teacher, for what may emerge in the course of discussion is not predictable: what emerges may depend in part on the particular memories, concerns and current experience of members of the group. It also depends on their willingness to participate – and this works both ways, some members being all too willing, others not engaged at all. Where the group is tired, or the day has been long, the threat may loom that nothing will emerge and the possibility of re-energising the group may be remote. The task of keeping the discussion directed, of treading the fine line between merely meandering and fruitfully digressing, may then give way to a more basic concern simply to keep things going.

Intuition

The teacher's principal task, in the conception of philosophy with which we work, is to promote fruitful discussion – 'fruitful' in that it is a source of learning. As has been hinted at above, this is not straightforward. The term 'enquiry' may suggest something linear and focused: the reality, however, at least where enquiry is undertaken in a group setting, is otherwise. Issues that arise for the teacher may include the following: should I allow X to continue talking?; should I try to draw Y into the discussion?; how, at this point, to lighten the atmosphere?; should I speak now, or allow space for others?; is now the time to introduce a different perspective?; would it be appropriate to mention my own experience here?; is this digression 'on task', although it is a digression?; would small groups for five minutes be productive?; should a summary be attempted, or would that risk misrepresenting the richness of what's been said?

In manoeuvring through these different possibilities, the teacher may have to draw on humour and imagination and has to be alert to the mood of the group and sensitive to the individual members. Since the kinds of question just noted typically require immediate decisions, responsive to context rather than thought through in advance, the practice of this sort of teaching may legitimately be termed 'intuitive'.

Respect

Respect is an intrinsic part of this process. This is not simply a moral point, although it is certainly at least that. It is intrinsic because truth is not a function of status: what is true (or apt, or well thought out, etc.) is independent of the speaker. Hence the process of philosophical enquiry presupposes careful consideration of what is said, however and by whomsoever it is said, and therefore also respect for any person's right to speak. 'Respect for persons' is, in particular, thus also intrinsic to the process. Respect should thus be thought of as a pre-condition of the process I am attempting to describe and, further, as promoting an atmosphere and ethos conducive to discussion.

Uncertainty and anxiety

In various ways, the process being described is characterised by uncertainty and anxiety. The extent to which the overall aim (noted above) may be achieved is uncertain – there is no way of measuring whether, or how much, a student's 'ability and disposition to reflect on and analyse aspects of practice' has been promoted; what will emerge in the course of any particular discussion is uncertain, as is, to an extent, the directedness of the discussion; questions of value, for example ethical dilemmas, do not typically throw up 'right' answers, so certainty here is elusive (although a student may arrive at answers which, for him or her, are persuasive). In particular, reflection on concepts, the meaning of which has hitherto been clear and taken for granted, is likely to promote a sense of uncertainty, a sense of the familiar world of language and concepts coming apart. (For example, in everyday practice the concept of 'breaking confidentiality' goes unquestioned, it is part of the common coinage of discourse; and yet how it should be understood is not clear.)

This 'uncertain' process it seems reasonable to suppose can be a source of anxiety. The worry which may be felt in any discussion group (do I contribute?, can I make my voice be heard?, will what I say come out as sensible?, will it be acknowledged or ignored?) may in philosophy be heightened by the focus of the enquiry, which, as I have indicated in outlining some of the concerns of philosophy, may call in question what has hitherto been felt as commonplace and obvious (as with conceptual analysis), or explore value issues where the possibility of a 'right' answer is remote (as with ethical dilemmas); and in which the only authority is well-reasoned argument.

Holding

Above I said that the task of the teacher is to promote fruitful discussion. It is now clear that there is the associated task of providing a context in which uncertainty and any anxiety can be held. One particular strategy we have used is providing a framework, in the form of agendas, for each session. (In order to be open to creative possibilities, it is made clear to the group that this framework can be subverted.) The framework includes detailed summaries of the previous week's discussion and picks up questions that, it seems, still need to be addressed. It also proposes a specific focus for the session. This serves the important function of keeping discussion directed and, by bridging the gap from one week to the next, particularly through the detailed summaries, illustrates that students' comments are not lost, but carried forward and valued as a basis for continuing discussion. More fundamentally, fruitful discussion, in which uncertainty is contained, requires a non-threatening context in which students are valued (this follows from the requirement of respect, discussed above). How such valuing may be expressed and experienced clearly has many modes. It is evident that, although the teacher can provide a significant model of valuing, by the ways in which he or she handles particular contributions or hesitations to contribute, providing a context in which uncertainty and anxiety can be held cannot merely be an individual achievement: the process of enquiry must, ultimately, be held by the ethos of the group as a whole.

DOING PHILOSOPHY: THE CONTENT

The content–process distinction is in some ways unsatisfactory since, as I have argued, 'process' is significantly part of the 'content'. 'Content' is used here narrowly, to designate some of the areas that have been explored in this particular course.

Some areas of study

Knowing and believing   The assumption here is that there is a practically important distinction between knowing and believing, knowledge being more secure and therefore a firmer base for authoritative practice than belief. (Like all assumptions, it is, of course, open to question!) If you know that p is true, as distinct from, say, merely thinking you know, then logically p is true. And even though what you say you know turns out to be true, you are open to the charge of having made a guess, or of having just been lucky, if you can't give good grounds for your claim. Hence the question, what are good enough grounds for knowledge? Discussing this and related questions gives students the opportunity to reflect on claims they may make, or come across, in practice. What kind of knowledge-based expertise is available? Can they know how others feel? On what basis? Is transference, say, a source of knowledge? Is intuition a form of knowing? And so on. (The area has been developed by some in a written assignment, addressing the question, 'do therapeutic child care workers know what they're doing?'.)

Respect for privacy   The assumption here is that, in general, respect for privacy is an important principle, but that it may in practice be in tension with the demands of communal living and in particular with the concern to work therapeutically. For example, a student reported a case where a psychiatrist wanted her to gain access to an anorexic girl's diary; other examples have been cases where drug use is suspected and the question arises whether or not to respect a young person's space. So discussion in this area gives scope to explore the dilemmas that may arise from this tension. (Some students have thought about the issue further in writing a critical appraisal of the claim 'Respect for privacy and the concern for therapy are mutually exclusive'.)

Confidentiality   In professional work generally, the principle of confidentiality is an important value. Is it also of fundamental importance in therapeutic child care? After all, confidentiality has to do with maintaining the boundary around shared secrets – but how does this differ from anti-therapeutic collusion? If it is an important principle, what is its scope, i.e. what should be kept confidential and from whom? In other words, if observing the principle of confidentiality implies 'protecting the boundary around shared secrets', what determines where this boundary is situated – the children's wishes, or rights?; others' need or right to know? Exploring this and the previous area involves the question of relations between worker and child or young person. Other dimensions of this are outlined below.

The professional relationship How should the relationship between worker and child or young person be conceived? As involving authority and power? As a friendship, or a partnership? Is it, properly, paternalistic? What, in any case, do these terms denote? And what qualities should characterise the relationship? It has been claimed (Bayles 1989) that the professional–client relationship should be marked by such virtues as loyalty, discretion, honesty and candour. Supposing this to be the case, dilemmas arise. A student mentioned, for example, the case of a child whose father was his grandfather: should the child be told? This would be 'candid' – but would it be harmful? In another case, a boy was required to leave because he was judged to be a leader in sexual abuse: other children wanted, perhaps needed, to know why he'd left. To tell them would be a breach of confidentiality and so not 'discreet' – but would it be beneficial? In a third, a worker was offered promotion which meant he would have to break off a fruitful therapeutic relationship with a boy: should this be seen as a lack of loyalty and, if so, would it be justifiable?

For reasons of lack of space, other areas of study can only be noted. Among these have been: conflict and compromise; coercion and control; personal identity; personal and professional boundaries; education and indoctrination. It is perhaps evident that all of these, and those areas that have been outlined in some detail, give rise to ethical debate: hence one underlying theme, impinging throughout the course, has been what criteria are there for doing the (morally) right thing?

PHILOSOPHY, TRAINING AND THE MATCHING PRINCIPLE

I noted at the start that, when the Reading MA was set up, 'it was not clear . . . how (philosophy) might contribute to the students' training; it was even less clear in what way it might exemplify the matching principle'. My description of the course illustrates, I hope, how both these issues have been clarified.

The open-ended, exploratory and in many respects intuitive approach, within a conception of philosophy as enquiry, in which, to be fruitful, students must feel valued and in which intrinsic uncertainty and (it may be) anxiety is held within a framework, key elements of which are the relationship between student and teacher and the ethos of the group as a whole – these features of the process surely provide parallels with the students' own practice; and the selection of areas of 'content' ensures that the enquiry is grounded in issues from practice, in particular in those issues felt to be significant by the student group.

How this may contribute to the students' training cannot, of course, be measured: as I noted above, 'the extent to which the overall aim . . . may be achieved is uncertain'. This is so, because the aim is not to convey bits of information but to develop an 'ability and disposition to reflect on and analyse aspects of their practice'. However, as we learn from students' own evaluations, at least for some the discussions are fruitful.

Three of these evaluations indicate that a positive assessment of the contribution of philosophy is justified. One student wrote, 'I've gained valuable experience in being able to argue cases with more confidence at work, which these sessions have helped me to do'; another student wrote that she appreciated the 'opportunities for shared exploration of issues only vaguely touched on (or avoided through anxiety) in work settings'; a third valued 'particularly those discussions where there were examples from the group's own experience or "everyday life" that I could relate to' and commented that 'thinking in a philosophical way was a new experience, which I struggled with, but felt it was valuable and I have myself been examining and questioning more closely, which has been a good thing'.

Chapter 10

Learning in the Experiential Group

Teresa Howard

The deepest links between training and practice need to be made at an 'inner world' level by each student both as an individual and as a group member and the main place in which such learning is encouraged on the MA programme is the Experiential Group. Here course members meet together each week without a formal agenda, but focusing on 'the connections and overlap between the personal and the professional, with an emphasis on personal development rather than academic learning', as they are told when applying for the course. My own role as convener of this group is to help them to make and understand these connections and to learn from personal experience (often at quite an intimate level) about many of the themes touched upon elsewhere in this book. In this chapter I will attempt to explain what I do and why I do it and how this work connects with the overall task of the course.

CONTEXT OF THE GROUP

The Experiential Group meets for an hour and a quarter every week in a specially designated room which remains constant for the whole of the course. It is called an Experiential Group because the principal mode of learning involved is learning from experience and this is achieved by continually working together at understanding what happens between all of us in the group as we talk together, making connections between past and present, between family and workplace and between inner and outer worlds. It is intense and demanding for everyone, but it offers course members the possibility of exceptionally valuable learning about self, work and each other. Chairs are arranged in a circle and the room made as comfortable as possible. The size of the group has varied over the years from seven up to the present fifteen, which has often made it a larger group for experiential work than is commonly used in some other approaches. Indeed, some would argue that work of this sort is best carried out in small groups of about six to eight people. Our view, however, has been that the larger size of this group gives it strength and added validity within the matching principle. The model of group work that I use is based on the concept of the median group, which has been described by de Maré (1991) and which itself is a development of group-analysis as applied to a setting of ten to thirty people. It is neither a small group nor a large group but somewhere between the two, and the size therefore matches well with the work groups or organisational settings of many of the participants, as well as with their extended family and social networks.

The distinctive principle upon which group-analytic theory is based is Foulkes' concept of the 'group matrix'. This is defined as 'the hypothetical web of communication and relationship that determines the meaning and significance of all events in the group and upon which all verbal and non-verbal communications exist' (Foulkes 1964: 292). Everything that happens in the group is related to the matrix. In contrast to other forms of group work, group-analysis focuses on the individual and the whole group *at the same time*. It as 'a form of psychotherapy by the group, of the group, including its conductor' (Foulkes 1975: 3). As the individual does not exist as an entity without a group, each person is seen as a nodal point in this web of communication and both individual and group are seen as having mutual influence on each other. The 'matrix' carries with it all the unconscious assumptions brought into the group by the individual members, assumptions which are usually described as transference from past important family relationships. In the median group, the matrix is seen as additionally including the transposition of large areas of experience from outside, in the world beyond the immediate family and it is through these associations that aspects of culture and society are included within the 'group mind' (de Maré 1991: 81).

The use of larger groups such as these in the training context is still seen as unorthodox in some quarters, although in fields such as training for group analysis (Lyndon 1997) and for therapeutic community practice (van der Linden 1988) it is well accepted. Indeed, Skynner (1974) and others have written persuasively of the value of training experiences in even larger groups, with seventy or more members. The rationale for the median group approach in particular is that it adds extra dimensions to the potential work of the group, for example by widening the context of the students' learning. In addition to their families of origin, the students metaphorically 'bring with them' (to think about in the group) the families of the young people with whom they work, as well as their work organisations. As all these levels of context are brought and worked with, there is constant movement between the inner world of the individual, the outer world of the course and society beyond. It is argued (de Maré 1991) that the advantage of this way of working is that it enables all these levels of context to be attended to and allows new relationships between them to be discovered. Gradually each student learns about these connections and finds their own authoritative voice in the group: a voice which is based on a deeper understanding of their own needs and how they came to be the people they are now. The outcome we are hoping for is that the students will in turn become better able to negotiate between the desperate personal needs of their young clients and the often *im*personal and sometimes even dehumanised, social structures of their working environment.

This approach can also enable learning to be derived from students' much earlier experiences on the *receiving* end of organisations such as schools, hospitals and care settings. Although many of us spend a large proportion of our formative lives in school and later in adulthood in various kinds of institutional settings which can at times be disturbing and unsatisfactory, therapeutic endeavours do not always directly evoke these experiences in the present. Even if such experiences do surface, they may sometimes be experienced (in smaller groups) as too overwhelming to attend to, whereas we have found that the 'larger than life' response of the larger group can help such feelings to be evoked, witnessed and ultimately contained.

For example, one student found herself getting in touch with the grief of an experience which she thought had been long forgotten. Many years ago she had been diagnosed as needing constant hospital care a few weeks after the birth of her baby. She was told that she could only receive treatment on the condition that she agreed to leave her baby at home. Initially, she experienced the group as if it was that same hospital ward, full of 'unsympathetic doctors'. As the dialogue evolved within the group, however, she was able to re-live and re-work her experience and another woman who had been the daughter in a similar situation was able to reassure her that it might still be possible to repair a relationship which appeared to have been damaged irretrievably.

Likewise, many of our students retain deeply painful and half-buried memories of experiences at school – often memories of being humiliated and bullied by teachers, which effectively disabled them from achieving their educational potential. It is only later and with enormous courage and determination (and the mutual support of the group), that they have eventually been able to face the lasting impact of such experiences and finally to overcome them during this period of professional training. Thus people who may have been brutally and inappropriately 'written off' even in primary school ultimately emerge from this programme with MA degrees!

Within the median group approach, therefore, students' associations to aspects of experience in the outside world beyond the group or family are not interpreted as defensive manoeuvres to avoid feeling in the here and now, as might sometimes happen in small group or individual therapy. In the median group approach *all* associations are used to help people find meaning for those traumatic experiences that may have occurred out in the world where there was perhaps no family protection. In contrast to insight, de Maré refers to this meaning-making process as acquiring 'outsight'.

The problem is that for many people these traumas are in themselves often very 'silencing'. Consequently the group can also become a silencing place, despite the fact that it can at last provide a place to speak about the original experience. The whole experience along with its silencing context gets transposed into the new larger group setting. For example, there have been several students who have had refugee experiences, or other versions of displacement and disorientation such as moving from one social class to another. Some of these individuals have been virtually silent at the beginning, except to voice doubts about whether they will complete the course. It is almost as though they are initially unable to trust the 'host culture' of the course and the university to accept their pain and difference.

Despite the positive potential of the median group approach, this size of group does undoubtedly evoke distinctive anxieties which need attending to and feeling unable to speak and the consequent fear of becoming mindless or paralysed with terror is the main one of these hazards. In our experience on this programme, such fears also tend to resonate powerfully with many people's experience of the larger groups in which they work. The problem for many profes-

sionals lies in making sense of these complex organisations and of
the often chaotic situations which arise in their practice. Most
organisations are at least median sized. However, as most people
find any group larger than about eight people potentially difficult,
they tend to avoid meeting in a larger group and it has been argued
that whole organisations, both in industry (Mumby, 1975) and in
care settings (Ward 1993b), are often structured to avoid dealing
with this anxiety. The anxiety does not disappear just because it is
defended against, however, and many people bring it with them
straight into the training context.

There is therefore an enormous potential benefit for these
students in learning more about these fears, by re-experiencing them
within the safe limits of a facilitated group in which they are not
judged and from which they cannot be sacked or ostracised for
daring to speak as they might fear in the workplace. The aim is that
learning to talk in an experiential median group setting will enable
students to cope with the anxiety of meeting and working in a
larger group and that as a result they will discover that the complex
and chaotic situations can be transformed, both in the present and
in future expectation. This experience is crucial because it opens the
way to the belief that, at times of crisis in their work, it may be both
necessary and possible to work with *all* those involved rather than
just to react to their own and others' anxiety and to act immediately
(and often mindlessly), alone.

HOW THE WORK OF THE GROUP DEVELOPS

A median group within a university setting may be seen, and is
often probably, experienced – as a 'counter-cultural' experience (de
Maré 1991: 108). Since there is no agenda apart from learning to
talk to each other and since the 'leader' does not lecture or chair as
in a tutorial or seminar, it is sometimes met with initial confusion.
Although, as we have seen, students are told in advance that the
Experiential Group is not a teaching or discussion group and that
the emphasis is on personal development rather than academic
learning, this information is not always understood and remembered. Only one or two students over the six years has had any prior
experience of being in any form of therapy or therapeutic group.
For most, it is a completely new experience; a bit like walking on
the moon.

Early sessions are often spent in tentative discovery and sometimes aggressive enquiry. Stories about other unsatisfactory group experiences abound. Suspicion is expressed about me and my role: 'What is this for?'; 'Why should anyone want to give us anything?'. For many it is the first time that they have ever sat in a circle without a formal agenda and at this stage the group can feel frightening for many reasons. Initially, there is often a dawning awareness that the unusual experience of having space just for themselves is so scary that they hardly know how to deal with it. Indeed, there is often a self-fulfilling prophesy that it will be uncomfortable and sometimes this prediction is based on past negative experiences in groups. Some students then behave in a way which may in fact contribute to a persecutory atmosphere, either by not speaking at all or by being very judgemental about other people's contributions.

Just speaking about whatever comes to mind seems so simple and yet it can be so terrifying, as the invitation just to talk freely about whatever comes to mind is sometimes paradoxically experienced as inhibiting. There is often an unspoken assumption that sitting in a circle means 'spilling your guts' and it takes time to realise that even ordinary enquiry about each other's wellbeing is difficult enough in the context of the larger group. When anxiety is high, particularly at the beginning of the life of a group, the convener should be seen to contain that anxiety as a way of making it feel safe enough for thoughts and feelings to be voiced (Skinner 1975). Behaving in this manner also models a way of being in the group that is facilitative. It is natural for people to feel afraid at the beginning, so it is important for the convener to acknowledge how it feels and to remind the group that this is a process that takes time to learn. Gradually students realise that through speaking they will feel less anxious and more acknowledged. The convener's first task is therefore to promote this realisation by encouraging members of the group to voice their thoughts. Initially many people tend to assume that, in a larger group, they must make some form of cleverly crafted statement and they tend to dismiss their everyday reactions to each other as though these were unimportant. In fact, the everyday is the key, since it is through people giving an airing in the group to quite simple expressions of feeling and thought that it can become a place of human encounter and a friendly and supportive atmosphere can begin to emerge.

As previous larger group experiences such as school, church and the sports team, get transposed into this setting, they can be brought to light and understood. In the early days of one cohort, there was an ongoing theme of illness being reported as a reason for absence – until each student remembered having difficulties starting school as small children. It appeared that the anxieties experienced when starting school had been re-enacted on the course with equivalent illnesses and could now be worked through. Previous educational experiences of having been punished for getting it wrong tend to live on in the present and for this reason the teaching staff of the programme and I are sometimes seen as the stern teachers who prevent people from speaking. For example, it sometimes happens early in a course that some students fail their first practice essay. This is often received as a shock and sometimes their response is to view the tutors as the enemy. Despite the constructive written feedback which tutors aim to provide, students sometimes assume that there will be no help until they get the essay right all by themselves, as if to say, 'I have to work everything out on my own. I will tell the group when I have found the solution rather than ask the group for help'. For these students the learning which can come from exploring this experience can prove pivotal. By using the group to reflect on their failure and their response to it in the light of previous experiences, both at home and at school, of receiving or more usually not receiving support and encouragement when in difficulty, a remarkable turnaround can be achieved.

THE ROLE OF THE GROUP CONVENER

In the group I take a role which might best be described as 'not . . . an interpreter, catalyst, or observer, but . . . a full participant in an evolving process' (Blackwell 1994: 44). I enter into the dialogue not as someone who assumes that she has an accurate view of reality but as someone whose main role is to attend. Essentially I am not a blank screen but a human being using my emotional responses to inform my understanding of what is going on. In the initial stages my main task is to help the group feel as safe as possible, until people can gradually begin to undertake more of this task for themselves, although there will still always be times when new material or events force me back into my original position. There are times when I am confused and do not know what is happening or what to do. Such times are always difficult, but by paying extra attention to apparent minutiae such as the feelings in my body and the fleeting thoughts that cross my mind, I have learnt that everything is in some way connected. Just as a plant that pops up as a lone flower in the ground may be joined with its unseen roots below to many others, I watch for patterns of behaviour and thought that recur to uncover buried connections. There are other times when what I do feels so in tune that I find myself registering an intense feeling of 'just rightness' about the moment, although I may still be unable (until much later) to explain the precise connections at a rational level – because I have been working with the unconscious.

I always pay close attention to the way people position them-selves in relation to each other in the group and I will sometimes comment directly on the way people who appear to have things in common, such as coming from similar workplaces or backgrounds, choose to sit together. Drawing attention in this way to feelings of closeness or distance that may be reflected in the obvious sub-groupings in the room is often seen as provocative, because most students are used to pretending first that such differences do not exist and second that their need for support is non-existent. The denial of difference, leading to a defensive 'pseudo-mutuality' to avoid pain, is paradoxically extremely destructive and can lead to unbearable and unmentionable pain (Wynne 1984: 298). For example, sometimes white students will relate to black students in a 'colour blind' mode, as if to say, 'You are the same as me. I don't notice your blackness'. When these obvious differences do start to be acknowledged and talked about, it can become an extremely painful process, as white students begin to feel the shame of their racist heritage and black students have to deal yet again with a dominant culture blotting out their heritage as though it did not exist.

Throughout this work, my role is one of being there and staying with a 'trial-error-and-adjustment' style of learning, metaphorically holding an arm to steady the new-found balance as previously buried pain is released and past experiences remembered and used to inform practice. Students themselves gradually learn to 'stay with' the process as it is, without invoking the need to punish either themselves or each other (or me!). Many find themselves, upon completion of the course, ready for promotion or for taking quite new directions in their career. They also learn that, with a bit of internalised support, life can change dramatically. One woman discovered that as a result of talking in the group about the impos-sibility of being allowed the time to go on one of the course residentials, she had metaphorically 'taken the whole group with her' and leapt over the hierarchy straight to her head of personnel, to see if it could be arranged. The head of personnel asked her where she had found the courage to ask her for help. She replied, 'The group on the course'. The response was, 'Well, if they can do that for you, you should go on the residential and I will arrange the cover for you'.

I work in the belief that every individual has an inner template in their mind, constructed from their unique experiences and giving rise to a set of unconscious assumptions about how the world works and how life should be lived. Because of the group's size and the mode of working, these 'worldview' assumptions tend to get projected onto the group. Consequently, there is a possibility of reworking them, often for the first time in the student's life and often to develop a greater freedom of choice. As the group evolves, it generates its own culture, which in turn gets internalised, restructuring the cultural assumptions linked to the template of each person's inner world. Instead of totally identifying with the unconscious assumptions which they have brought with them from their family and culture of origin, they can re-examine these assumptions from the perspective of the new multi-possibility creative culture of the group. When assumptions start bumping up against each other the group can become quite chaotic and disorienting, a bit like being in a rough sea. My role here in what can at times feel like a very upsetting process, is to be constantly aware of this 'meta-structure' and to interpret it by providing landmarks along the way. Having found their bearings, students may begin to see that the world holds new possibilities.

Beyond the usual skills needed by a group analyst, there are additional aspects of my role that arise from my working within a median group perspective. In this mode, the main task for group members is developing the ability first to think at all in the face of the enormous emotional forces that inevitably arise and second, through the dialogue that emerges, to find real personal meaning for their experience. As this larger setting is social, in contrast to the familial experience of the small group, it demands skills akin to those needed for the workplace (and thus the 'matching' with practice can be very close indeed). One example of these skills is the ability to express issues of high emotional concern in a way that will evoke helpful and constructive responses rather than damning and destructive ones: through experience and feedback this skill can be learned in the group and can then be developed into a most valuable asset in organisational life.

All of these experiences in the larger setting bring with them the difficulty of 'voicing the thought'. Mindful that in the work setting things inevitably need challenging not only with clients but with colleagues, the group gets used as a testing ground for the work environment. For example, if a group member starts to miss sessions, this tends to be viewed with increasing agitation, as it certainly would in the workplace – a residential child care setting, for instance. While those present wrestle with feelings of anger or resentment, group members also have an understanding of the real dilemmas of making the journey to the university, as well as a fear that their missing colleagues may not return. At the same time, there tends to be a growing awareness that the reasons given for absence may reflect deeper dilemmas about commitment, whether to the group itself, to other relationships, or to life in general. Reticence in challenging each other about such issues may also reflect people's fear of being challenged themselves. Occasionally, particularly in the early stages of the course, such fears stifle any free expression and students do leave with important things left unsaid. It is therefore critical to the healthy development of the group that I encourage people to find a way to give voice to their feelings, so that both the group as a whole and individuals can continue to develop.

HOW PEOPLE USE THE GROUP EXPERIENCE

As the ability to speak in the group becomes more fluent, stories often begin to emerge about people's childhood memories and their survival strategies – perhaps of making themselves scarce to avoid abuse, or of not getting too involved with others, in the hope of avoiding the pain either of being abandoned or of being left alive following the death of a parent. As time goes by it becomes more possible for people to acknowledge the pain of others' absence, whether in the present or in the past, until courage is eventually gained to talk directly in the present. In one group we discovered that every 'not-being-present' told a story that was inextricably wound into the reason these students were in this kind of work. Many had been faced with the death of, or separation from, a significant person, in their childhood, events which had drastically changed the pattern of their lives. These previously unacknowledged losses had often led to a way of being (and styles of working) which involved high emotional content but which avoided deeper emotional commitment. On joining this course they are immediately confronted with an expectation that they do commit themselves, not only to the work but to each other as people. Thus, an internal struggle can sometimes ensue, which may sometimes get played out through physical absence or weeks of silence in the group, but which will eventually be talked through, understood and learned from.

Reflecting on the difficulty that many of these students have had about 'engaging' led me to the realisation that some people go into this work as if to try to become the parent or carer they never had. Unconsciously recognising that their own childhood would have benefited from a relationship with somebody like their current selves, they work with children in this very special way, as one way of partly trying to repair this deficit. Many students discover long forgotten stories about themselves. Others risk the telling of too-painful-to-tell-stories for the first time, sometimes expecting to be told how stupid they had been originally, as if they had only 'got what they deserved'. They are, then, sometimes amazed to be told that nobody deserved the abusive or neglectful treatment they received. In the process, some students come to realise that – without being consciously aware of it – they have spent most of their professional lives working with young people whose experiences are almost identical to their own. Such self-learning often comes as a complete revelation, which leads on to a re-evaluation of both their personal lives and working practices. Likewise, many students arrive on the course with the assumption that being professional means always hiding your feelings and it is a revelation and a relief to them to discover that their gut response is an important indicator they can use to inform their practice. The group experience offers students the opportunity to gain conscious learning about many of these unconscious processes and through this learning to become more integrated as people and less 'driven' or defensive in their work.

CONCLUSION: WHY HAVE AN EXPERIENTIAL GROUP?

People sometimes ask, 'Why have an Experiential Group on an academic course? What is it for and what could students possibly learn from sitting around "navel gazing" for at least an hour every week?'. Our response might be, 'How can we expect people to learn about such intensely demanding and personal work unless they experience and reflect upon their learning in this very personal way?'. Our hope is that, by being in the group, students will experience a 'holding environment' for themselves (sometimes for the first time) and begin to realise what it is they are expecting from their clients. So, instead of attempting to explain to students how they should be with their clients we give them the opportunity of experiencing how it feels to 'be there' for others and to have others 'be there' for them. Thus, after realising how difficult it was for him to express his own feelings in the group, one student exclaimed in amazement, 'I expect those kids, who don't know me from Adam, to trust me completely by telling me about their most intimate and painful experiences as soon as they come through the door.'

Chapter 11

The function of the staff meeting

*Adrian Ward, Linnet McMahon, Paul Cain
and Teresa Howard*

In Part 2 we have each been giving our individual accounts of our work and of the conclusions which we draw from this work, as if we each functioned purely as individuals, popping up one after another to hold forth and then disappear. In reality, our work is far more closely linked than this impression implies and intentionally so: our aim is to 'match' a mode of practice in which teamwork is paramount and close communication essential. In order to do so, we need to work continually at our collective understanding of our task and at our respective contributions to this task. We therefore meet together at the end of each Thursday to review and plan our work and this meeting has evolved into playing a central function in the overall work of the programme. In this chapter we want to describe and analyse the functions of this meeting, especially in terms of its parallel with meetings in therapeutic practice, and to demonstrate how this aspect of 'matching' between practice and training can work.

THE STAFF MEETING IN EDUCATIONAL PROGRAMMES AND IN THERAPEUTIC PRACTICE

Most of the literature on vocational and professional education tends to underestimate or even completely ignore the importance of the staff meeting. It is often relegated to a largely invisible administrative function, perhaps because in some settings meetings do not happen, are infrequent or irregular, or are seen as purely administrative rather than as part of the educational endeavour. It may also be because for some teams meetings are difficult and awkward and therefore hard to write about constructively, while for others meetings are positive, hard work and are creative. But they are so much part of the system that people may not have recognised the value of studying the contribution of the meeting to the work of the team. Perhaps most training teams also like to think that the relative strengths and weaknesses of their teamwork are similarly invisible to their students: this is odd, because if we think of our own experiences as consumers of training programmes, most of us probably have a fairly shrewd idea about the teamwork of the staff running the programme and as to whether or not, for example, the staff appeared to communicate well with each other. Informal feedback from our MA students tends to confirm the impression that they are well aware of the dynamics of the staff team for better or for worse – and even when they are not consciously aware, we would argue that they are likely to be indirectly or unconsciously affected by unresolved staff tensions, just as children are affected by the marital tensions in an unhappy partnership even if they never actually witness their parents arguing.

Initially, as a group of staff running the Therapeutic Child Care programme we had similarly given relatively little focused thought to the role of our own staff meeting. The meeting seemed to work, we were in broad agreement on its style and timing and we just got on with it. This situation continued for a few years, until we were visited by two senior academic staff from a Russian university, who sat through a day of course work, including the Opening and Closing Meetings between staff and students. Our visitors looked intrigued but increasingly puzzled as the work of the day progressed, and informal discussion with them between sessions suggested that they had concerns about one or two students in particular and about the atmosphere in one of the seminars. They also had a general question about what they saw as the informal atmosphere between staff and students. (They were used to a system in which much more emphasis was placed on formal instruction.) On talking afterwards they said that the day's work finally made sense to them when they observed the staff meeting at the end of the day and saw how the staff team brought to each other's attention every one of the matters of concern which the visitors themselves had picked up during the day and much more besides. They also recognised how the team developed on from these observations, making links with themes which had arisen in previous weeks as well as with external events and with the internal dynamics of the university. The view of our visitors was that it was the work of this meeting which held together the work of the whole programme and it was at this point that we recognised as a team the full value of the meetings. In other words, until outsiders held up a mirror to us as a team we too had underestimated the function which the meeting played. We tell this story here not in order to make any grand claims about our own meetings, but to emphasise the fact that, although we were as a team conscious of valuing them, we had not paid sufficient attention to their function. Indeed there is much more that we have to learn as a team about how to work more effectively. More will be said about this later in the chapter.

The staff meeting in therapeutic practice

Whereas the staff meeting is fairly absent from the educational literature, it does receive considerable attention in the study of therapeutic work in group care settings and especially within the therapeutic community approach. We saw in Chapter 3 how the task of providing a 'holding environment' for young people depends largely on the staff themselves feeling supported and contained in a holding environment of their own, which will mainly be provided through a system for staff meetings, consultancy and supervision. This is not a simple matter, however and it has been widely recognised that a complicated pattern of relationships will develop between the staff as a team and the young people as a group. Hinshelwood (1987) has shown how the staff team may be collectively experienced as a 'transference object' by the patients in an adult therapeutic community and how the team will need to focus on understanding this dynamic and continually to renegotiate it with the community as a whole. We also know from the literature on family therapy that clinical teams will often 'reflect' dysfunctional aspects of the families whom they are treating – i.e. they will become similarly dysfunctional themselves (Berkowitz and Leff 1984). The lesson of this experience is that teams need to meet regularly to work at understanding their own responses to the unconscious as well as to the conscious challenges in their work and it is this focus which we have in mind in the ensuing discussion.

THE FUNCTION OF THE MEETING FOR THE TASK OF THE COURSE

Every type of meeting must first fulfil its practical function, which in the case of this meeting is to review and evaluate our day's work together, making sure that as a staff team we all know what has happened throughout the day, by piecing together what might otherwise remain disparate and unconnected. Thus we might discover that we need to exchange information about an individual student who has, for example, appeared to be distressed or withdrawn in the morning session but then might have been absent from an afternoon discussion and rejoined the group for the Experiential Group meeting. Some such information will have been conveyed through the day by the group as a whole, but very often key pieces of information are held by only one or two individuals. What we do with this information is another matter: usually it is enough for something just to be known for us all to hold it in mind for the following week's work. Thus the meeting informs our practice in a broad sense, although not always in an immediate sense. Sometimes, on the other hand, there are clearly 'things to do' with the information once we have worked at understanding its meaning – we may need to plan to contact the student in question or to watch out for a particular pattern or behaviour in the following week's work.

At times, the content of these discussions will focus upon individuals. However, at others it focuses on groups and sub-groups, or on atmospheres and resistances which have emerged. Sometimes the students will have felt to us more like a collection of individuals with pressing individual needs than a group and it is only by assembling their individual images at the end of the day that we can start to regain an image of the group as a whole. By contrast with, for example, some forms of group psychotherapy training, we do not attempt to place any injunction against course members communicating with each other outside the group. Indeed, this often seems something actively to foster rather than to discourage, with the necessary proviso that all such 'external' communications should be brought back into the internal life of the group so that all business is available for work in the public arena. Therefore, we acknowledge that students will also meet informally and telephone each other to do their own piecing together. In this way the total environment becomes the 'therapeutic milieu', in keeping with the therapeutic community model.

There is also a certain amount of practical business to be done in the staff meeting, such as the sharing of basic information, clarifying of communication between staff members and making decisions about how certain issues should be handled. On the other hand, we are clear that this meeting must not become a merely administrative one – there are other occasions when we can confer on administrative decisions and other 'business' matters, whereas there is no other occasion in the week when we can assemble to work together on our collective task with the students.

If the task of the course is to produce practitioners with an advanced level of understanding of their work, we can serve that task by working hard at our own understanding. In addition to the 'matching' element to which we have referred, there is also an element of direct modelling here for the students. We make it explicit to them that we meet and that we are trying to work in the way that we hope *they* will be able to work in their own establishments. It is important for them to know this. Of course there will be times when individuals or groups are angry with the staff team and probably believe that the staff meeting must be a peculiarly ineffective gathering, because it feels to them that they are not being well treated, or properly 'held'. The most that can be said about this is that we usually seem to know when this is happening, even if there may not be much that we can realistically do to resolve their anger. At other times the students, individually and/or collectively, may feel that the staff group is hostile to them, or indifferent to their troubles and struggles, or threatened by their complaints, etc. In reality, such feelings may well arise in staff members, but we have a responsibility to be aware of them and of where they may have come – whether from our personal counter-transferences or from feelings which we may have 'picked up' from the group and its dynamics.

Handling crisis

The true value of meetings emerges when a crisis develops and people need to consult together to make important decisions. For example, occasionally students may find themselves undergoing a personal crisis in relation to the impingement of their professional work upon their personal lives, or vice versa. At times like this extreme emotion or even behaviour may emerge either within the group (e.g. a verbal attack on a fellow student or a sudden collapse into depression), or at the margins of the group (e.g. a depressed student who disappeared from the day's work without explanation but leaving her 'baggage' in the group both literally and metaphorically). Here we may need to be able to communicate urgently with each other and with the students in order to decide upon a constructive response. Such events have been rare, but when they do happen the demands upon the whole group can be great because these events tend to find echoes with similar issues which everyone faces in some way or another and the success or otherwise of the team's holding of the group and the group's holding of itself (like a therapeutic community), will depend upon a well-practised ability to really communicate about our anxieties and our possible responses.

THE FUNCTION OF THE MEETING FOR THE STAFF THEMSELVES

It is important to recognise that a meeting such as this plays an important function for us as staff in helping us to maintain our morale and our ability to stay on task. The nature of this particular course is that a great deal of work is concentrated into one day: many things may happen for each of us as individual staff members, which are important for all of us to get to know about. The meeting thus plays an important function in helping us as a staff team to feel in sufficiently close communication with each other. We all recognise that we need each other's care and concern, because as in any sustained piece of groupwork or therapeutic practice, an individual staff member may 'collect' strong feelings of anger, depression, or guilt. Such feelings may really belong with an individual course member or with the group as a whole, but may have been projected onto the staff member.

Course members inevitably bring with them unresolved 'emotional baggage' from their personal lives and at times they may unconsciously project onto the staff team expectations and feelings arising from past experiences; the staff team thus becomes a 'transference object' (Hinshelwood 1987: 101) just as it may do in a therapeutic community. As a team therefore we need to work hard at recognising and responding to such projections if we are not to become enmeshed in them and caught up in, for instance, either retaliation or patronising sympathy when a course member expresses anger or frustration. Course members also often bring stories of very powerful experiences from the work setting, which can engender equally powerful counter-transference responses within the staff. These need to be understood and worked through in the staff team so that the students' experiences can be sufficiently held and understood by each member of staff. This process not only gives much needed support and insight to staff but also to students. It also limits the amount of unresolved distress that we all take home at the end of the day.

On a training programme such as this, there will inevitably be difficult and even painful times for the staff and occasionally we may feel that we have had a terrible day. We have tried to find solace in David Wallbridge's view that, when each student takes their turn to present a case or scenario within the 'seminar format', 'there is no such thing as a bad presentation' (Danbury and Wallbridge 1989). The argument is that, *whatever* content is presented and however the process of the presentation is managed, it all provides data upon which the group can work in order to extract the maximum learning. Likewise it is possible to argue that there is no such thing as a bad day's work on a training programme – although it can certainly feel as if there is! There is only a day on which things do not seem to work well and when people cannot understand why this is so or resolve it to everyone's satisfaction and are left feeling bad either about themselves or about each other (or even about the content, it might be added: Tom Main argued that people experience theory itself as an emotional 'object' about which they will have feelings). The task with which the group is left is one of working on the difficulty which has arisen and deriving maximum knowledge from it – and if necessary returning to it on the next day's work, just as one might have to do in practice. This is a particularly hard approach to sustain – when things appear to have gone wrong, it is much easier to get angry, attach blame or express frustration than it is to stay with the process and try to work at *why* things have happened rather than just repeatedly going over *what* has happened. The staff team is the heart of the enterprise and it is here that such difficulties will ultimately need to be faced and resolved.

At a more personal level, an unexpected spin-off from the meetings is that we have been able to learn from each other about each of our areas of expertise, both in terms of process and content. We represent different disciplines: our various specialisms include individual play therapy, residential child care, philosophy and group analysis. We are two men and two women, which brings a strength and balance to the team, although it also means that there is ample opportunity for us to be unconsciously 'split' by course members into 'good' and 'bad' mothers and fathers. On the other hand, we are all white, which means that we are missing a black perspective –

a most significant gap in our team, although it means that we have to 'kill our own snakes' in relation to confronting our own issues on anti-racist practice. We bring together a very wide range of personal, familial and cultural experiences, which is important in helping us to identify with the range of circumstances which we encounter in our work with the students. We bring this range of perspectives to bear upon our task, which can sometimes be challenging and sometimes very productive. There is thus a strong element of interprofessional work but also inter*personal* work in our collaborative effort, which might be described as a mixture of perspectives on a common concern, this being our shared task of training.

An additional function of the meeting was revealed when one of us, Linnet McMahon, joined the team. She now reflects on this experience:

> As a one-to-one play therapist joining an established training team, aware of the significance of the group but lacking the tools to understand the group process, I found that the staff meeting provided an essential induction. Initially confused, puzzled and sometimes alarmed or overwhelmed by unexpected personal resonances during the day's work, I gradually found the staff meeting helped me 'understand' the course. A particular issue for me was working at the place of my individual relationship as a tutor with a course member. For example, being more used to confidentiality in a one-to-one relationship I did not realise that holding on to some information risked setting up a collusive pairing which might inhibit the group task. On understanding this I initially questioned the value of any individual work and felt de-skilled. Over time I found that there was a place for it, for example in providing support to an anxious group member in order to help them go on to make use of the group. The staff meeting was the place where this was worked out.

Difficulties

In emphasizing the positive functions of this meeting we are not seeking to create the picture of a 'dream team' totally fulfilling its task. Far from it: like any other team we have times of difference and disaffection, of confusion, tension and hurt. Like any other team we sometimes have to work hard to resolve these difficulties and there have been times when it has not felt possible to resolve fully a difference. If we did not meet to work at them, the difficulties would presumably become stronger and would be enacted in conflicting messages given to students, which would in turn create further difficulties for us as a staff team. Our aim in writing this paper, then, is not to claim that we have achieved a perfect state (which would of course be false), but to suggest what we are learning *from* working together *about* working together.

CONCLUSION

We have tied our debate on the function of the staff meeting very specifically to our particular circumstances, whereas it may be objected that other teams in other circumstances may need very different patterns and types of meetings. We would agree: our argument is simply that, in applying the concept of the 'matching principle', we need to aim to 'match' not only those parts of a programme which involve direct contact with the students, but also the parts which just involve the staff. As we have seen earlier, the match does not have to be exact or total, but a good enough match can certainly help to establish a 'positive feedback loop' so that both staff and students feel validated in their work.

Chapter 12

On the experience of keeping a reflective journal while training

Deborah Best

The endeavour of engaging in therapeutic work with children, or in training for this work, is less a matter of reaching right answers than of learning to recognise helpful questions and finding ways to explore them. Reflective writing is one way of guiding and charting the process of exploration and of reaching insights to inform learning and practice. In this chapter I draw upon the experience of keeping a reflective journal over the four years since I became a part-time student on the Diploma/MA course in Therapeutic Child Care at Reading University. This course offers a variety of ways of nurturing the capacity for reflection as an essential skill in therapeutic work.

Keeping the journal became a way of managing and learning from the overlap between the three key areas of my life: as a teacher in a secondary special school unit for pupils with emotional and behavioural difficulties; as a student on an advanced professional training course; and as an individual with a personal world of self, family and others. Integrating those spheres through writing and reflecting on the learning process has led me to understand the creative potential of writing as a keenly appropriate tool for training in therapeutic child care. Its fitness for purpose can be explained in terms of some of the key concepts that contribute to the body of psychodynamic theory upon which therapeutic work is based and I use these concepts as points of reference in developing this chapter. First, I offer some thoughts on the principles and process of journal writing.

PURPOSE, FORM AND CONTENT OF THE JOURNAL

The place and purpose of the journal as coursework

To assist them in the tasks of monitoring their learning and of
developing their ability to reflect, students are asked to keep a
journal as a way of 'making connections, unravelling difficulties
and arriving at new understandings'. This means regular and
committed writing to record thoughts and feelings about every
aspect of work and development, leading to a reflective piece to
review progress and identify emerging themes. Although this reflective piece is submitted as coursework it is not subject to academic
assessment.

Students are referred to David Walker's chapter on 'Writing and
Reflection' (1985) in which he surveys the uses of writing for
learning in a variety of areas and quotes Rainer's review of thinkers
who have 'pointed out how the diary permits the writer to tap valuable inner resources' and who have 'recognised a need . . . to reflect
calmly upon knowledge that comes from within' (1980: 21). In this
book, I apply such insights to the role of reflective writing in
training for therapeutic practice.

As a reflective exercise the journal is more than a record of
events, feelings and insights; it is essentially a work-book, a dynamic
working document intended for review, rethinking, re-vision, most
effective when open to question and open to change. It becomes a
tool which is effectively an extension of the writer as learner. My
own journal reminds me: 'Rather than setting aside these parts of
my life I am freed to become aware of them and work with them as
living material; if this produces more questions than answers it
extends my chances of learning'.

An approach to keeping a journal: getting on with it, keeping at it

The approach which I have used is guided by Walker's full introduction to the methods of keeping a journal. In practical terms I have
found that a loose-leaf binder is a useful medium because it allows
pages to be inserted to record secondary reflections after review. It
also allows for the inclusion of photographs, drawings and
diagrams, letters (both unsent and received), poetry, or any other
material that seems fitting. The papers are best kept in a place
which is private yet readily accessible for work.

The business of writing I began by following the advice simply to 'get on with it': without worrying too much about details of expression I used it as a release, a place to dump the detritus of the working day (whether as brief comments or accounts of incidents), in a paradoxical process of letting go whilst holding on to feelings in a place where I might later recognise and acknowledge them. I used it to record interactions and develop insights that arose from reading and study day discussions, as well as to think about the connections between work, study and personal life.

Initially I found the suggestion of setting regular times for writing and review somewhat irksome, according to how drained or energised I might find myself at the end of a working or study day. Several adaptive solutions appeared: I could write more briefly; once in the journal habit I could reflect as if committing thoughts to paper and store them in memory until I could manage to write; and I could reflect on the significance of gaps and lapses between entries. Yet the better I come to understand the process of reflective writing, the more importance I attach to allowing regular time for writing and review when it can be managed, for reliability must foster a more complete learning experience.

The journal as a tool for developing learning

Although the course offers students specific opportunities to discuss thoughts and issues arising from journal writing, the process is essentially personal. Knowing that there is no right or wrong way to keep a journal and that it is a very personal document, gave me confidence which allowed it to flow and to grow. The opportunity for further review and for writing a reflective paper encouraged me to continue and to use reflective enquiry later as an aid to research.

Setting side-by-side those spheres of my life which in my mind were liable to get muddled gave me a way both of thinking about them separately and of being able to see how they related to and reflected on one another. I gained a clearer idea of who I was and what I was bringing to my work.

I have found it helpful to try to understand this process in terms of the stages of development towards integration: experience, realisation, symbolisation and conceptualisation (Dockar-Drysdale 1990). Reflecting on experience is a way of realising and confirming it, then expression through symbols and images (including words and metaphors) stimulates thinking as a means of understanding and retaining its significance (meaning and value).

How the journal helps the student-practitioner

Keeping this observation in mind, I will consider the concept of reflective writing as an instrument for holding and containment and as a medium for managing transitional experience. The way in which it thereby helps me to understand immediate events and their meanings (both overt and unconscious) may be inferred from the illustrative sequence of journal entries and review comments. These lead into an exploration of the journal's more experimental role in developing deeper reflections, conceived in terms of psychotherapeutic space, potential space and attunement.

There have been elements of all of these in my experience of writing a training journal and in many respects they are inseparable. In a field where the worker herself is so much part of the process of the work, the practical and the perceptual are woven into one texture, the search for deeper meaning serves evident purpose. If, after Jung, 'I try to see the line which leads through my life into the world and out of the world again' both may be fed by the current of meaning flowing through the connections thus made.

HOLDING AND HOLDING IN MIND

Initially, the process of writing seemed to satisfy a need both for catharsis and for confirmation. Writing can have a 'holding' function just as the simple maternal act of physical holding can relieve a baby's anxiety or distress: if the emotion is received, making the baby feel real, her existence confirmed (Winnicott 1960a). I found that to commit to paper even the most awful incidents, or feelings of anger, frustration or annihilation, I had first to bring them to mind and then to express them. Thought and emotion tumbled out together, caught up in the tide of recall; yet when they reached the calmer waters of record, I could look again and begin to see them separately. By putting them 'on hold' in a place where I could return to deal with them later, I had taken the first step towards reflection and away from the risk of reactive response that comes of putting feelings out of mind.

There can be a powerful need to forget painful episodes and uncomfortable thoughts, particularly those that we are afraid or ashamed to speak about. My early experience of the Experiential Group sometimes left me feeling quite lonely and vulnerable, which was difficult to confess even to myself. Putting this in writing showed that the problem was alive in my own mind and gave a starting-point for the reflection that would enable me to talk about it.

Another way of dealing with feelings too painful to contemplate is to repel the risk of hurt by recounting outward events unreflectively to a listener (willing or not), showering anxiety into words liable to form a barrier which shields the real source of anxiety. As I began to entrust to the journal material that otherwise I might have repressed or expelled in an unfocused way, I was able to notice such strategies as an unhelpful defence against anxiety; and because the distress was being held, I had a better chance of calm reflection which, in itself, alleviated my feelings of helplessness.

So the journal performed a holding role for me directly, but it also extended my capacity to hold in mind the young people with whom I work. It became a place where I could set down some of my anxieties about work and keep safe my ability to think.

REVIEW AND CONTAINMENT

Describing the journal as a container is to draw on the notion of a mother acting as a container for her baby's feelings; first by receiving and holding his communications and then by helping him to manage them by returning them in bearable form. Gradually the baby learns to contain and manage his own feelings (Bion 1962).

Putting words on paper fixes a version of reality, but at the same time makes it available for reconsideration. Sometimes the very process of writing may prompt subtle shifts in perspective; then re-reading – receiving back that material – allows the thoughts and feelings to return in modified form, making it more possible to reconsider them.

Reviewing alerted me to underlying issues, for example if the presentation betrayed a discrepancy between content and expression. Where the telling of powerful content was flat, without emotion, was this to make powerful feelings more tolerable by denying what needed to be noticed and acted upon? On the other hand, how could I explain strong feelings expressed about seemingly trivial events? Some unreflective pieces carried a sense of 'stuckness' that suggested the need for deeper work.

When an intense account left me feeling 'bombarded and confused, unable to think and wanting to take cover', I had to ask myself whether I could tolerate those feelings and how I could begin to think about them. Review helped me to identify feelings and freed me to think more creatively.

Reviewing some sections left me unsure whether I had seen a picture of the outside world or a reflection from within, until I learnt to select passages like frames from a film-strip and concentrate on them. Reviewing selectively encouraged more focused writing, which in turn yielded more accessible material and more opportunity for reflection. Just as a container is designed to limit or prevent spillage, the journal can channel material so that it is neither lost in the unconscious nor liable to flood areas of life where it does not belong. I have found, for example, that mapping critical incidents or unidentified feelings provides a means of tracking them so that I can recognise a pattern or recurrence and think of possible responses to use next time around.

Serving as a container for material from the different areas of my life, the journal helped me to manage the transitions between them and it is to its function as a transitional tool that I turn now.

JOURNAL AS TRANSITIONAL TOOL

I see the journal as having the ego-strengthening function of a transitional object (Winnicott 1971), for the writing arose from and served as a connection to a training which was teaching me to understand my other worlds in a new way. It became instrumental in supporting transitions between all the areas of life and learning and in making connections meaningful.

The most difficult transition for me was from the challenge and stimulation of the study day back to the world of work. I needed to internalise that experience and those relationships, to grasp new concepts, to hold on to the meaning of the day's work, to reflect on my personal learning. Because the ethos of my workplace favoured a behaviour management approach to our task, I did not expect a shared comprehension of the concepts let alone the personal understandings that had come my way, nor easily to convey them to my colleagues. So, to store that experience I would make notes to sustain me in that other working world.

Worries about work could be admitted in the safe place of the writing as a step to being aired on the study day. Likewise, insights from study could help me to understand some of my own family dynamics and I could be aware of the risks of muddling them with my work.

As a transitional tool the journal allows the writer to reflect upon and learn to integrate meanings attached to separate spheres, in a way which may be best understood by referring to my own journal.

JOURNAL ENTRIES AND REVIEW COMMENTS

I have selected a sequence of entries concerning the complex question of the role of the worker and setting which offer containment; this is a matter for constant appraisal and for awareness of issues such as transference.

20 October: To hold and contain is like performing a parental role, but FN (educational psychologist) was right that time: 'You are not that child's mother'. Sharply accurate. She named something she saw going on and let me leave it – what a relief (for me). Where did that put the real mother/child relationship, after all? Glad not to have to be 'good' mother replacing 'bad' mother if that's what I was trying to do; not OK to try to do (be) that, when all you (I) can be at home is a mixed mother. Try a different role.

13 November: Talking in 'tutor' about new pupil to join – some negatives from Josie who sees her in the street. Matthew: 'You see we're a family, me and Josie, like I'm her brother, we get on well like brother and sister, we don't want no newcomers coming and causing trouble. It was better here when we first started'. But its only weeks and they talk as if it were the dawn of time. Good to have group identity, even some family feel, but have to treat the distinctions carefully.

17 November: Matt angry about letter-writing exercise, not wanting teaching. Is this transference i.e. am I like mother who tries to direct, not wanted aged fifteen? Keep firm, patient.

18 November: Trudy has joined the group. She has only one arm; she says she needs lipsalve. Mum left seven weeks ago. Would rather ask Mum than Dad, who she lives with now. How to help her – not myself, too obvious, but too easy if that's what I jump to doing. Not my feelings, how to help her to manage hers.

23 November: Feeling burdened, low. Matt not working so well: 'I should be out doing a job, not in school. It'd be OK if you paid me'. Hard to find energy to prepare work/offer holding. And what about my own children and what do they think/feel about our pupils and me working with them?

25 November: Minibus: Matt, as if going on family holiday: 'When will we get there Mum?'. Also earlier, having made coffee for Trudy, 'it's like being at home, in a family, sitting in the kitchen with a cup of coffee'. Review comments: How to challenge, explore, clarify 'Mum' and family remarks, beside expectations of school, staff, themselves. How to respond: How far am I responsible? Winnicott writing on transference, negative transference: important to stay in role, so pupils not confused, so especially those whose mothers have been uncertain do not try to manipulate and repeat behaviour patterns that have got child into place s/he is in now; need to be more mature, respect child enough to take beyond that stage.

1 December: Matt: 'You can't tell me what to do, you're not my Mum'. Review comment: Still the 'Mum' theme and still confusion, take care not to make more than there is already . . . . Does he not do what his Mum tells him either?! Why do I ask myself this question? Still needs thinking through his/my transference and how to handle it.

These (abridged) entries enabled me to identify and work through some of the concerns about transference and appropriate holding relationships for effective work, they also allowed me to question their place *vis-à-vis* family and other personal claims. This process was helped when I found links with reading material and with other learning from training, a context where, as I recorded later, other student practitioners faced similar uncomfortable questions.

While allowing thoughtful working through of practice issues the reflective process also helps to nourish the necessary personal resources by preserving a psychotherapeutic space, as I describe next.

JOURNAL AS PSYCHOTHERAPEUTIC SPACE

In writing about psychoanalytic work with children, Monica Lanyado (1991) focuses on the therapeutic space created within the worker's mind and the means of creating and protecting that space. In her own practice she prepares for sessions by note-writing and thinking as a way of coping with the painful emotionality they may evoke; likewise she places great value on personal, detailed and honest note-taking about an encounter and 'the way I feel and felt about it' (Lanyado 1991: 33). In the pursuit of increasing one's ability to withstand emotional onslaught she commends this exercise particularly where the worker does not have training analysis or is unable to share her work with colleagues. In identifying with this position, as a student and a teacher I found that using the committed space of the journal outside myself, as it were, helped me to find a corresponding space within my own mind.

Learning through experience how this might happen, reflecting on it and thinking about it, gave me a better understanding of the concept of containment and of how a baby develops the capacity to contain and integrate his own good and bad feelings. It showed how I too could 'make . . . chaotic experiences into elements of emotional experience that can be thought about' (Copley and Forryan 1987: 254).

In writing of the journal as psychotherapeutic space, with physical dimensions (time, place) to suggest its therapeutic function, I distinguish it from the aspect in which (for me) it also represents potential space (Winnicott 1971).

REFLECTIVE WRITING AS POTENTIAL SPACE

The potential space of the journal resides in its creative possibilities for the interplay of experience, memory, imagination and thought. It comes of a sort of relaxed attentiveness which gives rise to symbols and truthful images released within the freedom of the focused form.

I notice that while my symbols (images and metaphors) represent cultural phenomena of the external world, most spring from the play area of my own mind. Often they reflect the play area of my outward life, as when I used for myself the metaphor of a: 'solo circus performer, compulsively spinning the plates of my three busy worlds, making constant small adjustments to keep them in motion. I maintain equilibrium not only by concentrating on the spinning but by preserving the spaces in between. Writing is a way of doing this'.

The metaphor arises from my memory of a workshop for refugee children and presented itself as a symbol which helped me to conceptualise my own experience of managing difficult but satisfying work.

In providing a non-directive play experience for a child, a carer's task is to use the potential space it offers to help the child discover who he really is: his true self rather than his false or hidden self (Winnicott 1960b). Likewise the journal is a safe place to play creatively, away from the serious business of work and academic encounter.

An extract from the written review of my first year's writing shows how I used that space for exploration of the process of growing up and for playing with the possibilities that I was eventually able to think about:

> I find an underlying theme of the reflective work between my various selves: mother, wife, teacher, student, friend and other struggling adult selves and these in a reflective process with my own child-self. The experiential work offered a chance for me to find a way to grow up and this theme of growing up is woven through my writing.
>
> The wish 'to grow up' must, I suppose, be universal, implying independence, integration, selfhood. This is paradoxical when set alongside the yearning to return to the original state of 'integration' within the womb. My own wish in searching for maturity was for some kind of magic transformation, shedding the childish aspects of my 'self'. I needed to do this to meet the needs of the children I work with. What has changed, I think, is my realisation that my child-self has to be acknowledged and nurtured as an integral part of what I am now. It is easier to accept my own needs, before I can hope to take responsibility for the needs of others, or to distinguish mine from theirs.

This change in perspective was the outcome of a variety of experiences and realisations in my training which the play area of the journal allowed space to explore and confirm. It proved directly valuable in understanding my relationship to my work. In this case conceptualisation came through discursive writing, but could equally arise from developing a sort of dialogue.

REFLECTION AS ATTUNEMENT

Engaging reflectively with the journal in recording and review can develop into a dialogue which I see as a version of attunement (Stern 1985). This nurtures emotional understanding which in turn can facilitate thinking.

The journal extracts I use to illustrate how this has worked for me will also show the effectiveness of the form in drawing together into a meaningful pattern the threads which connect work, study and personal life.

Thinking about the concept of attunement and patterns of response in infancy stimulated a process of creative exploration which evoked a childhood memory of (literal) attunement:

> Aged about seven or eight, I am standing on a bright summer's morning, brimming with the very sunlight that makes a broad path to our feet. Beside and behind me are some thirty other children, all alert to our music teacher as she purses her lips, 'Hmm'. We respond, reaching back to her with our hummed note. She smiles encouragement, then rises on tip-toe to conduct us in the sing-song of a mounting scale, leading our learning. My face follows hers, as I feel my whole being intensely involved in that moment of singing which is still within me now.

When that interlude found its way into my journal it showed me how reflection can bring past experience, including body memory, effectively into play. It allowed a surprise to happen, as imagination subsumed reason and put me in touch with an element of self that is both 'me' and 'not-me'. It gave insight which touched the core of my work, as questions flowed from it: 'Am I in any sense a singing teacher? What concentrated attentiveness can I give? How do I respond? Can I hear the music behind the words? Is there a tune at all, or do I hear silence? And if so, what does it say?'.

The academic exercise of understanding (conceptualising) attunement was achieved by reflecting on earlier experience, helping me to integrate it into my understanding of my current practice. I later recognised this process at work in sharing a two-part play – a dialogue – with a boy who had previously been unwilling to read aloud: his expressive response to using the play suggested that it worked as a version of attunement, developing both cognitive and affective skills. Recorded reflection showed good experience realised, symbolised and stored as an integrated part of the self to make it.

WRITING, REFLECTING AND PSYCHIC TRUTH

With practice I found that reflective writing gave confidence, feeding both emotional and expressive fluency and engendered a kind of meditative searching for psychic truth.

It became a means of nurturing personal growth necessary to healthy professional development. As I wrote, 'If we reflect deeply and face what we find, what we discover will be true for us. We need to be able to do this to grow and to learn'. Truth-seeking is not the least important use of journal writing, for it offers the chance for safe, honest exploration, for the student/worker herself as much as for those she works with. As Bion (1965) says, 'healthy mental growth depends on truth as the living organism depends on food'.

CONCLUSION

It might be raised as an objection to reflective writing that it could encourage self-deception and excessive introspection. The risk exists, but if recognised it can remind the writer to keep questioning within and outside the written form. I realise too that this form may not seem immediately helpful to every student in the way it happened to help me and that it takes time. By inclination and experience I found the form familiar, although it took a particular set of circumstances to begin: the need to cope with learning to learn through experience; a working environment unable to offer containment or reflective practice; the time to give to it. These personal considerations aside I believe there are clear educational grounds for making reflective writing an integral part of training for professional practice.

In my introduction I presented reflective writing as a process of integration and I have demonstrated variously the way writing can foster emotional growth and learning. I have also shown how a reflective journal can fulfil the need for holding and containment and act as a transitional tool; how it can provide a psychotherapeutic space, encompass a potential space and facilitate attunement. Although elucidated separately, these functions are interactive and interdependent. To have presented my understandings in this way is more than a convenient form of description, however; it is an explanation of the effectiveness and validation of the use of reflective writing in training. For this is an exercise which enables the student to rehearse and experience, to realise and understand, the concepts which are at the heart of psychoanalytically-based therapeutic work. By establishing and developing its use in training, students can set out from a sound base upon that continuing course of enquiry which is professional practice.

Part 3

Returning to practice
Applying the learning

INTRODUCTION TO PART 3

In arguing that training should match practice, we have summarised in Part 1 our understanding of the theory and practice of therapeutic child care and shown in Part 2 how we have tailored our training efforts to fit this model and what happens when using such an approach. What matters most, however, is what happens when people apply their learning to their professional practice. In Part 3, therefore, we offer some evidence about outcomes, showing how those who have experienced this approach have been able to apply it in their own work settings.

Some of these examples come from people working in the specialised setting of a therapeutic community, while the others show applications in less specialised settings – family centres, children's homes and an educational withdrawal unit. We have been especially keen to encourage cross-fertilisation between these more specialised and less specialised settings, in the belief that each has something to learn from the other.

Our hope is also that these chapters will help to bring the theoretical material to life by showing how these understandings have contributed to the help provided to real children in real circumstances.

Chapter 13

Alice and her blanket: a case study

Ros Wheeler

'Alice' was born to a very young married couple who had a volatile relationship; her early life experiences were characterised by living in a chaotic household where alcohol and drug abuse were rife and from which her father was often absent. From the time of Alice's birth her mother became increasingly pre-occupied with her own childhood experiences of severe physical, sexual and emotional abuse, later acknowledging, 'I cried when she was born because I knew what happened to little girls'. There was a highly ambivalent relationship between mother and daughter.

The care of Alice engendered concern amongst involved professionals almost from the very beginning. Stress in the household continued to increase with the arrival of a second child 'Carly' a couple of years later, which led to the permanent departure of their father (who was later to die in a car accident) and the further disintegration of their mother's capacity to cope. Concern grew during a series of non-accidental injuries to both young children who subsequently were placed on the Child Protection register, their mother very reluctantly accepting social work help. Alice's mother soon remarried but her partner proved to be a very violent man and over the next few years Alice, Carly and their mother had recourse to women's refuges or friends' houses to escape his violence. These incidents alternated with periods of intense reconciliation. Medical and school professionals continued to express concern about Alice who was reported as being frozen and 'watchful'.

After a particularly violent incident where Alice (aged about five) witnessed and tried to stop her stepfather seriously wounding her mother with a knife, her mother had a complete breakdown and was hospitalised, their stepfather arrested and Alice and Carly taken into care. Alice was extremely disruptive and defiant towards the foster parents with whom they were placed and began to display self-harming behaviour. Alice began to disclose sexual abuse by a number of male 'babysitters'. After three failed foster placements social workers concluded that Alice was in need of specialist help. She was placed in a therapeutic community (the Caldecott Community) in a small group where she could have intensive therapeutic treatment.

On arrival at the unit Alice presented as a very well-defended child. It became apparent that she had experienced some 'good enough' care, although the inconsistent and unreliable environment in which she had lived had probably meant that these experiences were incomplete. Dockar-Drysdale (1990: 115) comments, 'Babies can be deprived . . . by the failure of the mother to become preoccupied with the baby or by the actual absence of the mother'. Alice had experienced a degree of both these forms of deprivation, but nevertheless she seemed to have experienced sufficient 'good enough' care to facilitate the formation of a fragile 'false self' – a way of surviving emotionally by complying excessively with whatever was expected of her, but at the cost of feeling 'real'. As Winnicott describes,

the false self sets up as real and it is this that observers tend to think is the real person. In living relationships . . . and friendships however the false self begins to fail. In situations in which what is expected is a whole person the false self has some essential lacking . . . the true self is hidden.

(Winnicott 1965a: 142–3)

It was not only that Alice was so fragilely integrated but that her sense of self had not yet 'gained stability' (Dockar-Drysdale 1990: 37); she presented a complex picture to work with. The false self 'shell' concealed but scarcely contained her rage and profound disappointment in grown ups. The origins of this false self lay in her experience of a world in which children existed to gratify the needs of grown-ups, in the case of her mother for nurturance and self-esteem and in the case of male carers for the gratification of sexual impulses and desires.

An important part of this false self was Alice's apparently deep sense of futility which was reflected in her envy, paradoxical in nature. Alice frequently envied other children's possessions or experiences and would try to make them hers by coercion or stealing, yet if her attempts were to succeed she felt futile; it was as if other people's things were only desirable because they were someone else's.

ALICE'S BLANKET

Evolution

From the very beginning Alice seemed to know what was right for her. Dockar-Drysdale comments on working with emotionally deprived boys: 'The boy concerned will actually tell us what he needs, which we then provide . . . the provision of symbolic experience leads him back to the beginning of life' (1990: 31). In Alice's case her 'blanket' is symbolic. It has been significant since Alice found an old piece of soft brushed cotton sheeting and her keyworker Liz spent hours appliqueing a small brown velvet rabbit, green velvet grass and blue velvet sky on to it (despite the fact that Liz was not remotely competent at sewing). The end result was a real 'labour of love' and perhaps this was the most tangible quality to it. Alice was delighted with her blanket and would carry it with her everywhere (except to school).

After two years of being cared for by Liz during which her blanket was of enormous importance Liz left the unit and I became Alice's keyworker. Alice was distraught at the loss of Liz and went through a long period of mourning and depression. During this period of grief Alice's treatment of her blanket was significant; once she left it on the beach after a group outing to the seaside and one of the grown ups as well as a number of the young people returned to the beach to retrieve the blanket (thankfully it had not been swept out to sea). Dockar-Drysdale comments: 'The transitional object or group of objects may speak on behalf of their owners, in a way which brings the therapist to realization concerning the children' (1990: 35). If this is the case then the abandonment of the blanket on the beach may 'speak' of Alice's feelings of having been abandoned by Liz.

Second, Alice began to mutilate and destroy her blanket, making well-worn holes worse. I repeatedly sewed them up because it seemed to me that Alice was very angry at Liz for leaving and was attempting to destroy her good experience of being cared for by Liz which her blanket symbolised; it felt important that her destructiveness was contained. Dockar-Drysdale makes it clear that such objects must 'Never . . . be washed (the smell is always important) but the slightest hole needs to be mended at once by the therapist' (1990: 39). The attacks on the blanket eventually subsided and it remained intact. Alice rarely asked for her blanket to be washed and it was often grubby as it was dragged all over the floor inside and outside. At times Alice would like me to spray it with the perfume I wear and the blanket increasingly developed a life of its own, although Alice scarcely spoke of this.

The blanket continued to be important for Alice and she soon acquired a piece of pink and white cotton jersey from Jane the team manager who was not only a close friend of Liz's but also someone who meant a lot to Alice. I offered to sew this on to the existing blanket and Alice agreed that she would like this; thus the blanket became approximately 2.3 metres long and 0.6 metres wide. Then Alice 'borrowed' a white silk scarf from me and did not return it. A little while later I found a piece of soft cotton at home and on impulse embroidered Alice's initial on the corner and gave it to her. Alice was delighted as she had wanted me to make her something special for a while and I had not been able to work out the right thing. She had wanted me to make her a soft toy as I had done for other children I was involved with but I had resisted this as I felt the gift needed to be spontaneous and individual; giving her a soft toy would possibly have been to collude with her envy of the other children I was working with.

The shared nature of the care of the blanket has been noted by Dockar-Drysdale from her own experiences: 'Frequently there is a shared responsibility for the transitional object between the owner and the therapist. This arises easily and naturally, because the therapist helps in the caring for the transitional object' (1990: 35–6). Once the embroidered fabric was sewn on Alice's blanket was about 3 metres long and knotted up with the silk scarf which was rapidly falling to pieces from being rubbed and fondled.

Use and theoretical understanding

It is important to point out that Alice's blanket was not a comforter; the way it had been created and its use in terms of timing and tactile experience meant that it was a 'transitional object'. Alice had a 'Peter Rabbit' soft toy which she used as a comforter but this was two dimensional in its emotional quality as opposed to her blanket which was three dimensional through being invested with

emotional meaning born of experience. Winnicott wrote about transitional objects (or phenomena):

1   The infant assumes rights over the object, and we agree to this
    assumption. [. . .]
2   The object is affectionately cuddled as well as excitedly loved
    and mutilated.
3   It must never change unless changed by the infant.
4   It must survive instinctual loving and also hating.
5   Yet it must seem to the infant to give warmth, or to move, or
    to have texture or to do something that seems to show it has
    vitality or reality of its own.
6   It comes from without our point of view, but not so from the
    point of view of the baby. Neither does it come from within, it
    is not a hallucination.
7   Its fate is to be gradually allowed to be decathected so that in
    the course of years it becomes not so much forgotten as rele-
    gated to limbo . . . it loses meaning.

(Winnicott 1971: 5)

Each evening after school Alice would fetch her blanket from her
room and would either sit doing an activity or talk to people whilst
'playing' with her blanket. This 'playing' involved Alice holding her
blanket securely between third and fourth fingers while rubbing it
between her forefinger and thumb, or else sucking her thumb and
rubbing her blanket around the tip of her nose and her upper lip. At
these times there is a faraway look in her eyes which is reminiscent
of the way a baby looks when contentedly feeding at its mother's
breast; indeed Dockar-Drysdale notes that, 'The use of a transitional object has much in common with the baby at the breast'
(1990: 41).

Alice's blanket stood for her experience of being mothered and
Alice had not yet 'realised' enough good care to be able to relin-
quish this. It seems likely that Alice had not yet fully separated out
of the primary mother/baby unit and that to some extent her experience of separation from her mother/was more akin to a 'rupturing'
of the primary state of unity of mother and infant. It seemed as if
by collecting together parts of her blanket from significant females
that she was trying to finish this off properly and she would achieve
this in her own good time.

Alice had become quite fragilely integrated and needed time for her 'self' to be consolidated. At this stage she could make good use of a transitional object, as is reflected in the writing of Dockar-Drysdale,

> the transitional object belongs to that stage in a baby's evolvement when he is beginning to separate out from his mother . . . . One would think of this important process taking place near the end of the first year of life. The transitional object bridges the gap between mother and child. This is an illusory bridge, but nevertheless the transitional object is real.
>
> (Dockar-Drysdale 1990: 37)

Alice used her blanket many times to communicate with me, for example on the occasion where I had been asked to take special care of a particularly demanding girl in the group and the children were informed while I was on holiday. The first morning back I was confronted by a very angry Alice who thrust her blanket at me and told me to 'put it in the bin'. I was very surprised and refused to do so. Alice became even angrier and demanded that I do so because it was her blanket and she did not want it any more. I still refused but pointed out that she looked rather angry and asked what was really bothering her. After a while Alice was able to say that her blanket needed repairing but as I was becoming involved with another child I would not have time so I 'may as well throw it away'. I was able to reassure Alice that I would have time for her and to agree that her blanket needed repairing.

In this situation it was important for me to recognise that Alice was communicating symbolically through the use of her blanket rather than taking her demand to throw away her blanket at face value. To have ignored or been oblivious to the symbolic communication would have meant that an essential part of Alice's inner emotional life would have been treated in a trivialising manner and would have given Alice a powerful symbolic message that she was not valued and could be 'thrown away' like rubbish. On reflection I realised that the demand to throw her blanket away had aroused painful feelings in me; feelings of rejection and of being 'rubbished' by Alice and it was important that I contained these feelings so that they did not affect my response to Alice.

I was able to do this because I had developed sufficient understanding of the symbolic meaning of Alice's blanket through reading and discussion with more experienced team members as well as receiving training myself. This training emphasised the importance of recognising the symbolic nature of children communications as well as the crucial role played by the feelings of the carers. This meant that the importance of reflecting on one's own feelings was recognised so that being in touch with or getting in touch with the feelings aroused in me by Alice was a skill I had been encouraged to develop. It was because of this that I was able to make an informed response rather than a reaction to feeling 'rubbished'. I had been able to develop an understanding of how Alice's blanket formed part of the whole picture of her emotional development as well as its symbolic importance and I was able to recognise the value of allowing her a specific area in which she could regress to the point of failure – that is, back to the stage in her emotional development at which things had broken down. This planned and localised regression gradually enabled Alice to begin functioning in other areas, for example, she was able to reach a sufficient level of achievement in a special needs school so that she was eventually able to go on to become integrated into mainstream school.

CONCLUSION

The theoretical knowledge relating to child development and the evolution of the inner world of the child must become a cornerstone of any training for residential carers working with emotionally deprived children. These concepts form a vital part of understanding and catering for the emotional needs of children in residential care, the meeting of which facilitates the emotional evolvement of the child.

Chapter 14

Therapeutic work in an educational setting

Deborah Best

In this chapter I consider the possibilities of applying learning about therapeutic work within an educational setting. The discussion begins in general terms then focuses on some details of my own experience within the constraints and potential offered by my particular workplace.

I work as a teacher in a small unit attached to a local authority secondary school for children with emotional and behavioural difficulties, the school itself being organised broadly on behaviour management principles. Since my own approach is guided by a training grounded in psychodynamic theory and practice, the discrepancy between those perspectives suggests that I do not offer to describe the integrated work of a therapeutic community. However, I doubt that my circumstance is unique and believe that my attempts to make connections between the ideas derived from training and my own task as a teacher are worthwhile, both for the work that is accomplished and in helping me to make sense of what I am trying to do. I regard 'making sense' as a key benefit of learning to use informed thought and reflection to gain insight into the meaning of a therapeutic encounter, making it valid in turn for the young people with whom I work.

I hope that my experience will be helpful to others whose intuition leads them to seek ways of working therapeutically in situations both where this may not be the expected approach as well as where it is a common endeavour. In view of current trends in school exclusions and the need for appropriate alternative provision there is an urgent need for clear thinking about the nature of that provision.

This discussion begins by examining the relationship between education and therapy and the notion of working therapeutically in an educational setting. It refers also to the links between emotional development and the capacity for thinking and learning. In describing the work of my own unit I will refer briefly to issues of structure and management and identify therapeutic aspects of our task performance under the broad terms of the environment, the working processes of teaching and learning and their content. In presenting examples I preserve confidentiality by altering names.

THE EMOTIONAL BASIS OF LEARNING

It is widely recognised that the capacity for learning depends on a basis of emotional safety and trust. Children with early experiences of deprivation and disruption to the processes of cognitive and emotional development are likely to lack the internal strength for tackling the developmental tasks presented by the outer world of school. So when the outcome is failure and rejection within the school system, culminating in exclusion and referral to special schools and units, it further depletes any shred of emotional safety or trust. Often their documented histories hint at the deprivation, distress and chaos of the inner worlds of such children. When they bring those worlds to school with them, in minds so assailed by worries and muddles that little space or capacity exists for thinking or learning, it is the teacher's first task to receive and hold on to what they bring. To then be effective in facilitating thinking and learning entails a process of developing meaning and of providing safe starting-points for the work of exploring the world beyond the self.

It follows that any teacher attempting this work needs a high level of awareness and clarity about her own feelings if she is to think clearly about her task. Certainly, when I became a part-time student of Therapeutic Child Care I was soon aware of the confusion and doubt attendant on the role of learner and found it salutary to recognise and learn ways of managing those feelings. Equally, I was alerted to some of the cognitive and emotional challenges facing my pupils.

TEACHING AND THERAPY

If we understand therapy in its simplest terms as a helping and healing process, which can enable a child to change enough to be able to cope and grow as an autonomous person (Bruggen and O'Brian 1987) it can be understood as a form of learning. The teacher's task is close to that of the therapist: 'To create situations in which children or young adults . . . can learn is, in fact, to be concerned with bringing about change' (Richardson 1973: 18). Whilst the tasks of bringing about cognitive change – in thinking and reasoning – differ from those needed to bring about affective change – in feeling and intuition – the skills required are interdependent (Barber 1988). My own understanding of working in a therapeutic way in an educational setting is to engage in a nurturing process that can facilitate these interlinked aspects of development for the purposes of growth, enrichment and autonomy.

In making the connection between the roles of teacher and therapist it is important to answer the anxieties of those who fear that 'working therapeutically' implies a risk of ill-defined and possibly dangerous dabbling. We need to be clear about what it is we are trying to do, how we might go about it and what it is realistic to suppose we might achieve. We need to recognise the boundaries set by our roles and working environments and be informed by our training and support systems. To use a psychodynamic approach to inform and help in carrying out therapeutic work that is essentially based in another profession (teaching) is quite different from undertaking the specialised role of a psychotherapist (Copley and Forryan 1987); anyone working in this way does require a firm base in that other profession.

In an educational institution the primary task must be about enabling learners to develop the capacity to think, acquire skills and knowledge, on the one hand, and about promoting a process of maturation that will allow autonomy and survival in the community, on the other (Menzies Lyth 1988; Richardson 1973). This task cannot be evaded since, 'Children who are not taught are entitled to think that they are too dull, too bad or too mad for their teachers to take their education seriously and it is doubtful if parents can have much confidence in special education if no education is done' (Wilson and Evans 1980: 130). Staff should be able to offer reliable relationships that will foster a process of communication, teaching and learning, brought about through a high professional standard of preparation, presentation and recording. The principles underlying this process will be those which are valid in any good school.

I have found it helpful also to apply aspects of psychoanalytic understanding to my school setting and to my personal practice. I would suggest that teachers of children with emotional and behavioural difficulties are uniquely placed to provide therapeutic help within the context of their work and that they should be enabled by an appropriate training based in psychoanalytic ideas and practice to make sense of what they do and to do it better. This approach, which implies an understanding of behaviour as communication and an awareness of the value of open communication in identifying and managing feelings should not preclude so much as provide a key to managing behaviour in school settings. An alternative solution of offering specialist psychotherapeutic help, is unlikely to match the need among the growing numbers of troubled children in our schools, besides which it is often difficult to engage youngsters in what may be feared as elitist individual work.

In describing my experience of working in a school unit and my understanding of it I hope to show how I have found my own training helpful.

THE SCHOOL UNIT

Mansbridge House is a unit for up to twenty-one pupils aged fourteen to sixteen, in their final year or two years of compulsory education. It is attached to Reading Alternative School, a special secondary provision for pupils with emotional and behavioural difficulties; the two sites are about two kilometres apart and beyond some staff training sessions and certain administrative matters contact is minimal. The unit is staffed by three teachers, a teaching assistant, a part-time secretary and a lunchtime helper.

The pupils are referred by the local authority schools' psychological service usually directly after exclusion from mainstream school (often after exclusion from several schools) or following a period of part-time education through the home and hospital education service. The gaps and discontinuities apparent from their educational records frequently reflect similar early personal and family histories; rarely do pupils live with both natural parents; most are in the care of their mothers, sometimes with a partner, while a number live with father alone. All have experienced loss and disturbance within the family unit and the emotional pain which this suggests; some are known to have suffered physical or sexual abuse. The additional stresses attendant on adolescence together with the demands of the academic curriculum too often evince the classic reactions of flight or fight: truancy or disruptive behaviour, either of which is likely to end in exclusion from mainstream school and transfer to alternative provision such as our unit. It is our task to work with

those youngsters in ways which I will outline. First though, I offer
some thoughts about working within the organisation.

STRUCTURE AND MANAGEMENT

I address this issue first not only because it holds the key to sound
work in any setting but also to signal my realisation that problems
in this area present costly constraints both on the workers and the
work. As Butlin states, 'Therapy cannot exist without
management . . . . To provide treatment is required a good but flexible management structure within which a thought out, theoretically
based therapeutic programme can be contained and hence pursued
for the benefit of all involved' (1975: 286). My own workaday experience did not match that nor any other ideal scenario described in
the literature as an 'integrated treatment system' (Miller 1992),
within which 'every aspect of the community's daily functions (is)
integrated and illuminated by psycho-social understanding' and
where 'nothing less than a total approach . . . will suffice' (Rose
1993). Yet I discovered that the group learning approach used on
my MA training was integrated and allowed for recognising and
managing the difficulties presented by untidy interpersonal
dynamics and uncomfortable personal learning.

To bring those pieces of theoretical and experiential learning to
bear within my own work setting seemed like an impossible task, yet
it did help me to understand the discrepancies and to find ways of
working with what was there. Even if some elements seemed anti-
therapeutic and I was aware that what we were able to deliver was
less than the best, I believed useful work was still possible. A 'good
enough mother' (Winnicott 1971) makes adaptations to her child's
needs, yet where she does this within a less than satisfactory family
her efforts are not necessarily in vain for she may by communicating
her own hopefulness engender enough hope in her child to
encourage growth and change.

A significant support in managing my own role during and since
training has been the use of reflective writing. I describe this in
Chapter 12.

ENVIRONMENT

In thinking about the environment for learning and teaching I include provision both in terms of physical space and of emotional holding and containment.

The large Edwardian house where the unit is based retains the sense of a home; as well as classrooms (including an art room) it has a comfortable common room combined with a kitchen area. There is a small office but no separate staff room. The sense of welcome and the feeling of a comprehensible size and space also emphasise to some pupils the fact that – as some pupils say – 'it is a house, not a proper school', highlighting the inherent difficulty of offering an appropriate balance of containment and challenge in all aspects of our work. It matters that the building should be well cared for and classrooms should be attractive and well organised; it is also important that the work should be appropriately adventurous.

Through being constantly available the staff offer a sense of safety and of holding and although some pupils complain that they have little privacy and little chance to break rules, most are relieved to have reliable support. This is achieved through attention to the detail of daily life, whether in teaching time or in-between times.

The sense of safety comes not only from the presence of caring staff, but also from an ethos in which there are clear boundaries and expectations of behaviour. To be caring does not mean merely 'being nice' or making children (or ourselves) 'feel better', but to have an attitude of genuine concern and to be consistent and reliable both individually and as a group. The ability to resist attempts by pupils to create or exploit splits in the staff group is essential to its holding function.

At one time such an attempt became evident within the context of the provision of food and drinks. Pupils are allowed to make hot drinks and toast and have worked out a scale of charges to cover the cost. A situation developed whereby some staff sometimes offered to pay for certain pupils, until some pupils seemed to expect it and were unwilling to pay, demanding treats by bullying the staff. With this went a sense of unease as if pupils were becoming afraid of their own greed and subversive power; some staff seemed to be colluding in a divisive process. The pupils' behaviour was an overt reflection (acting out) of hidden divisions among the staff. Once the problem was faced openly a solution was found which satisfied even the most reluctant payers. (All pupils were to put payments into a clear sealed jar.) More importantly this had the effect of improving communication within the staff group, the lack of which had allowed a variety of anti-therapeutic strategies to develop. Reliable control not only relieves children of the impulse to make constant demands but also makes it possible for them to internalise their own models of control.

It might be tempting to dismiss this sort of incident as an irritating administrative problem created by a few devious and manipulative pupils and to be solved by a behaviour management strategy; yet this would ignore the unconscious impulses which were driving the difficulty. The experience of observing and exploring within the training group made me aware of the power of unconscious communication within and between groups, led me to question what might be going on and suggested a way forward.

It is perhaps not so surprising that food should become a focus for conflicting feelings, since it is such a significant provision. Although the unit cannot provide full meals, at lunchtime pupils choose from a menu of snacks which they drew up from suggestions made at a unit meeting. They are also able to eat meals they have prepared during cookery lessons. A few find it hard to cope with eating in a group, especially at first and it is taken as an important sign of emotional recovery when they decide to take the risk of accepting and sharing food.

Birthdays offer one of many opportunities for celebrating and giving individual recognition through sharing a cake and receiving a card. Others include taking photographs of activities and achievements, or displaying work. Many attach great value to their ongoing 'profile' folders of work, to building up their own record of achievement and to entering for exams which will earn public accreditation. The tangible evidence of success is therapeutic in itself because it presents to the young person a new sense of self and identity and helps to dispel the sense of failure and fear of mindlessness.

THE PROCESS OF TEACHING AND LEARNING

The teaching environment communicates some of the most important messages which provide the sense of safety and good order needed for thinking and learning in formal situations. Those situations are planned in such a way as to make relationships and the academic or practical tasks manageable. Tutor groups of seven pupils, which are also the base teaching unit, offer the possibility of attachment and alliance with the tutor and identification with others as part of that group. The building of those relationships takes time, constant communication and a developing sense of shared responsibility; through them individual and co-operative learning become possible.

In a unit where attendance is uncertain, either through absence or through work experience, progressive learning in a group is difficult so some teachers prefer to plan individual programmes of study to enable each child to work at their own pace. While this has the benefit of special provision, there is also a social and academic need for shared experience and the stimulus of exchanging ideas. Both methods are possible within a carefully planned timetable. In the following section I will describe examples of work within the curriculum which I believe has been helpful to some pupils as well as to my understanding of them.

WORKING THROUGH THE CURRICULUM

Limitations of size and resourcing prevent delivery of the full National Curriculum (to which all pupils are entitled); however, the curriculum does provide a useful structure which gives scope for appropriate specialised work. I focus here chiefly on communication and creative work particularly in English.

Some children with emotional difficulties find oral communication more difficult than drawing or writing. While autobiographical work and family history help most to think about and value themselves, it requires a particular kind of attentiveness in the teacher and a stage of readiness in the child for experiences to be thought about and given meaning. Often oblique and symbolic communication are the first step towards self-understanding, as happened with Matthew, aged fifteen.

Matthew's drawing of a minute desolate figure in a colourless barren landscape suggested to me his sense of being powerless and lost in a hostile world. He also produced a repetitive doodle of a man's head with the top open like a lid through which the contents were escaping, leading me to wonder whether this linked with his habit of wearing the hood of his duffel coat, even indoors. Both communications became clearer when I came across Winnicott's observation (1958) that helmets and hoods can be important in giving reassurance that the self will not escape through the top of the head. This is associated with a fear of not living in the body, of regression to insanity. Just such a fear was expressed in this poem which became a starting-point for Matthew to speak openly about his fantasies.

I Remember

> I can remember when I was a young lad
>   All I wanted was to grow up big like my dad
> Now I'm getting older and I take time to think
> Oh! What I'd give to reverse time and shrink
> Go back to the days when all the problems I had
>   Was what I would swop for my marbles
>   I still have those marbles to this day
> But sometimes I feel like I'm going to lose them

By sensing that his earlier communications had been accepted at a symbolic level Matthew gained the courage to enter into open dialogue, to work through some of his anxieties and sense of isolation.

We had long recognised among our pupils a common fear of being, or being thought of as insane or stupid. My training encouraged me to reflect on this cluster of communications and by attending to them enable Matthew to give meaning to the content of his mind, allowing him to manage his fear of the terrors of empty nothingness.

My second example is of the unexpectedly therapeutic effect of a piece of group learning, which also showed me what has proved to be an effective approach to anti-discriminatory work. Following the theme of racism, which was chosen by Rebecca and agreed by the group, we had read about Martin Luther King and watched a moving video which included coverage of his speech, 'I have a dream'. Later that morning this discussion emerged between Adrian – usually timid and withdrawn – Andrea – normally adamant against using dictionaries – and Rebecca:

Adrian: What was that word? – deprived – What does it mean? What do they mean, those words . . . like desegregation, humiliation, anti-discrimination?

Andrea: We need to get the big dictionary from the office! . . . Being made to go without something, being separated.

Rebecca: You're sad, doing all these long words . . . . What's the point?

Andrea: So I can understand anyone, anyone at all. I'll know what people are saying. It stops you being humiliated.

Adrian: Because then no-one will be able to look down on us!

Andrea: If a school inspector comes in here, whatever they say, you'll know those long words, you won't need to be humiliated. Or if a police car stops and they want to question me, I'll say 'Certainly officer!'.

Adrian: Yes, if you really want to, you can do it! Like the woman in the video, she said he made them feel they *were* somebody.

It became evident that the work had resonated at a deep level, enabling these young people to recognise their own predicament, to realise the meaning for themselves, to express it and to show empathy with others. The fervour of enquiry which this fired astonished me and gave a glimpse of a reservoir of hitherto hidden potential.

This discussion recalled for me those times during training when an exercise or an experience in the group had enabled me (or another student) to realise and conceptualise a hidden personal truth. What had been a stumbling block was transformed to a place from which to set out with new self-understanding and confidence.

Just as group identity can be strengthened by its focus on a piece of learning, an individual child can use her work as a means to contain and keep together her mind and her sense of self, investing the work with significance beyond its intrinsic meaning and purpose. I have come to understand this in terms of a transitional object, made available by the teacher but given meaning by the child, to provide a thread of security and continuity. I have known some deeply troubled delinquent youngsters, who seemed to hang on to their school work as the central skein in a web which they extended to include teachers, parents, social workers, youth justice officers, work experience employers, in the hope that they could provide the necessary holding; the central notion of school work was a way of warding off the threat of disintegration. This work might equally be almost any aspect of school, from basic skills, creative artwork or simply the identity of being a learner at school.

It is paradoxical that creative work is sometimes given low priority for pupils who have missed a lot of school and need to 'catch up', for it can release blocked channels of communication, enabling symbolisation and a means for self-realisation. Many sense its importance: 'This (art and craftwork) is my favourite, because you can make things all afternoon'; 'I love this subject and wish we could do it every day.' For children whose destructive impulses are often overwhelming, expressing their creativity whether practically or imaginatively (music, drama) can be vital in building up their sense of self and their belief in their own capacity to make reparation. Paintings, models, clay and papier-mâché work, friendship bracelets, greetings cards or soft toys are evidence not only of creativity but of a deep reparative impulse which is an important source of mental growth and activity. This is realised not only in the process but also in the outcome, for much of what is created is given as gifts to parents, teachers or friends.

CONCLUSION

I have offered a partial and personal view of therapeutic work in a particular educational setting and indicated some ways in which my training has become (literally) essential to my approach to my work. I have said little of the pain and difficulty it involves, but I believe that it is made more manageable by reflecting on the process and applying psychoanalytic understandings and experience to discover meaning; this approach can make a real difference to the outcome of such work. Although it is but one element in what are often complex and difficult lives, it would be wrong to underestimate either the responsibility or the potential for the good that it affords.

Marion Bennathan reminds us that, 'attending school is a very important part of a child's life. It is not only about acquiring intellectual skills and knowledge. It is about learning to live with other people . . . . Young people in trouble . . . may have no other social network. School for them is the representative of the wider society. Its importance in their lives is hard to exaggerate' (1992: 37).

There need not be any counsel of perfection, but the work requires a willingness to try to understand and bring out the best in the young people so as to help improve their chances of living their lives with a measure of hope, enjoyment and a sense of meaning. The contribution that specialised training has made to my own practice persuades me that it should be made available to the many teachers working in what has become a significant field, as yet too little understood.

Chapter 15

Therapeutic work in daily living settings

Linnet McMahon[1]

There is an aura around the notion of therapy which leads many workers in child care to undervalue the task which they do and to assume that therapy is something done only by experts or in therapeutic communities. This belief is shared by managers, policy makers and the public at large. It is assumed that any kindly soul with (or more often without) a basic training in general child care can look after children and young people, however deprived and damaged. A senior staff member of a children's home where some excellent work is done with individual children once said to me that 'of course' they could not do the therapeutic work done by therapeutic communities. Certainly the resources available to each are not equivalent; although resources matter they are not the whole story. This staff member went on to express her sadness and frustration that her voice was rarely heard when field social workers were making plans for the future of children whom she had got to know well and whose emotional difficulties she had gone some way towards alleviating. She needed support in her underlying recognition that the work she was doing was important and was indeed therapeutic.

Comparable scenarios exist elsewhere. A family centre worker may be involved in productive day-to-day relationships with children and parents. Foster parents can have an intimate knowledge and sound understanding of their foster child. Some children's teachers in schools, psychiatric nurses in hospitals and adolescent units, or residential care workers with learning disabled children or young

---

1 With Michele Alfred, Nyasha Gwatidzo, Matt Vince, Janet Vale, Viv Dacre and Mark Adams.

people, have similar skills and work in ways that provide immense support and help. Yet the expectation common to all these workers, held of them and often also by them, is that they should provide good enough child care but leave therapeutic work to the 'experts'.

As the first part of the book has shown, workers involved with children with emotional difficulties are not starting from the same point as those caring for children who are not damaged, so that provision of good enough child care, although essential, will not be sufficient. There is repair work to be done. Although some thera-peutic interventions (such as family therapy, play therapy, psychotherapy) may be formally structured to occur at certain times and places and by people with specific skills, working alongside a child or family in the prolonged experience of daily life presents its own opportunities for therapeutic management and communica-tion. Therapeutic care of emotionally damaged children requires more of the worker than providing good basic child care and under the right conditions can flourish not only in therapeutic communi-ties but in all sorts of places.

In the examples of therapeutic practice which follow, students from a number of daily living settings, which are not formally thera-peutic communities, demonstrate the integration of theoretical and experiential learning as they reflect on and manage their work.

PROVIDING A HOLDING ENVIRONMENT FOR A CHILD IN A RESIDENTIAL CHILDREN'S HOME

In the following case study, manager Michele Alfred shows how she enabled her team in a local authority children's home to provide a 'holding environment' offering primary experience to a severely disturbed boy.

Eight-year-old Wayne was a stocky unattractive boy who was difficult to warm to. He was placed in a local authority children's home after his foster placement, his fourteenth move, had broken down after his violent sexual assault on a four-year-old. He had previously been living with his father who had a history of violence, although he had spent his early years with his mother, mainly in different women's refuges. On his arrival in the chil-dren's home Wayne stood in the doorway and urinated at the staff there to greet him. He spat, kicked, head-butted and screamed his way through the day, interspersed with idyllic behaviour and profuse apologies to those around whom he had hurt. His mood swings were extreme and, as one worker put it, 'When he goes he's quite frightening – like that child in *The Exorcist*'.

Staff were initially concerned for the safety of other children and were encouraged to hang on to that concern but at the same time re-examine their own feelings both as individuals and as a team and draw on their acquired knowledge and skills to work with Wayne, in the belief that in time they could succeed, at least in part. After several staff meetings allocated to thinking about Wayne, staff became excited at the prospect of working with such open disturbance in a structured, shared and open way, involving a team approach with structured individual supervisions. We decided that come what may we would try to hang on to Wayne. We saw him as an 'archipelago' child (Dockar-Drysdale 1968a) and understood that he too found his panic states very frightening. We gave him a clear message that aggression towards others was not acceptable and that we would stop him, by holding him physically if necesary. When he panicked we made sure we never left him alone, held him if necessary and communicated with him throughout.

We felt that we needed to do things for Wayne as he showed no control over everyday matters. He would run a bath and deliberately let it overflow; he would lose his toothbrush every day and not clean his teeth when a new one was produced; he would pour half a bottle of ketchup over his dinner and then slurp his food up with his fingers. Staff started to run his bath for him, clean his teeth for him and ask him if he had wiped his bottom when he had been to the toilet, giving him undivided attention. I managed to argue for extra staffing hours so that the other children would not feel displaced. Someone was with him during all his waking hours, doing things with him and for him. His whole day was organised for him, trying to make things uncompetitive and achievable, encouraging his interest in art, swimming and growing things. We bought boxing gloves and a punch bag in the hope that he could channel his aggression. We gave him a wendy house, sleeping bag and tent so that he could hide himself away in his bedroom. We sat beside him on the floor (due to his destroying all his furniture) reading him bedside stories and singing lullabies at bedtime.

After some months Wayne became inwardly and outwardly a

much happier child. His violent outbursts diminished greatly. His replacement furniture in his room remained undamaged and he started to put down roots. His interest in growing things was used to help him relate to other children, who had until then seen him as a 'nut case'. His healthy response to one of the staff one night was 'I'm not going to let her wind me up you know' and he promptly had a bath and came out managing himself well.

A team approach made possible such sensitive and responsive care for Wayne, with its attention to reliability and continuity and the provision of 'complete experiences' – a holding environment. Wayne's good experiences enabled him to hold on to enough good feelings in order to start to think. He went on to be helped to use symbolic communication to think about and focus his anger. Only then was it decided 'to start some life work with him so that he can have some order and clarity of his life down on paper'. The staff who had followed his progress so far were in a good position to judge when the time was right to help him conceptualise his experience. Michele Alfred describes the impact of her learning on the Therapeutic Child Care course:

I find my learning to be very exciting; it gives me encouragement to forge ahead when supervising staff in their work with the children. The concept of a 'holding environment' is all embracing and feels right and good to me and my staff and to what we as a team feel most comfortable with.

THE EMOTIONAL EXPERIENCE OF CONTAINMENT – RACE, CULTURE AND IDENTITY IN RESIDENTIAL CARE

Angry and violent children out of touch with the source of their emotions can be very frightening to work with. The worker's task, so powerfully described by Dockar-Drysdale, is to experience repeated annihilations by the child, not simply to empathise with the child's pain but to feel it personally and to survive with their concern for the child undiminished. Out of this come the beginnings of hope within the child that they too may have a future. That this is possible was demonstrated in the work with Wayne. The theme is continued in the following case study by Nyasha Gwatidzo, then manager of a residential unit specialising in work with black children. The added dimension in this instance was the need to work with race and cultural difference, which involved the worker's reflections on her own feelings as a black woman manager.

Femi is a thirteen-year-old black girl. She was taken from West Africa to Britain when she was about nine. It was clear that she had suffered a lot. In Africa she was never told who her parents were or who she was. She was then uprooted to an alien culture where for two years she relied solely on a family she did not know in a situation she was not clear about, where she was treated as a maid and sexually abused. On being found and taken into care she was moved round a number of residential units and foster placements, all of which broke down, mainly because of her behaviour. At one stage she was moved ten times in two months, causing her increasing distress and a sense of hopelessness. She was referred to our therapeutic unit which has a black African woman manager and staff who are mainly black and female, from a wide range of cultures. It was agreed that Femi should move into the unit in a planned way so that a structure for her daily care was in place and everyone involved would be clear on all the details.

On our first meeting I was left with the feeling of having met a toddler who giggled inappropriately and I wondered if she could understand what I said. Soon after her arrival Femi fought with another resident and broke all the windows and some furniture in her bedroom, hurt the staff on duty and had to be restrained for about two hours before she finally collapsed and fell asleep. The next morning she refused to take responsibility for the damage she had caused, but later asked 'If it is true I did this can you help me to remember such events'. She also said, 'someone who is not me takes over when I get angry and I am scared'.

Femi frequently ran away, sometimes being brought back by the police. Each time she would beg me to end her placement saying, 'You are the manager, tell A (the social worker) that Femi is a horrible girl and we cannot cope with her behaviour'. I refused and told her we could cope. Once she lost her temper and broke the glass in the door and generally caused such extensive damage that the police were called. The police did not want to return her to us as she was making allegations. They wanted to press charges for criminal damage, which I refused to do, telling them she was not a criminal and I insisted that she come back. She returned, only to attack me for having agreed not to end her placement. It was then I decided that we would not call the police again and that we quickly needed to come up with some kind of safety net for her to feel held by us.

Femi clearly did not like herself. She was very depressed and wanted to remain detached from everyone. She asked staff to buy her pornographic material. She attempted suicide by drinking cleaning fluid and some paracetamol. Her level of distress was touching everyone within the unit. As a team we felt that she really needed our commitment and that ending her placement would only make her situation worse. Her daily living experience had to be structured through activities and individual attention. The dramatherapist built some trust through Femi's interest in singing and dancing and art therapy was a way for her to talk about her life in Africa. We tried to encourage Femi's attachment to her keyworker. Femi found it difficult to trust this attention and remained aggressive, depressed and anxious, keeping everyone at a distance. We had to understand her level of distress and not reject her.

The staff group felt that Femi was 'workable' but the need for her to be restrained for long periods caused much anxiety and stress. No one spoke her language and none of us knew much about her religion or culture. It left me feeling that although I am black African I did not understand all that was going on for her. Femi was also verbalising her internal racism towards staff. She was faced with all these 'black mothers' whom she could not make use of. This made her very angry with us and she did not know how to respond except by lashing out. She said to me one day that she wished she had never been born and that I was the main cause of her problems because I would not reject her like everyone else would.

Femi is still with us six months later but what a struggle it has been for the team and what powerful feelings she has evoked in us. In my work with Femi I became involved with her, passing through a phase in which I was vulnerable as the mother is. I remember feeling greatly concerned when she first ran away and crying when phoned at midnight to be told she had not returned. I believe that Femi aroused some feelings which touched me on a personal level, so that I was trying to create a personal holding environment. In attempting the 'mothering' of Femi I found myself struggling with lots of issues and my ambivalence was shared by the team. I was left with Winnicott's idea of maternal pre-occupation and Femi needing this level of attention. Femi no longer runs away and her outbursts are minimal. She has stopped asking me to move her and has finally unpacked her things.

BEARING THE REALITY OF LOSS – THE WORKER'S USE OF SELF

The work of thinking and communicating about the reality of past experiences often involves painful loss issues. In the preceding examples course members have given some indication of the painful feelings which may be aroused for the worker and of how a team may be managed to provide the holding environment for the workers, which helps them avoid some of the defences against these feelings that would impede the therapeutic task. A related experiential aspect of training is about bringing understanding of past personal experience to bear appropriately on a current work situation. Matt Vince, senior worker in a private residential unit for abused and neglected girls, describes how his own experience of loss helped him in the therapeutic task of working with a young person's feelings of loss.

As a residential social worker, one of the most important tools I feel I can use when assisting a child or young person in dealing with a situation of loss is my ability to reflect on and utilise my own experience of loss. In addition to the 'normal and necessary losses' that have occurred throughout my life I have experienced the loss of my mother who died from cancer when I was twelve years old. Reflecting on my various abilities and inabilities to cope with this loss and the carefully considered use of my own memories and experiences of the emotional and psychological difficulties that this loss has presented for me has, I feel, enabled me to empathise with those young people in our care that have experienced similar situations. In my opinion this has increased my ability to sensitively assist and guide them to some extent towards their own resolution of the emotional difficulties that this loss has created for them.

The emotional damage and crippling of a child or young person, brought on by an inability in the child to experience a period of healthy mourning or grieving for the lost parent, due to a lack of appropriate or sufficient support and attention to the needs of the child by their remaining parent or significant adult, can be healed to some extent through the actions and responses of a residential staff team willing and able to listen to, withstand and act upon the pain communicated by the child.

Sandra's father had died following a short illness when she was between four and seven. Aged fourteen when she came to us, from a Middle-Eastern refugee family in which she had experienced sexual and physical abuse, her behaviour to men was either excessively flirtatious and sexualised, or highly dismissive, leaving us feeling uneasy, powerless and worthless, in the words of one male worker 'like a lump of shit'. At the same time she recounted constantly a story of her father as a hero-like figure who, had he lived, would have saved her from the abuse she suffered. Interestingly while telling this story Sandra often referred to her father in the present tense, as though he were still living. I felt this meant that Sandra had not accepted the loss of her father and her fantasy was that one day he would return. As members of the team confronted Sally about her dismissive behaviour her story telling increased, as if she were testing the team members to see who was strong enough to withstand the uncomfortable feelings she evoked and who would therefore be able to withstand the pain of her experience of her father's death, if or when she felt able to share this.

One evening, after Sandra had been particularly dismissive and verbally abusive towards me throughout the afternoon shift and I had confronted her about this several times, she became withdrawn and tearful as bedtime approached, refusing offers of comfort from team members. She went to the front door-step and began smoking, a forbidden action that she knew would provoke a rebuke. In an attempt to break this pattern of negative attention seeking, I offered to sit with her on the wall opposite the unit (where smoking was allowed) whilst she had her cigarette and she accepted. I asked her why she seemed to want me to be annoyed with her and said how horrible it felt for me to have to be always telling her off. This developed into a conversation in which Sandra spoke of her confusion about her situation, her sadness at being separated from her brother and her family and her feelings of loneliness and despair. When I asked her whether we could help her feel less alone she burst into tears and cried 'no, because you can't bring my father back!'. She cried inconsolably and after a while we returned to sit in the lounge.

The intensity of Sandra's distress felt to me to be greater than we had experienced before and I was left feeling that her present sadness was uncontrolled and genuine, in contrast with her previous displays of emotion that had seemed controlled and feigned. In a lengthy conversation I encouraged Sandra to begin a process of separating the reality of her memories of her father and the events surrounding his death, from the fantasy that she had created to fill the missing pieces and make his death more comfortable. I asked questions about the nicest thing she could remember about her father, what he most enjoyed, what she remembered their doing together. I asked her 'what memory of your father you would prefer to forget?' and this seemed to help her connect with her true memories surounding the actual moment of seeing her father die. At one point I asked 'if you could have one wish what would you wish for? and she replied, looking at the nearby Christmas tree, 'that when I open my presents my father will be inside and will jump up and hug me'.

This was obviously a very painful and exhausting exercise for both of us and required very sensitive handling. It seemed to have been a positive experience for Sandra, who engaged with various members of the team over the following months, sharing her memories and feelings about her father's death. In particular she reached a point at which she could state that she hated her mother for not having been there to help her cope with her father's death, for not giving her information that she needed concerning why, how and where he died and for not having been good enough to fill some of the empty spaces in her life that his death had left.

This account demonstrates not only the worker's skill in opportunity-led work but also his capacity to use his own experiences, which he developed further through his experiential learning on the course.

THERAPEUTIC CONTAINMENT OF PARENT AND CHILD IN A FAMILY CENTRE

The work described so far has focused on providing emotional containment for an individual child. In work in family centres a recurring issue is how to manage the apparent conflict between the needs of child and parent. Workers can feel very split, preferring to work either with the child or with the parent and blaming the other for 'inadequate parenting' or 'appalling behaviour'. The neediness for emotional support of both can often lead to envy and rivalry in which meeting the needs of one appears to be at the expense of the other. At the very least there is often a dilemma over timing. Providing a holding environment for the whole family then becomes difficult. While effective long-term help to the child may involve meeting some of the parent's needs and restoring or developing their ability to provide good enough parenting the child has immediate needs which, if not met, put development at even greater risk. Janet Vale, a senior social worker in a family centre, gives the following account of how she was able to offer emotional containment to help both parent *and* child.

A model which is particularly appropriate to work in family centres is parent–infant psychotherapy, which assumes that there is no such thing as individual psychopathology in infancy but that problems will be related to the parent–child relationship. Selma Fraiberg (1980) uses this model to understand how the parental past may interfere with the present mother–infant relationship. She suggests that a parent's feelings from a past relationship can sometimes be transferred to the child. The child has come to represent a figure from the parent's past or a part of the parent's hidden self. These 'ghosts in the nursery' prevent the parent from being able to respond appropriately to their own child's needs. In therapeutic work the parent is worked with in the presence of the child and attention is focused on the child's development. The child's presence ensures that the parent's feelings for the child are available for interpretation. Fraiberg combines this interpretation with a number of interventions which aim to support the parent emotionally by emphasising, for example, the parent's importance to the child.

An intervention using aspects of the infant–parent psychotherapy model involved my work with Sally, a young mother who has a son Mark, aged eighteen months. At first, Sally was very unsure about the centre and said that she might not stay. Sally said that one problem was that her little boy was 'terribly naughty'. When I asked, how he was naughty, she was not clear, except that she said that he would not do as she asked. As we talked he sat wide awake in his pushchair. Sally did not want him to get out and run around as she was afraid that he would be naughty. Though I felt uncomfortable about this myself he did not appear to be distressed at all. Later Sally did sit him on her lap for a while.

From our conversation I found out that Sally lived at home with her parents after some years of being independent and felt trapped by her responsibility for Mark. She felt isolated during the day as her parents were out much of the time. I also got the impression that Sally seemed to see herself as a 'naughty girl' because she was a single parent which her parents might disapprove of. I noted that Sally's concern about the family centre was that the day was structured and that there were a number of 'rules' or guidelines for parents.

The next time Sally came to the centre she allowed Mark to go and play, although she was anxious if he went too far away from her. However, when he did come back to her side she scolded him for being naughty and interrupting her by putting his head on her lap. I gently suggested that a little boy of Mark's age may well go off for a while and come back to his mum if he's a little uncertain about the world, because going back to mum makes him feel secure.

On her next visit Sally said that she found the centre too restrictive and not what she wanted. However she had found a local mother and toddlers group to go to where she could meet people. I said that if this is what she wanted it was fine by me. She looked surprised briefly and then relieved. During the day both Sally and Mark were much more relaxed, Mark playing freely around the centre with Sally being freely available for him. Once Mark lost Sally and cried. Sally came to him, cuddled him and talked to him.

For the first two visits, keeping Mark restricted and under total parental control seemed to be enacting something from how she felt about her own relationship with her parents, that is, restricted and controlled because she was a 'bad girl'. Somehow by talking about these feelings, having attention drawn to Mark's stage of emotional development and her importance to him and finally being able to make her own 'adult' decision without my 'parental' disapproval, helped their relationship appear to move on, at least a little.

The worker's emotional 'holding' helped the mother start to take her own decisions about staying at the family centre and moving on to another group. The worker's attention to the feelings of not only mother but also her child helped the mother begin to provide a similar containment for her child, providing a more secure base out of which some autonomy becomes possible.

A 'HOLDING ENVIRONMENT' FOR REFLECTIVE PRACTICE IN A FAMILY CENTRE

If the worker is to offer the kind of containment just described she needs the support of a holding environment that can manage the potentially overwhelming feelings arising from being with damaged people. Viv Dacre describes how she applied her learning about reflection and the reflection process to the task of managing a family centre:

> Planned structures for staff support can help people hold on to and bear the feelings which the work involves. One way to ensure that this happens in family centres is to give time and space for these feelings to be explored. This can take place in training sessions or in supervision (both planned and impromptu), consultation and in team meetings. Exploring feelings through reflection can promote understanding and self-awareness. As a manager I found that keeping a personal journal helped to bring clarity to my thinking, particularly when trying to face difficult issues in an honest way.
>
> Understanding of the reflection process, in which 'the processes at work currently in the relationship between client and worker are often reflected in the relationship between worker and supervisor' (Mattinson 1975: 11), can further help the individual worker or team to make the connections between what is happening within different groups, for example, the family group and the staff group. There needs to be a mechanism through which a team can identify and understand this process. As a family centre manager, I give time at the beginning and end of each day for the whole team to plan and evaluate the work of the day. Workers also use these meetings to talk about concerns and anxieties about things that have happened and to gain insight into some of the dynamics at work within the centre as a whole. There are certainly times in these meetings when it is possible for us to find 'reflective' connections between feelings within the team and equivalent feelings which seem to belong within the group of families. Where we do find these connections, we can

often use what we discover to help us decide how to respond to what is happening. At other times it is more difficult to make these connections – but even here, the reason for the difficulty is sometimes to do with the team feeling stuck or 'blocked', which may itself reflect issues that the families are bringing with them.

FROM CHAOS TO CONFIDENCE

A manager's reflective practice in managing change in a national health service setting

Mark Adams, a clinical nurse manager, used the course requirement to write a research dissertation to reflect on the experience of managing a major change in the service. He drew on his training experience of using reflection and group process:

As senior manager of a nursing team I was experiencing at a local level the repercussions of national organizational upheaval. The problem facing me was how to bring together two disparate child and adolescent psychiatric teams which needed to merge for organisational reasons and integrate them into a single team, to create sound and focused nursing practice – despite the teams also having to relocate to an unsuitable and institutional setting. I needed to learn how to observe myself as manager within the team, the culture and the subsystems. The key to managing my subjectivity was reflection.

For five months I kept a journal, including general observations on the following: 'why is this issue important to me?; what am I attempting to shape?; how can I get beyond my own personal understanding of the situation?'. The journal was organised into sections on outside events and pressures, on what I heard, saw and thought about inside events, behaviours and activities and reflections on how I was affected by my observations, by my feelings of love, hate, resentment, respect and identification. It included speculation about the meaning of events and about my thoughts and actions in the context of the change. These recordings helped me be attentive to everyday practice. Writing down what felt worrying provided further opportunity to make sense of events and place the anxiety where it belonged. It also helped me to look at my own personal bias and increase my self-awareness. Part of the learning involved thinking about the defences which I as a manager mobilise to cope with excessive anxiety, so that I could try to avoid irrational and destructive behaviour. For example it became important to me to understand my relationship with the two teams, one of which felt to me 'familiar and safe' and the other 'strange and dangerous'. I used regular meetings with an external supervisor to bring issues arising from my journal and explore those problems together.

It became helpful for me to place feelings, thoughts and actions within the context of myself, the team and the organization as a whole. In this way I was able to ensure that I could differentiate myself from the environment and establish my own identity as a manager. These times formed a part in the cycle of action, reflection and action. They also created an opportunity for me to look back within myself and at how I was caring for my own mental health, a kind of ensuring that the child within me gets looked after.

My participation moved from a position of isolation, distance and being peripheral to the experience, an 'alone' state, to a position closer to the experience and one creating conditions for deeper involvement, in which assumptions within the teams about what they do were more effectively challenged. As a manager my own change process involved a long journey from the experience of not coping through to a feeling of coping and ultimately a position of confidence.

CONCLUSION

This chapter has indicated some opportunities for therapeutic work with children and young people occurring in everyday living. Because daily life is messy and complicated with plenty of scope for disruption and interruption and a guarantee that difficult and painful feelings will be involved, there is a clear need to work within the active support of a setting which provides a holding environment for workers as well as for children and families. The holding environment of the Therapeutic Child Care course provides an opportunity for reflection on emotional as well as intellectual processes and helps students learn about the meaning in practice of emotional holding and containment.

Chapter 16

Using the situation
Management perspectives and their potential in staff development and training

John Diamond

This chapter explores the use of management perspectives in a therapeutic school. I explain how these perspectives are developed from a critical 'observational' position at the 'boundary' of the treatment task of the school. I discuss the task of this area and the use of forms of observation including counter-transference in psychoanalysis as a relevant model for monitoring and diagnosing resistance to task performance. I go on to explain how the material gained from this perspective can be used for training purposes and give examples of this work. This chapter attends to the experience and the problems of maintaining a combined role, based on my own experiences of being in a dual role of leader and trainer.

THE MULBERRY BUSH SCHOOL

The Mulberry Bush is a school which exists specifically to provide for the care, education and residential treatment of up to thirty-six seriously emotionally-damaged boys and girls, aged five to twelve, who have failed to develop a secure sense of ego integration and identity. Consequently, these children are often unable to manage themselves in age-appropriate ways or allow others to do so for them. They are, in Winnicott's terms, unintegrated (Winnicott 1965a). The children who come to the school have suffered serious and repeated interruptions to their emotional care and nurture at an early age. Often this has been due to neglect or physical, emotional or sexual abuse which has led to the development of severe behavioural problems. Many of the children have never moved beyond primitive levels of development and functioning. Due to this 'early environment failure' and at times to later traumatic experiences, they are often chaotic, impulsive, unpredictable and unable either to accept being one of a group or to allow a group to operate without disruption. Such behaviours are often present to an extreme degree.

The therapeutic provision of the school is based on psychodynamic principles largely as developed by Winnicott and the school's founder, Barbara Dockar-Drysdale. Staff consciously use themselves to develop relationships and through teamwork provide a planned environment and predictable pattern from day to day, thus establishing a reliable structure of emotional containment for the children. This ensures that the conditions exist for the child to experience having their genuine physical, emotional and psychological needs met. The school offers education for previously ineducable children and a space for damaged children to experience a secure sense of childhood, where the child will have stability of self and placement, be offered good relationships, be respected and be offered a model for respecting others.

THE ROLE OF THE HEAD OF RESIDENTIAL THERAPY

As head of residential therapy in the school, I am leader of the residential treatment task. This role requires me to maintain a strategic view of effective maintenance and the steady development of this task system. My managerial responsibilities are for the deployment and training of staff to run and maintain the high quality of the treatment task. Through this work, resistance from care staff to the complex task is inevitably encountered. This resistance arises mainly from the anxieties of working closely with such troubled children. My role is to monitor the task through regular contact with the teams via attending team meetings, supervising the team leaders of the four teams and through my training role in induction and training groups. These times allow me to have direct contact with the day-to-day dynamics, anxieties and pressures of the work.

Several writers, e.g. Turquet (1974), Lampen (1986) and Miller (1989) have analysed aspects of the role of leadership, which include, among other things, the janus-like function, or 'management at the boundary' (Zagier Roberts 1994) which requires both an internal and external perspective on the organisation. These writers have also highlighted the management of anxiety as a function of the leader's role:

inherent in every task – and institutions are set up to perform tasks – there is anxiety, pain and confusion arising from attempting to perform the task; and that institutions defend themselves against this anxiety by structuring themselves and their working practices and ultimately their staff relations in such a way as unconsciously to defend themselves against the anxiety inherent in the task.

(Obholzer 1987: 201)

So what are the anxieties inherent in the task of residential treatment of unintegrated children? By definition these children are not sufficient containers of their own anxieties; some in fact live in a permanent state of impending terror. These strong, indeed overwhelming, feelings are inevitably projected onto the adults who live and work alongside them and these feelings will be received in different ways. The anxieties that unintegrated children produce in the adults who work with them are within the realm of the normally unknowable. They may induce fears of disintegration, loss of a sense of self, loss of control, emptiness and deep fears of separation, loss and annihilation. Much of this material is 'transmitted' at an unconscious level and manifests itself by adults carrying 'uncomfortable' feelings on behalf of the children. The defences employed by adults against such overpowering feelings include avoidance through emotional distancing, denial, fight/flight and pairing.

In an environment where regressive behaviours are often the primary emotional currency, there is a constant tug to reduce all work and thinking capacities to levels of confusion. This can also be unconsciously adopted as a resistance to performing a clear task, to defend against the primary anxieties mentioned above. However, when they live with this doubt and uncertainty about providing purposeful activity, workers can then find themselves struggling with secondary anxieties such as their own usefulness and relevance. For this reason it is essential that workers have times to think and talk about the impact of the task on themselves. In our school, regular team process meetings and induction meetings for new staff provide a regular opportunity for this work.

Throughout the daily routines of living alongside the children, adults are engaged in the process of managing difficult behaviours and verbally reflecting these behaviours back to the children within the context in which they have been received. Over time the child will learn to internalise the feeling and thinking responses of adults as 'containers'. This form of management and its modifying influence allows the child to take in caring and growth enhancing experiences. However, even the most experienced workers at times will have their abilities as containers of disturbance worn thin by this constant emotional attrition. Then they can become unwilling and unwitting receptacles for this emotive material.

A function of my management role is to be in a position of oversight, which allows for observation of these (internal) dynamics. This 'observer ego' position can be used to recognise, intervene in and diagnose problems within the organisation. The theoretical model for this observational and diagnostic position is that of counter-transference in psychoanalysis. Paula Heimann's influential paper 'On Counter-transference' (1950) proposed that the emotional response of the therapist to the patient gave clues to the internal world of the patient's object relations: 'My thesis is that the analyst's emotional response to his patient within the analytic situation represents one of the most important tools for the work. The analyst's counter-transference is an important instrument of research into the patient's unconscious' (1950: 81).

In the same way as in psychotherapy, the manager at the boundary position within an institutional setting is able to tune into the dynamics either of the organisation as a large group or of a component group and in this way the material received allows for a personal emotional response to aspects of the organisation's 'unconscious'. The response gives clues to the emotional state of the workplace and in this way becomes the 'instrument of research'.

From this position it is possible to uncover and have sight of a range of dynamics and how they may deviate from the primary task of treatment. These could be represented in, for example, problems of team communication, or problems of distance regulation between adults and children. Within this diagnostic function the area of analysis is the interface of the group with their task. The task for the manager is restoring the staff to effective working roles and relationships, so that dysfunction is 'repaired' and the most effective way of maintaining the task continues. The various forums of group supervision and process meetings are probably the most direct and organic ways of bringing about change and repair. However, this peripheral and interpretive position occupied by the leader will inevitably be limited in its objective ability to some extent by internal dynamics in which the leader is involved. Consequently another diagnostic eye is needed, 'further out' to allow for any 'short-sightedness'. This is the role of consultation.

The prototype for my role of managing the therapeutic task is the dyadic relationship, in which the mother provides a flexible form of emotional containment for the range of feelings projected by the infant. Through the process of reverie, being in tune with (the needs of) the infant, she is able to regulate the strength of these feelings and then reflect them back in a modified and more manageable and acceptable form. Thus, the fundamental form of managing strong feelings is based on holding and reflecting back. This ability to monitor the needs of the child at differing distances is crucial. In theory both the parent and manager have to provide the appropriate conditions for the development of the child.

Within residential work the task of management has to include the maintenance of a high standard of service, as well as training and development which ensure the evolution of the system. The trainer/manager strives to understand the conscious and unconscious dynamics of the institution, through the reception of feeling, its processing and the transmission back of a supportive or modified message. From this position it is possible to see problems within the system and to provide a regular forum to act as the container and to develop critical and informed insight within the care teams.

DEVELOPING A REFLECTIVE PRACTICE AS A TRAINING METHOD

My own introduction to the idea of reflective practice came from the postgraduate course in Therapeutic Child Care at the University of Reading. Throughout the design and practice of the course, there is a strong emphasis on matching the mode of training to the mode of practice, known as the 'matching principle'. In this way, the working methods of the students and staff will reflect some of the working methods in the therapeutic community. Consequently the dynamics of the student group became part of the material for learning and the group itself became a central forum for problem solving and resolution of its own difficulties. This had direct relevance to my own experience of group care work and helped me realise the possibilities of harnessing the potential of the group for creating an evolving system of care practice.

Psychoanalytically-based therapeutic work necessarily involves a strong focus on process issues – the ways in which individuals and group affect each other over time both consciously and unconsciously and the developing awareness and understanding which people can discover through these interactions. Training on the other hand, necessarily concentrates more on the intellectual frameworks which will inform this understanding and awareness and has traditionally focused less on process; thus the risk of dislocation of practice and training.

(Ward 1995b: 190)

Increasingly within the school there are children with high degrees of behavioural disturbance, who express and enact their experiences through chaotic and often apparently mindless actions. The degree, intensity and regularity of behavioural management workers are involved in continues to be a big issue. Therefore, the need for maintaining ways of understanding and consciously using the self to think about, manage and moderate these behaviours is essential. The matching principle addresses the practice–training gap. By using elements of process within training, practice issues can be made accessible and help reconnect the trainee/worker to the context of a meaningful task and purposeful group.

The following section explains the role of the head of residential therapy in incident analysis and resolution and the strategies which can be used to develop understanding and learning based on difficult experiences. The range of strategies mentioned in the incident analysis are ones used at the school and are used to examine approaches to the communication and management of such incidents. They are not intended to be the only strategies available.

Example 1: an incident involving individuals within a group setting

John arrives for work at 8 a.m. feeling at ease with the events of yesterday, in a good mood and conscious of bringing this side of himself into the living group where he will be helping to get the children up. He goes into Ralph's room gently, says good morning to the half-awake child and waits to see what response he will receive. No answer. He proceeds gently to open the curtains and tells Ralph he has run a bath for him. Ralph responds with strong verbal abuse. John responds gently, 'OK Ralph, I can hear that you are a bit angry. Shall I leave you alone for a bit? Maybe then you can tell me what is bothering you'. More swearing. John decides to move away;

he is followed by chanted abuse which is so loud that all the other children cannot fail to hear it. John returns and tries again using the tactic of not getting ruffled. Maybe this approach will contain the anger and 'defuse' Ralph. 'I will get your clothes out ready for you Ralph'. 'I'm not getting dressed'. He swears aggressively, a pillow swings out and catches John in the corner of the eye, causing soreness and temporary loss of sight. Ralph is now full of glee, shouting to the other children, 'Ha, ha, I've hurt him'. It is now 8.15 a.m. John, far from feeling good about himself or his work, is feeling abused, hurt and is so angry that he has to take himself out of the situation to calm down.

The resolution of this particular incident was made easier due to John's confidence as an experienced care worker. After a short break, John was able to return to the dormitory to talk with Ralph about his outburst, with the knowledge that this behaviour meant that Ralph was anxious about something and unable to hold these feelings. In John's absence Pat, another care worker, had taken over the management of Ralph, telling him he would not be doing anything else until the adults had time to talk and decide the best course of action to help him with his angry feelings.

John talked with Ralph, first about his feelings of being hurt when he had come to help him start the day properly. He then asked Ralph if he knew what had made him be so angry and behave in this way. Eventually, Ralph was able to explain that it was his mother's birthday and he had not sent a card or had any contact with her over the last week. Ralph's overwhelming and confused feelings of guilt mixed with feelings of separation and loss had been intolerable and found some temporary relief through converting the feelings into aggressive behaviour.

John's work allowed Ralph to verbalise his feelings and create meaning where there had previously been confusion, enabling him eventually to apologise to John; the re-establishment of their relationship allowed Ralph to re-engage with the routines of the day.

THE ROLE OF THE HEAD OF RESIDENTIAL THERAPY IN INCIDENT ANALYSIS AND STRUCTURED RESOLUTION

The therapeutic resolution of this incident, where both child and adult learn from and achieve some insight into their behaviour, thoughts and feelings, could take various routes. As head of residential therapy in the school I could be either directly involved in this process, or monitor it at a greater distance. Often the most useful way of working is to be involved closely with detailed work, but maintain an ability to return to the boundary position. In most cases the resolution of an incident would be worked on by the team under the direction of the team leader. If I am to take over this work there would need to be clearly agreed reasons. The incident will always be reported in the group log book and if it is a serious incident, it will also be recorded in the school incident book and the head of residential therapy informed.

Once the team has established that they can and should do the work in resolving the incident, the head of residential therapy can liaise with other groups to ensure that the team has some protected space within the day for this work to be carried out. In this way, being 'inward' looking from my boundary position, I can help provide the conditions for the work to take place. If the incident is more serious, perhaps one in a series of violent episodes and the team is concerned about their ability to provide the right form of containment and therapeutic provision for the child, my role may become 'outward' looking from my boundary position, to include work with the parents/carers and social worker of the child to explain and discuss the child's situation.

Within my role of monitoring the work of the treatment groups, I would try to understand the incident in relation to the task of the group. This would include questions such as, what does this incident say about the emotional state and stage of the child?; the contact between the adult and child, i.e. was the adult working too closely in or too distant?; what can be learned about the management of this child at this time of day? It may be useful to write a management programme, or to use a context profile (Dockar-Drysdale 1990) to help clarify these issues.

The information needed to answer these questions will often be written up by the adult in the account of the incident. My boundary position also allows some 'neutrality' and it is not uncommon for me to talk with the adult involved and the child, to hear their versions of the incident. Whether the process for the resolution of the incident is managed by the team leader or the head of residential therapy it will usually follow a pattern, which is likely to include the following stages:

1 A space will be provided for the child, supervised by an adult, to make the child aware of the seriousness of the incident – a space

for thinking, which may be facilitated by asking the child what they were feeling at the time, whether they were aware of how hurtful their behaviour felt to the adult, etc. The task is to help the child get in touch with any feelings or concern or depression and to hold these feelings. Often children will want to find ways of making reparation by writing a note or making a card for the adult involved.

2 For the adult to be offered space to regain their composure and be offered the support of another adult to be attentive to their feelings. Sometimes a colleague who is a friend provides the right support, at other times a more senior and experienced member of staff may be required to talk through the incident in a counselling role and to represent the authority of the school in re-establishing an appropriate boundary within which to re-engage with the work.

3 After the incident an 'on line' team meeting will often be held to discuss the events of the incident and the feelings of the team. Inevitably feelings of anger, despair, anxiety will be expressed. The team leader or head of residential therapy will ensure that these concerns are listened to carefully and ensure that within the process of resolving the incident, retaliatory feelings will be understood, but only non-punitive methods of resolution will be used. This will include discussion about the right balance of separation and close contact with the child in which clear communication of real feelings from adult to child and child to adult, will be supported. A well-managed resolution requires that a sense of order, concern, clarity and justice are present.

4 A meeting with the group of children will be held, with an experienced adult group leader convening the meeting and as many staff members as required to create an ordered forum for discussion of the incident. Children's thoughts and feelings will be carefully listened to and any denial of concern will be acknowledged and reflected back in a way that the children holding those feelings will be able to make sense of. This may involve the removal of a child from the meeting if those feelings are so overwhelming that the child can only disrupt the meeting. The task of the meeting will be to help children hold their feelings, with an emphasis on the children reaching concern for all those involved.

5 It may be useful to revisit the events of the incident after a period of time has passed using a meeting such as the team process meeting. This space may provide fresh insights into the incident

from all concerned and allow a sense of adult community and purpose to be re-established. This meeting will be facilitated by either the team leader or myself. Sometimes the greater distance of my role allows for a broader range of discussion to take place, by freeing the team leader for the duration of the meeting to share the same level with other team members.

6 If the adult involved feels in need of more support and the opportunity to talk more about the impact of the incident, I am in a position to be able to organise a session or series of sessions with the school's therapeutic consultant.

Fortunately, incidents such as this do not occur every day and this example highlights a particularly emotionally-charged incident. It shows the speed in which a mature adult world can be reduced to a sense of meaninglessness and irrationality. Increasingly, there are children who will actively attempt to destroy and negate the experience of workers engaged in the most basic child care activities. In the face of such ceaseless attack, the possibilities of providing even a 'good enough' experience requires Herculean effort.

The daily oscillations of despair, anxiety and anger are communications, albeit subtle ones and we are easily caught in the reality of the negative action, instead of being able to hold this and also recognise the feeling as a communication from the child about their present emotional state. The concept of 'helicoptering' (Hawkins and Shohet 1989: 37) is a useful one – trying to objectify the situation by viewing it from the outside; developing this skill is a useful analytic and diagnostic position. The concept of 'negative capability' from Keats (1952) can be useful too. Bion (1984) developed this idea within psychoanalytic practice to help manage the stress of the unknown. Hence, in the work adults have to be supported to stay with uncertainty and not knowing in order to begin to make the next and necessary step of making sense of chaos and finding meaning in the apparently meaningless.

Example 2: feelings aroused within a group over an organisational issue

Several years ago in a complicated time when the school made its first moves away from a model of a traditional large group organisation towards developing a model of small group living, the question was debated of what level of responsibility for clothes care should and could the children be allowed to take was debated. This was polarised between those staff who felt 'none' and those who felt 'some'. This indecision found a place in what was known then as the 'green dormitory'. For those in the staff team who said 'none' it was felt preferable that the children's clothes should remain in locked cupboards, with the only access controlled by key holding adults. It was true that some children did damage clothes, but the rationale for this form of clothes management was that it stopped children with 'caretaker' defences from reinforcing these defences through self-provision and self-management. This is a false self syndrome, where one part of the child takes over a caretaking role, to care for and defend the fragile and undeveloped real self. As Dockar-Drysdale states, 'Treatment as with a false self child involves the caretaker handing over the little real self to the therapist' (1990: 182).

As I came to see it, a sense of loss of control was being played out in the need to lock up the clothes. However, the less accessible feeling might be to do with anxiety and a sense of dislocation in the overall change process. The cupboard discussion provides a concrete issue on which to project feelings about loss and change. Anxiety about the children's destructive and manipulative behaviours seem to mask the reality of adults' unconscious infantile anger and sense of loss of control over this degree of change.

At this time the only open forum for discussion of whole school issues was the fortnightly whole school process meeting. A heated debate took place about clothes care in which I was able to put forward my own tentative interpretation of the situation. Within this forum at this stage of the school's development there seemed little ability for us as a group of workers to recognise or learn from our own shortcomings and blind spots. However, I was able to continue to work with this as an issue in the induction group, to inform future practice and the newly formed small teams continued to discuss the issue in their own team meetings. Eventually, the issue was worked through and after a period of a few months individual chests of drawers were introduced to the children. Since then these have been accepted and the deliberate damaging of clothes has become a relatively rare event.

In this situation recognition of the potential 'us and them' culture, based on polarisation and splitting, is an important issue for discussion within the team and as an issue for training. This might include some painful recognition of aspects of the children's behaviour as the adults' disowned chaotic areas. The anxiety created by the regressive tendencies of workers within a system at a 'paranoid/schizoid' position of development creates the risk of a projection and the conditions for a self-fulfilling prophecy that children will function by destructive acts.

This projection needs much work to be seen for what it is – a construct based on persecutory anxiety. Consequently, there is a need to shift the emphasis from the regressed or immature aspects of the children towards emphasis, validation and support of the children's functioning aspects (and the corresponding structures for adults, including training and development, to accomplish this). A fundamental error based on a defence against the anxiety of chaos is to deal by full-frontal attack with developed ego functions or defences, as though they have to be dismantled. The phenomenon of the 'caretaker' defence was one such issue within the school at a particular point in the change process.

The school has, of course, moved on from this stage, but I believe it does highlight how regressive tendencies become powerful unconscious motivators of decision-making within living groups. With awareness, regression can be positively constructed as a meeting place where the adult encounters the child as an emotional baby/toddler, in order to go forward.

This example highlights the importance of using the material of the work to help forge links between the experiences of individuals and the larger group systems of which they are a part. The use of such a situation analysis within training should help to develop analytic understanding of events, so that a non-judgemental approach can be used to make sense both of the unconscious motivation of adults and children and of their behaviours within the dynamics of the organisation. This is, of course, easier to theorise about than to do!

SOME THOUGHTS ABOUT TRAINING

Tom Main has some astute psychoanalytic insights into the difficulties of developing a practical training programme:

> Difficulties in the learning process seem to lie in three areas. The difficulty of understanding the knowledge itself (because it may require considerable intellectual effort by the ego) is the first and the one recognised by almost everybody. The difficulty that a fact or theory becomes an internal object subject to all the vicissi-

tudes of object relations and of diffused energies is the second . . . the third is that of training methods which are well studied only by educationalists.

(Main 1990: 62)

In a task where the management of anxiety is an essential and core personal and institutional requirement and where emotional and physical tiredness are component parts of the work, the provision of a heavy theoretical training is likely to create as many problems as it might solve. The use of a regular time that provides protected space away from the demands of the work and allows time for thinking and reflection in a relaxed manner, will provide more appropriate conditions for the internalisation and processing of information. The use of experiential learning through live material and group exercises, allows for a sense of adult community to be re-established, reduces competitiveness which is powerfully played out through deprivation and provides the possibility of purposeful fun alongside deep learning about the self and the task.

In a group care setting where such personal growth and learning for all are the ultimate goals of people's efforts, the group can provide a supporting, containing and reflective function that is able to develop and improve its individual members and hence its therapeutic service in a manner that matches the most effective form of change, that of 'always becoming' (Bettelheim 1950), an organic progress whether in the maturation of the group itself, the individual, the educational area or the institution.

Such a training programme should be able to aid the development of a learning culture within the school, which provides a model of progressive development and which through the function of anxiety management (that converts unconscious anxiety into conscious communication) can challenge the defences, such as those identified by Menzies Lyth (1988) in her early papers, that hinder the development of task performance in therapeutic enterprises. Hawkins and Shohet also identify eleven key attributes of the learning/development culture. A broad description is as follows:

This is clearly the culture in which supervision most flourishes. It is built on a belief system that a great deal of social work and indeed counselling and therapy is about creating the environment and relationships in which clients learn about themselves and their environment, in a way that leaves them with more options than they arrived with. Further, it believes that social workers, counsellors and therapists, etc. are best able to facilitate others to learn if they are supported in constantly learning and developing themselves. An organisation that is learning and developing right from the top of the organisation to the bottom is far more likely to be meeting the needs of the clients, because it is also meeting the needs of the staff.

(Hawkins and Shohet 1989: 137)

The training model we continue to develop at the Mulberry Bush is based on these principles. It is intended to provide a model of progressive development for staff involved in the professional disciplines of therapeutic child care and education. It is a three-year programme covering theoretical and practical issues, whose objectives of the programme are: to enable care workers to develop an empathic understanding of the emotional and physical needs of emotionally damaged children; to provide workers with information on the important and relevant topics discussed; to enable workers to develop and consider both personal and social attitudes and form judgements on the issues; to learn from the process of group learning, where necessary being prepared to explore the material that has blocked this learning process.

There are particular tensions and problems inherent in a combined role of trainer and manager. These arise from the need to be able to move from one 'boundary' position to another to be able to carry out the different tasks. In my managerial role being at a peripheral boundary position allows for a useful objective distance to be created between myself and the care teams. In my training role I am further 'inside' the school and providing a time to share thoughts and ideas. This creates a different perspective on my work and consequently different expectations and projections. This shift in boundary position requires a different form of emotional engagement. The use of one's personal authority and ability to direct work are parts of both the managerial and training function, but have to be used in a different way.

Within training I am aware of the need to be clear about the presentation and structure of the session, as well as the process issues which are encountered in the experiential parts. The ability simultaneously to provide direction and hold emotions requires intense pre-occupation. Providing a thinking space requires a particular attunement if the group is going to experience the training as useful and productive, providing the conditions for a 'good feed' is an apt analogy. Preparation for the training session, i.e. making notes on the theme, structure and timing as well as photocopying and having materials available, has to be done within the running of the day, alongside the inevitable breakdowns, crises and levels of anxiety; this work requires a particular level of determination if it is to be done properly.

Finally, in my role of trainer, there is an important balance between being able to give the right amount of information including aspects of theory in a way that is accessible to all present and the converse, to fail to provide the right amount of information, leaving workers feeling let down or having not learnt anything. The right balance and model lies in an ability confidently to provide knowledge where it is needed and to be seen to be flexible enough to allow other viewpoints and feedback from the group to reformulate ideas and information where appropriate so that the session models the sort of exchange that happens in teams when thinking about meeting the needs of the children.

CONCLUSION

This chapter has set out to define the position of 'managing at the boundary' of the care and treatment task of the Mulberry Bush school. I have shown how this position can be used to observe and then intervene and 'repair' problems caused by resistance to the task of working closely with such troubled children. I have explained and given examples of how working with high levels of disturbance and regressive behaviours creates anxieties which are quickly converted into resistance to carrying out the work. I have also explained the importance of creating group training and meeting times within the working week, where incidents and the impact of the work can be discussed. Through the use of the group, problems can be resolved and learning from these experiences can take place. In this way, the events of daily life in the school observed through my role, can be fed back and constructively used as training material.

Part 4

Conclusions

Chapter 17

On 'reflection'

Adrian Ward

Our concern in this book has been to explore the relationship between theory and practice in the training of child care workers and particularly to focus on what we have called the 'matching principle': the proposition that the mode of training should 'reflect' or match the mode of practice. We have covered a lot of ground as we have moved gradually from an overview of some of the relevant theory-base in Part 1, through the detail of the matching between training and practice on a particular programme in Part 2 and finally into some examples of how participants in this programme have applied their learning back into practice in Part 3.

The reality is that the relationship between theory and practice is not always an easy one: sometimes the demands of practice seem to outstrip the reach of the available theory and sometimes the theory can simply feel remote or inadequately expressed. The responsibility of trainers (and writers) is continually to explore and renegotiate this relationship and ultimately to try to bring the two closer together. In our own case as editors, as we have reviewed and revised the various chapters of this book, some aspects of these connections have become clearer while others have become even more elusive. In particular, it has become evident that we and our contributors have been using the term 'reflection' in a number of different ways – which is no real surprise, since in the literature on therapeutic practice this term is used with a very wide range of meanings. Sometimes, as in the discussion of the 'reflection process' in Chapter 6, we have defined our usage quite fully, while in other places we have made only passing reference to the distinctions between the different usages.

In order to conclude this part of the discussion, therefore, I want to re-examine this pre-occupation with reflection, which has been emerging as a central theme in the relationship between theory and practice. I will outline the chief distinctions between the ways in which the term or concept of reflection is encountered in training for therapeutic work and will comment briefly on the range of implications of each set of meanings, showing how we have provided opportunities for students to learn from experience about the different types of reflection. In some cases I am drawing on usage of the actual term 'reflection', while in other cases related terms such as 'mirroring' and 'attunement' have been used and occasionally quite different terms may have been used to refer to closely-related phenomena. It may help the reader to keep track of the discussion if I begin by listing the various meanings of reflection:

1 Individual reflection on self
2 Reflection of another: mimesis
3 'Reflecting back' to another
4 The (unconscious) reflection process in supervision
5 Dramatization/enactment/resonance:
     mutual unconscious reflection in the group
6 Role play/sculpting/dramatherapy:
     conscious use of reflection in the group
7 The matching principle: aiming to facilitate reflection

INDIVIDUAL REFLECTION ON SELF

Here 'reflection' is used to refer to the individual process of thinking things over, turning them over in your mind to re-evaluate them and perhaps to make new connections. This sort of reflection has been defined as: 'those intellectual and affective activities in which individuals engage to explore their experiences in order to lead to new understandings and appreciations' (Boud *et al.* 1985: 19). It has been said to often involve correcting a previous imbalance of the elements of thought and feeling in the decision-making process and to consist of three elements: returning to experience, attending to feelings and re-evaluating experience. Thus one might say, 'On second thoughts, I have decided to . . .'.

The professional application of this type of reflection is found in the concept of the reflective practitioner (Schön 1983). Schön argues that contemporary professional practice requires the ability to reflect on the relationship between theory and practice and makes distinctions between 'reflection-*on*-action' (transforming theory in the light of learning from past experience) and 'reflection-*in*-action' (improvising during the course of intervention). Here the practitioner might say, 'as this situation unfolds, I realise that I need to take this sort of action'. These concepts have been usefully applied to the training of teachers and of nursing staff among others and more recently to social work training (Gould and Taylor 1996). In practice, the concept of opportunity-led work offers a framework for a type of reflection-in-action, while in the training setting, among the methods which we have used to help students develop these reflective abilities are the use of the reflective journal (see Chapter 12) and the use of the Opening and Closing Meetings (Chapter 7); we have also encouraged students to incorporate such reflection in their research work. The concept of reflective practice is undoubtedly an attractive and useful one, although what is potentially confusing is that much of what has recently been written about it appears to imply that reflection is a single and easily definable concept, overlooking the wide range of other meanings which we shall be considering in this chapter.

REFLECTION OF ANOTHER: MIMESIS

In this second category 'reflection' refers to the use of mimicry (either consciously or unconsciously) to show someone how we think they look or behave. This phenomenon is seen as a powerful element in early social learning and in psychoanalytic theory several writers have explored the roles of various forms of mimesis in early child development. Winnicott, for example, describes the infant using the mother's face as if it were a mirror, finding in her responses to him a reflection of himself and therefore an image of his own emerging identity – which he gradually incorporates as his self-image. Likewise the French psychoanalytic writer Lacan (1977) writes on 'the mirror stage' in infant development. Evidence from research into attachment and earliest relationships (Brazelton and Cramer 1991; Stern 1985) confirms the empirical basis for such interpretation of parent–infant relationships and Murray (1996) makes explicit the link with Winnicott's ideas.

The act of mimesis – the live and simultaneous recreation of another's behaviour – might be interpreted as signifying, 'I want to be like you, to be in harmony/unity with you and I want you to see that and know it', or alternatively: 'I find myself "reflected" in you and I am learning about myself in the process – I notice things which you do or say and I recognise them as versions of characteristics of my own'. Mimesis continues throughout life as a basic paradigm of social interaction: thus for example we may unconsciously 'mirror' a partner's or colleague's body-language. It is also related to the phenomenon by which some couples grow to look more and more alike, or some owners are said to grow to resemble their dogs (or is it the dogs who are chosen because they look like their owners?).

In the training context, this form of reflection may be said to happen in terms of the element of modelling which is often present, although frequently unacknowledged. Such modelling may be based on the student's observation of tutors, supervisors or peers. Thus the student might say: 'I've noticed how X handles similar situations and I'll see if the same thing will work for me' (see Chapter 18 for further discussion of modelling).

'REFLECTING BACK' TO ANOTHER

Third, but related to the second meaning, the term reflection is used in counselling and psychotherapy with the specific meaning of repeating back to somebody what you think you have heard them saying (or what you have understood them to be communicating in play or other symbolic ways), in order first to check your own understanding and second to help them be clear about what they are saying, or to give them feedback about how they are coming across. This form of reflection has been described as 'immediate shared retrospection' and a distinction has been made between the purely verbal reflection of content and the fuller reflection of feeling, in which the counsellor additionally aims to reflect back the tone of voice, body language and other non-verbal elements (Nelson-Jones 1983: 54).

Reflection here is a conscious device employed as a means towards an end and it involves a balance between elements of paraphrase and interpretation, e.g. first, 'What I hear you saying is this: . . .' and second, 'Is *this* what you are really trying to say: . . . ?', or even, 'What I think you *really* mean is this: . . .'. The various schools of counselling and therapy place differing emphases on the value of paraphrase and interpretation and of course individual counsellors will vary their style according to what they feel is appropriate for the situation. It may be that this conscious reflecting back is such an effective tool in the helping process because it offers the client not only the opportunity to re-examine the cognitive and affective content of the communication but also a sense of validation at a behavioural level through mimesis.

In the training context, there will often be some element of this form of 'reflecting back' in the way that tutors respond to issues posed by students in tutorials or seminars and some element of it in the various patterns of interaction which occur in the context of the whole group.

THE (UNCONSCIOUS) REFLECTION PROCESS IN SUPERVISION

We saw in Chapter 6 that the term 'the reflection process' is used in the context of psychotherapeutic work to refer to the phenomenon by which workers may bring into supervision (of counselling, psychotherapy, etc.) unconscious material which relates to their own reaction to the transference which they are experiencing from their clients. Mattinson (1975) and others have described this process as it operates in the supervision of casework and individual psychotherapy and in particular have shown how an understanding of it can not only help to maximise the learning from supervision, but can also facilitate the resolution back in the casework situation of the anxiety or difficulty which was originally being expressed. In this analysis, the reflection process is seen as an integral and inevitable part of both supervision and practice (see Hawkins and Shohet 1989). This form of reflection might be interpreted as signifying: 'I (worker) will do to you (supervisor) what my client does to me, so that you shall know how it feels to be in my shoes, or so that you can show me or tell me what to do, or so that you will suffer as I have done. I will do this in the hope that you will then be better able to help me sort out the difficulty which I have got into in my work'.

The unconscious reflection process has also been observed in other settings, e.g. in family therapy, where it has been argued that clinical teams may 'reflect family dysfunction' (Berkowitz and Leff 1984). Here again it is argued that an awareness of the process can be used productively in therapeutic work if it is accompanied by a willingness on the part of the therapeutic team to examine their own inter-relationships as these are affected by the dynamics of the families with whom they work. We also considered in Chapter 3 the potential confusions which can arise when these unconscious processes operate between all the different players in the group care setting.

In the training context we have seen (Chapter 8) how students can be helped to learn more about the reflection process through the use of the 'seminar format' (Danbury and Wallbridge 1989), as well as through the developing awareness of such processes which gradually emerges from the regular use of other elements such as the Experiential Group and the Opening and Closing Meetings. We have also commented (Chapter 11) on how as a staff team we have needed to draw on our understanding of this process in our work on holding together and interpreting the 'work of the day'. We would argue that this further learning about the reflection process is an essential component of training for therapeutic work and one which is often underestimated by those who write about the 'reflective practitioner' (often seen as drawing predominantly just on the *conscious* elements of reflection).

DRAMATISATION/ENACTMENT/RESONANCE: MUTUAL UNCONSCIOUS REFLECTION IN THE GROUP

Another version of unconscious reflection can be found in the literature on group analysis (Foulkes 1964). This is the equivalent phenomenon in group settings to the 'reflection process' outlined above and it has been most productively described in the literature on therapeutic communities. It refers to the process by which people unwillingly or unwittingly become actors in each other's working-out of phantasy and anxiety (Hinshelwood 1987). This is a complex and powerful phenomenon, which becomes the focus of much diagnostic and interventive effort in therapeutic community work; it involves the realisation, verbalisation and ultimate resolution of what has been or is being enacted. It may relate to immediate events in people's lives or in the group's experience and/or to much earlier or deeper material in people's unconscious, and it thus offers the possibility of bridging between the conscious and the unconscious. It implies the statement: 'I seem to have become caught up in acting out a role on your behalf, or in relation to a number of other roles which you and other people are acting'; or alternatively, 'The way you are behaving reminds me of some other important person in my life: it's almost as if you had become this person. Perhaps if I can try to understand how you are now affecting me I may be able to learn more about that other relationship'.

In the training context, much of what develops through the use of groups such as the Experiential Group offers the opportunity both to experience and to learn about this form of reflection, as people discover the dramatisations in which they become involved and learn more about what sorts of situations and people have which sorts of resonance for them. A further variation on the theme of unconscious reflection focuses on the external rather than the internal.

The unconscious mirroring of external events

It has long been argued in the group-analytic literature (see Foulkes 1975; de Maré 1991) that people's behaviour, and especially their behaviour in groups and meetings, may unconsciously reflect not only their here-and-now pre-occupations in relation to the group's task, but also their broader experience of 'macro-issues' in society. There is also evidence of the particular force with which such phenomena may arise where a society is in violent upheaval – (see papers on Northern Ireland (Benson 1992), on the former Yugoslavia (Trampuz 1993) and on Russia (Semyonova 1993)). In the training context, we have become especially aware of this element at certain times of civil unrest, political uncertainty or upheaval or public tragedy and we have heard powerful evidence at such times of some of the ways in which such phenomena have appeared to affect the work of those in group care settings.

ROLE PLAY/SCULPTING/DRAMATHERAPY

Conscious use of reflection in the group

The distinction between the conscious and the unconscious elements in reflection become apparent again when we consider the use of devices such as role play and dramatherapy. Such devices involve the deliberate and planned harnessing of the resources of the group to enact a situation presented or described by an individual or group, in order to clarify and thereby hopefully resolve conflicts, confusions, etc. (Jennings 1990). This meaning of reflection implies the statement: 'If it helps you, I/we will agree to act or improvise according to the role(s) which you will assign me/us, within the structure (and especially the time-limit) of a therapeutic exercise'. The place of such devices in training for professional practice is well established and we have seen some versions of such an approach in the work described in Chapter 8.

THE MATCHING PRINCIPLE

Aiming to facilitate reflection

One further version of reflection may be found in the concept of the matching principle, as advanced in this book, i.e. the proposition that the model of training should 'reflect' or match the mode of practice. This implies the statement by the trainers: 'if you are going to learn appropriately about handling this work problem, we must recreate in here some of the conditions out there'. This book has offered a range of thoughts as to why and how such 'matching' may be both appropriate and productive. In particular we have argued that it can facilitate the operation of both the conscious and the unconscious reflection processes and we have offered some detailed illustrations of where we feel this has happened. Some further aspects and applications of the matching principle will be discussed in the final chapter.

OVERVIEW

I have made some attempt to draw connections and contrasts between these different types of reflection. It will be seen, for example, that the term is sometimes used to denote conscious and deliberate strategy on the part of a therapist and sometimes to refer to unconscious phenomena arising out of the interactions between the parties. Equally, the focus varies between individual reflection, one-to-one relationships and relationships within and between groups. Sometimes the setting for the reflection is practice itself, sometimes training or supervision and sometimes the connections between all of these. It is no coincidence, of course, that similar terms are used for all these various phenomena – but at the same time, if the distinctions are not kept clear, there is scope for real confusion and distortion, as if we were in the hall of mirrors. After all, each of these versions of 'reflection' is just a metaphor intended to help us understand the complicated patterns of thought, emotion and their communication which arise within and between people, and such metaphors can only ever contribute a certain amount to our understanding. Beyond that contribution, we are left to puzzle out the patterns and their meanings and the metaphor can help us no more.

Chapter 18

Applying the matching principle
A comparative view

Adrian Ward

Our argument in this book has been that the 'matching principle', upon which we have based our work, is applicable as a general principle, well beyond the particular circumstances of the MA programme we have been describing. Indeed, we argue that this principle often operates at an implicit rather than an explicit level – people designing professional training programmes often appear to come up with models which do match practice, without necessarily having striven consciously to do so. We would say that it is likely to be productive if this process is made explicit rather than being left implicit, because this should allow for a closer and more effective match where this is needed and perhaps for *less* of a match where there may be aspects of the mode of practice which are seen as less desirable. These propositions remain to be tested and our hope is that others may feel motivated to apply the principle explicitly to their own course design and to report on the outcomes. Our final task here, therefore, is to offer some pointers as to how this might be done, by setting out some aspects of the process of course design and by drawing comparisons where possible with other modes of training and practice where these have been made evident in the literature.

ANALYSING THE FIELD OF PRACTICE: CONTENT AND PROCESS

First, the application of the matching principle depends upon a preliminary analysis of the mode of practice in question. In the case study presented here, our analysis of the group care context for therapeutic practice (Chapters 1–6) highlighted the concept of the 'holding environment' and the application of this concept through the therapeutic community approach in particular. The rest of our discussion has flowed from this analysis. In other cases quite different concepts and assumptions might emerge from the analysis of other modes of practice and thus lead to a different 'match' in the design for training. For example, whereas most of our students work predominantly with children and young adolescents, we might have needed to match for quite different patterns if most of them had been working with older adolescent and young adults. Certainly those of our students who have come from such settings have some-times brought quite different personal and professional pre-occupations, such as facing a deep and almost existential despair about the value of their lives, which seemed to connect directly with the key issues facing their clients.

One might have hoped to have found detailed discussions of such connections between the dynamics of training and of practice in the relevant literature, but unfortunately these have been comparatively rare until very recently and are often incomplete when they do appear. However, some fascinating glimpses have now been offered in the collections edited by Yelloly and Henkel (1995) and Gould and Taylor (1996). In the former, for instance, a chapter by Hughes and Pengelly (1995) offers several examples of difficulties arising and being resolved in the training of child protection workers. Here the trainers found themselves on one occasion driven towards a somewhat defensive position of enforcing authority with the students and on another occasion at risk of being drawn into collu-sion with them against a senior manager. Both of these patterns appear to have strong parallels with equivalent pressures in the practice of child protection, where the tensions between authority and collusion and the negotiation of workable partnership in situa-tions of unequal power, present a continuing challenge. It is not clear from these examples to what extent the design of the training programme took explicit account of the need to plan for an overt match with the mode of practice in question, but the authors' discussion of how the ensuing difficulties were resolved suggests that some matching was at least implicit.

An example of matching for 'care management': Enquiry and Action Learning

A different approach again is taken by Taylor *et al.* (1996) and Burgess (1992), both of whom have written about 'Enquiry and

Action Learning' (EAL) in social work education. As described by Taylor and Burgess, the mode of practice for which people are being prepared under this approach appears to be predominantly a 'problem-solving' version of the field social work task. Students are encouraged to assess a range of typical social work and community work scenarios with which they are presented in the classroom and then to locate the appropriate resources to help them address the problem which they have defined – resources such as specialist knowledge and skills, for instance. The staff (known as facilitators) see their responsibility as providing opportunities for students to discover how to solve these problems in the hope that, en route, they will develop their skills in assessment, resource location and mobilisation, and service monitoring and evaluation. In terms of content (e.g. knowledge and skills for practice), the EAL approach appears to match fairly exactly with some aspects of the field social work task, especially as this has evolved under 'care management' principles.

In terms of process, there also appears to be a good match. Students in the EAL model work in small groups of ten people known as 'study groups', which change in membership every term for two years. These study groups are drawn from a much larger total cohort of eighty students from two different courses; thus a student might work in six completely new groupings over the two years. After the first term, when groups are 'balanced' by the staff for race and gender, groups become self-selecting on the basis of special interests and learning preferences – at an acknowledged risk that these groupings may 'replicate patterns of power and oppression in society at large' (Taylor *et al.* 1986: 86).

These arrangements appear to produce a pattern of continually changing group membership which probably matches quite well with organisational realities in some field social work offices – although not, perhaps, with the ways in which such services might ideally be organised. Indeed, this is quite a different pattern from that which is usually aimed for in the therapeutic communities for young people. Here continuity of staffing and consistency of approach, slowly evolving over time, are given a high priority. Thus, the Therapeutic Child Care course requires students to work within the same group and with what is essentially the same team of staff consistently over the two years. The composition of the group only changes if a student or staff member decides to leave or occasionally if a student from a previous cohort who has suspended her studies rejoins the course. The match with practice is a close one.

Relationships develop and evolve over time – people get to know each other well and have to learn how to work with people whom they like as well as those whom they don't. Absences from the group and other variations from the norm such as late arrivals and early departures from the day's work, are evident to all and may be examined for their significance to the group as a whole or to individuals. The whole group thus works together at its identity as a large group throughout the programme, reflecting the emphasis on the reality of the large group in group care settings (Ward 1993b).

In some respects, while EAL appears to be a model that matches some aspects of care management in social work very closely, it would probably not be so well matched to preparing students for aspects of longer-term therapeutic work such as providing emotional containment and reflecting on the meanings of unconscious communications – aspects which, of course, are increasingly seen in some quarters as not part of the field social work task anyway. In other respects, there are several similarities between the assumptions underlying the EAL approach and those upon which we have drawn in this book and the above comments, far from being intended to compare the respective worth of the two programmes, are designed to show how in each programme the matching principle operates at the levels of both content and process.

DECIDING ON THE ELEMENTS TO BE IMPORTED INTO COURSE DESIGN

In the light of the above discussion, it is clear that the preliminary analysis of the relevant mode of practice will lead to some selectivity and especially to some consideration of what should not be matched – either because it is not viewed as relevant or appropriate for the student's intended field of practice or because it may be an aspect of practice which tends to inhibit rather than enable effective work. One Therapeutic Child Care student clarified very early in his training that since some organisational aspects of his practice in a therapeutic community for adolescents (e.g. long working hours and a relentless pace of work) served to compound the inherently stressful nature of the work, he would not find it helpful to have these 'matched' in his training experience.

The discussion of EAL also highlights the need to be clear about what precisely it is that we are trying to match. Is it the mode of practice as the books say it should be, or as the operational manual declares it to be, or as we – staff or students – would like it to be? At the level of conscious learning this is a familiar dilemma for those teaching about professional practice – if you teach about good practice people sometimes object that it can't be done like that in the real world and if you describe how awful practice can be they will rightly object that this is too depressing. This is a particularly poignant debate in the case of residential care, which (in the UK at least) has been viewed as a 'Cinderella service' – undernourished, unrecognised and scapegoated – and as a setting in which good practice is simply not possible.

The reality is that these three apparently different versions of the mode of practice actually overlap: practice is never exactly as the books or theory would suggest it should be, nor is it usually the same as the operational manual says it is and it does not often work in the way that we would wish it to. In reality there is always a struggle to achieve good practice and even to agree within a staff team and an organisation as to what this should be. The solution to this problem is probably that, rather than attempting to be absolutist in our view about which version of the mode of practice we should be aiming to match, we should simply aim to re-create conditions which will be sufficiently familiar to the students and sufficiently close to some consensus about the theory base, to allow for unconscious connections to be made and eventually for some aspect of them to be realised. We are not aiming to set up an exact model but a 'good enough' match with lived experience so that learning can take place.

The selectivity required in applying the matching principle also means being clear about some of the dilemmas and policy options which arise in practice. In our case we have been matching elements of both therapeutic community and group analytic practice. The assumptive worlds of these models of practice are fairly close to each other, but there are also many variants within and between them. For example, in group analysis, group members are usually discouraged from having any contact with each other outside the group meetings, whereas in the therapeutic community it is self-evident that people will talk to each other about important matters outside formal group sessions and that indeed much valuable work may be done by this means. We have tended to follow the latter assumption, but we have also adopted the practice in many therapeutic communities, whereby people are strongly encouraged to bring all such important discussions back into the group, so that individuals are not left holding key information which others do not know about and which might then risk inhibiting or confusing the work of the group.

Likewise, in some therapeutic communities for adults, members are *dis*couraged from having individual therapeutic relationships with staff members, whereas in those for children and adolescents there will often be a very strong emphasis on such relationships. We have therefore had to decide how far to encourage individual tutorial discussions between students and their tutors (which is the norm in many forms of professional education) and how far to promote or even insist upon a culture of self-disclosure in the group. When a student discloses to a tutor something which they have not yet talked about in the group, they are usually encouraged to 'bring it to the group' as soon as they are ready to do so; thus we promote full use of the group, while still allowing for some individual work. Our rationale for this policy is that, while our group members are indeed working with children, we (the teaching staff) are working with them as adults and we need to be especially clear about retaining a model based upon the principles of adult education rather than risking setting up a patronising or paternalistic alternative.

A NOTE ON 'MODELLING' AND THE DISTINCTION BETWEEN CONSCIOUS AND UNCONSCIOUS ELEMENTS IN MATCHING

At this stage it is as well to emphasise that the idea of matching is about more than just conscious replication or 'the modelling of good practice', as it might be seen in some quarters. Our argument is that within any form of professional practice there are also *un*conscious processes going on, which are often hard to detect but which certainly have an impact and which may account for some of the strange and even distressing things that happen in practice. Because they are hard to detect, these processes can be especially hard for people to learn about and correspondingly hard to teach about. Our experience is that you cannot *make* people realise things at this level, whether in therapy or in training: you can only create situations in which you hope they will experience them for themselves and then achieve their own realisations. In the training context, therefore, we aim to construct opportunities for such things to happen. Our main way of doing so is to begin by creating parallels between the conscious structures of practice and of training and then to develop and exploit the opportunities for learning about the unconscious processes as these arise. It is what happens and how it happens within the structures which matters, rather than the detailed modelling of any particular structure.

Nevertheless, there is inevitably a certain amount of 'modelling' involved. As a staff team we are well aware that students naturally observe and comment upon the work of the staff team, whether in terms of the consistency of our approach, or of congruence between what we say and how we act. They do this partly to see whether we can be trusted and partly to discover whether it is actually possible to act in the ways which we recommend. Although we naturally aim for consistency and congruence, it is when we fail to meet their expectations in such matters that some of the strongest and most productive dialogues can take place – if we can keep our nerve and avoid getting too defensive. Powerful learning is possible if it can be acknowledged that as the staff of the course we are only human and that we are subject to the same inner world processes as anyone else. Thus, for example, if a seminar sequence receives a negative evaluation from a group of students, we may be likely to defend ourselves against the pain of rejection by unconsciously retaliating in some way, even if we try to avoid doing so. If all of this happened at an overt and conscious level, that might be manageable, but of course it is much more likely to happen at an unconscious level and through indirect routes, which means that it will take a lot of unravelling if it is to be learned from. The link with 'modelling' is that, if we as a staff team can show that we have the flexibility, resilience and understanding to acknowledge our role in difficulties such as this, we will be modelling good practice to the students who will be faced with equivalent challenges in their own work. Such modelling appears to have been part of what Hughes and Pengelly (1995) offered to their students in the 'child protection' examples quoted earlier in this chapter. To some extent both sides may wish to deny the extent to which modelling operates – perhaps because both sides feel uncomfortable with acknowledging the unconscious dependency which it implies – and it is clearly a staff responsibility to recognise and overcome any resistance on their own part.

The acknowledgement of the fallibility and humanity of the trainer may therefore appear to involve a paradoxical position in relation to 'modelling': on the one hand, the trainer may wish to underplay the type of modelling which is implied by a pedagogical and didactic approach to the training task, while on the other hand he or she may in effect be offering a powerful model of a different sort – a model of the professional as reflective and responsive, but also vulnerable. This paradox of modelling may be inevitable in training for reflective practice and it may need to be supported by a reframing of the training task itself, from one of didactic instruction to one of mutual enquiry and reflection.

CONTINUAL EVOLUTION AND MONITORING

It will also be evident from this case study that whereas some elements in the design for process can be implemented right from the start, others tend to evolve naturally out of the continual re-examination of the design which is set in motion from the beginning. In our case this has happened partly through ongoing discussions in the Opening and Closing Meetings and partly through formal evaluations of the programme and discussion in staff meetings and further changes are yet to evolve. It would be a mistake to assume that everything can be designed to 'match' perfectly right from the start and in fact there is another match here with practice. Bettelheim (1950) argued that therapeutic units for children should expect to be continually in 'a state of becoming', because the nature of the work is that there is always a continually evolving group of young people who are themselves always in a state of transition. Since practice involves continually struggling towards goals which are never fully realised, so training creates parallel struggles.

Ongoing review does not always solve the problems it identifies, however. One cohort of students recognised several months before the end of the programme that they would find the ending of the course difficult and would value an extra opportunity to work on this. An extra day's work was duly added to the programme towards the end of the relevant summer term and the students took responsibility for planning and managing the day's work. It appeared that useful work was then done on the day and yet this group's ending still appeared to be unsatisfactory, with several students experiencing great difficulties in completing their studies. Perhaps the difficulties would have been even greater if they had not done the extra work, but certainly the mere fact of review and replanning had not in itself guaranteed a 'happy ending'.

If the continual monitoring and the evolution to which it

contributes, is to be effective, then both staff and students need to be clear about what it is that they are monitoring and why. It is therefore important that the operation of the matching principle is made explicit and is justified from the outset, so that people can consider the extent to which their training experience does indeed match with their practice.

AND FINALLY

Having come this far, we should acknowledge the limitations of the concept of the matching principle. As we stated in our introductory chapter, there is in fact not much that is new about it: we have simply adapted and tried to articulate an approach to thinking about training which other and wiser colleagues have used in the past. It is a principle we have found interesting to explore and fruitful to apply in the particular context described in this book. Others may have drawn upon quite different principles and may have had very different experiences in the process. We would be delighted to learn more about these experiences from those who may have travelled some equivalent journey. We began this book with a question about the distance between practice and training and our concern throughout has been to suggest some ways in which this distance might be reduced: there will be other ways and other outcomes, but our hope is that the outcome from this book may be some further exchange of views and experiences between the training and practice communities.

Recommended reading

ON LEARNING FOR PROFESSIONAL PRACTICE

Boud, D., Keogh, R. and Walker, D. (1985) *Reflection: Turning Learning into Experience*, London: Kogan Page.

Gould, N. and Taylor, I. (1996) *Reflective Learning for Social Work: Research, Theory and Practice*, Aldershot: Arena.

Saltzberger-Wittenberg, I., Henry, G. and Osborne, E. (1983) *The Emotional Experience of Teaching and Learning*, London: Routledge & Kegan Paul.

Schön, D.A. (1987) *Educating the Reflective Practitioner*, San Francisco, CA: Jossey-Bass

Yelloly, M. and Henkel, M. (eds) (1995) *Learning and Teaching in Social Work: Towards Reflective Practice*, London and Pennsylvania, PN: Jessica Kingsley.

ON THERAPEUTIC CHILD CARE

Copley, B. and Forryan, B. (1987) *Therapeutic Work with Children and Young People*, London: Robert Royce; repr. London: Cassell, 1997.

Dockar-Drysdale, B. (1990) *The Provision of Primary Experience: Winnicottian Work with Children and Adolescents*, London: Free Association.

—— (1993) *Therapy and Consultation in Child Care*, London: Free Association.

Greenhalgh, P. (1993) *Emotional Growth and Learning*, London: Routledge.

Menzies Lyth, I. (1990) *Containing Anxiety in Institutions: Selected Essays Vol. 1.*, London: Free Association.

Rose, M. (1990) *Healing Hurt Minds: The Peper Harow Experience*, London: Tavistock and Routledge.

ON PSYCHOANALYSIS AND ITS APPLICATIONS IN PRACTICE

Hinshelwood, R. (1987) *What Happens in Groups: Psychoanalysis, the Individual and the Community*, London: Free Association.

Miller, E.J. (1993) *From Dependency to Autonomy: Studies in Organisation and Change*, London: Free Association.

Obholzer, A. and Roberts, V.Z. (eds) (1994) *The Unconscious at Work: Individual and Organizational Stress in the Human Services*, London: Routledge.

Shapiro, E.R. and Carr, A.W (1991) *Lost in Familiar Places: Creating Connections Between the Individual and Society*, New Haven, CT and London: Yale University Press.

Bibliography

Adler, J. (1981) *Fundamentals of Group Child Care*, Cambridge, MA: Ballinger.

Ainsworth, F. (1981) 'The Training of Personnel for Group Care with Children', in Ainsworth, F. and Fulcher, L. (eds) *Group Care for Children: Concepts and issues*, London: Tavistock.

Aldgate, J. and Simmonds, J. (eds) (1988) *Direct Work with Children*, London: Batsford and British Agencies for Adoption and Fostering.

Alvarez, A. (1992) *Live Company: Psychoanalytic Psychotherapy with Autistic, Borderline, Deprived and Abused Children*, London: Routledge.

Andreou, C. (1992) 'Inner and Outer Reality in Children and Adolescents', Chapter 10 in J. Kareem and R. Littlewood, *Intercultural Therapy*, Oxford: Blackwell.

Argyris, C. and Schön, D. (1978) *Organizational Learning: A Theory of Action Perspectives*, Reading, MA: Addison Wesley.

Atherton, J. (1989) *Interpreting Residential Life: Values to Practise*, London: Tavistock and Routledge.

Balbernie, R. (1966) *Residential Work with Children*, London: Pergamon.

Baldwin, N. (1991) *The Power to Care in Children's Homes: Experiences of Residential Workers*, Aldershot: Avebury.

Bales, R.F. (1953) 'The Equilibrium Problem in Small Groups', in T. Parsons, R.F. Bales and E.A. Shils (eds) *Working Papers in the Theory of Actions*, Glencoe: Free Press.

Banks, N (1992) 'Techniques for direct identity work with black children', *Adoption and Fostering* 16 (3): 19–25.

Barber, P. (1988) 'Learning to Grow', *International Journal of Therapeutic Communities* 9 (2):101–8.

Barn, R. (1993) *Black Children in the Public Care System*, London: Batsford.

Bateson, G. (1972) *Steps Towards an Ecology of Mind*, New York: Ballantine.

Bayles, M. (1989) *Professional Ethics*, Belmont, CA: Wadsworth, 2nd edn.

Beedell, C. (1970) *Residential Life with Children*, London: Routledge & Kegan Paul.

—— (1993) *Poor Starts, Lost Opportunities, Hopeful Outcomes*, London: Charterhouse Group.

Beker, J. (1972) *Critical Incidents in Child Care*, New York: Behavioural Publications.

Bennathan, M. (1992) 'The Care and Education of Troubled Children', *Therapeutic Care and Education* 1 (1): 37–49.

Benson, J. (1992) 'The Group Turned Inwards: A Consideration of Some Group Phenomena as Reflective of the Northern Irish Situation', *Groupwork* 5 (3): 5–18.

Berkowitz, R. and Leff, J. (1984) 'Clinical Teams Reflect Family Dysfunction', *Journal of Family Therapy* 6: 79–89.

Berridge, D. (1994) 'Foster and Residential Care Re-assessed', *Children and Society* 8 (2): 132–50.

Bettelheim, B. (1950) *Love is Not Enough*, New York: Free Press.

Bion, W. (1962) *Learning from Experience*, London: Heinemann.

—— (1965) *Transformations, Change from Learning to Growth*, London: Heinemann; repr. in B. Copley and B. Forryan, *Therapeutic Work with Children and Young People*, London: Robert Royce, 1987: 254.

—— (1967) *Second Thoughts: Selected Papers on Psychoanalysis*, New York: Jason Aronson.

—— (1984) *Attention and Interpretation*, London: Maresfield Library.

Blackwell, R. (1994) 'The Psyche and the System', in D. Brown and L. Zinkin (eds) *The Psyche and the Social World: Developments in Group-Analytic Theory*, London and New York: Routledge.

Bloomfield, I. (1987) 'Co-Therapists Group at University College Hospital', *Group Analysis* 20 (4): 319–31.

Bohm, D. (1985) *Unfolding Meaning: A Weekend of Dialogue with David Bohm*, London and New York: Ark Books.

Boud, D., Keogh, R. and Walker, D. (1985) *Reflection: Turning Learning into Experience*, London: Kogan Page

Bowlby, J. *Attachment and Loss*: vol. 1, *Attachment* (1969, 2nd edn 1982), vol. 2, *Separation* (1973), vol. 3, *Loss* (1980), London: Tavistock.

Brazelton, T.B. and Cramer, B. (1991) *The Earliest Relationship*, London: Karnac.

Brearley, M. (1994) 'Captains and Cricket Teams, Therapist and Group', *Group Analysis* 27: 231–49.

Brendtro, L.K. and Ness, A.E. (1983) 'The Life-Space Interview: A Re-Examination', in Brendtro, L.K., Ness, A.E. *et al.*, *Re-Educating Troubled Youth: Environments for Teaching and Treatment*, New York: Aldine.

Bridgeland, M. (1971) *Pioneer Work with Maladjusted Children: A Study of the Development of Therapeutic Education*, London: Staples Press.

Brodie, R.D. (1972) 'Some Aspects of Psychotherapy in a Residential Treatment Centre', in G.H. Weber and B.J. Haberlein (eds) *Residential Treatment of Emotionally Disturbed Children*, New York: Behavioural Publications.

Bruggen, P. and O'Brian, C. (1987) *Helping Families: Systems, Residential and Agency Responsibility*, London: Faber & Faber.

Bruner, J. (1983) *Child's Talk*, Oxford: Oxford University Press.

Bullock, R. (1992) *Residential Care for Children: What we Know and Don't know*, London: National Children's Home.

Bullock, R., Little, M. and Millham, S. (1993) *Residential Care for Children: A Review of the Research*, London: HMSO.

Burgess, H. (1992) *Problem-Led Learning for Social Work: The Enquiry and Action Approach*, London: Whiting and Birch.

Butler, B. and Elliott, D. (1985) *Teaching and Learning for Practice*, Aldershot: Gower.

Butlin, E. (1975) 'Institutionalization, Management Structure and Therapy in Residential Work with Emotionally Disturbed Children', *British Journal of Social Work* 5 (3): 283–95.

Calam, R. and Franchi, C. (1987) *Child Abuse and its Consequences: Observational Approaches*, Cambridge: Cambridge University Press.

Centre for Staff Development in Higher Education/Central Council for Education and Training in Social Work (1986) *Focus on Adolescence*, trigger videos and trainers' notes, London: Contact Productions.

Charles, M., Rashid, S., and Thoburn, J. (1992) 'The Placement of Black Children with Permanent New Families', *Adoption and Fostering* 16 (3): 13–19.

Cividini-Stranic, E. and Klain, E. (1984) 'Advantages and Disadvantages of Co-Therapy', *Group Analysis* 18 (2): 156–9.

Clough, R. (1982) *Residential Work*, London: Macmillan.

Copley, B. and Forryan, B. (1987) *Therapeutic Work with Children and Young People*, London: Robert Royce; repr. London: Cassell, 1997.

Coulshed, V. (1990) *Management in Social Work*, London: Macmillan.

Cross, J. (1990) 'Therapeutic Experience: The Nature of the Therapeutic Community for Emotionally Deprived and Disturbed Children', in C. Fees (ed.) *Residential Experience*, Birmingham: Association of Workers for Maladjusted Children: 91–112.

Danbury, H. and Wallbridge, D. (1989) 'Directive Teaching and Gut Learning: The Seminar Technique and its Use in Video-Based Role-Play Learning', *Journal of Social Work Practice*, May: 53–67.

Davis, M. and Wallbridges, D. (1981) *Boundary and Space*, Harmondsworth: Penguin.

Davison, A.J. (1995) *Residential Care: The Provision of Quality Care in Residential and Educational Group Care Settings*, Aldershot: Arena.

de Maré, P. (1991) *Koinonia*, London: Karnac Books.

Department of Health and Social Security (1985) *Social Work Decisions in Child Care: Recent Research Findings and their Implications*, London: HMSO.

—— (1991) *The Children Act Guidance and Regulations*, vol. 4, *Residential Care*, London: HMSO.

Department of Health and Social Security and Parker, R. (1991) *Patterns and Outcomes in Child Placement: Messages from Current Research and Their Implications*, London: HMSO.

Devereux, G. (1967) *From Anxiety to Method in the Behaviour Science*, The Hague: Moulton.

Dimmock, B. (1993) *Working with Troubled and Troublesome Young People in Residential Settings: A Directory of Training Materials*, Open University and the Department of Health and Social Security.

Dockar-Drysdale, B. (1968a) *Therapy in Child Care*, London: Longman.

—— (1968b) 'Role and Function', in *Therapy in Child Care*, London: Longman; repr. *Therapy and Consultation in Child Care*, London: Free Association, 1993.

—— (1973) *Consultation in Child Care*, London: Longman.

—— (1990) *The Provision of Primary Experience Winnicottian Work with Children and Adolescents*, London: Free Association.

—— (1993) *Therapy and Consultation in Child Care*, London: Free Association.

Dunn, J. (1984) *Brothers and Sisters*, London: Fontana.

Erikson, E.H. (1965) *Childhood and Society*, Harmondsworth: Penguin.

Fahlberg, V. (ed.) (1990) *Residential Treatment: a Tapestry of Many Therapies*, Indianapolis, IN: Perspectives Press.

—— (1982) *Child Development*, London: Batsford and British Agencies for Adoption and Fostering.

Fonagy, P. (1996) 'Attachment and Theory of Mind: Overlapping Constructs?', paper to Association of Child Psychology and Psychiatry, Conference: 'Bonding and Attachment: Current Issues', Regent's College, London, 26 June.

Forehand, R. and McMahon, R. (1981) *Helping the Non-Compliant Child: A Clinician's Guide to Parent Training*, New York and London: Guilford Press.

Foulkes, S.H. (1964) *Therapeutic Group Analysis*, London: Allen & Unwin.

—— (1975) *Group-Analytic Psychotherapy*, London: Gordon and Breach.

Fraiberg, S. (1959) *The Magic Years*, New York: Scribner's.

—— (1980) *Clinical Studies in Infant Mental Health*, London: Tavistock.

Gadamer, H.G. (1981) *Truth and Method*, London: Sheed and Ward; cited in M. Jones, 'Education and Racism', *Journal of Philosophy of Education* 19 (2): 223–34, 1985.

Gould, N. and Taylor, I. (1996) *Reflective Learning for Social Work: Research, Theory and Practice*, Aldershot: Arena.

Greenberg, M., Cichetti, D. and Cummings, E. (eds) (1990) *Attachment in the Pre-School Years*, Chicago, IL: Chicago University Press.

Greenhalgh, P. (1994) *Emotional Growth and Learning*, London: Routledge.

Harris, H. and Lipman, A. (1984) 'Gender and the Pursuit of Respectability: Dilemmas of Daily Life in a Home for Adolescents', *British Journal of Social Work* 14: 265–76.

Hawkins, P. and Shohet, R. (1989) *Supervision in the Helping Professions*, Milton Keynes: Open University.

Heimann, P. (1950) 'On Counter-Transference', *International Journal of Psychoanalysis* 31: 81–4.

Hinshelwood, R. (1987) *What Happens in Groups: Psychoanalysis, the Individual and the Community*, London: Free Association.

Hughes, L. and Pengelly, P. (1995) 'Who cares if the room is cold? Practicalities, Projections and the Trainer's Authority', in M. Yelloly and

M. Henkel (eds) *Learning and Teaching in Social Work: Towards Reflective Practice*, London and Pennsylvania, PN: Jessica Kingsley.

Jennings, S. (1990) *Dramatherapy with Families, Groups and Individuals: Waiting in the Wings*, London: Jessica Kingsley.

Jewett, C. (1994) *Helping Children Cope with Separation and Loss*, London: Batsford and British Agencies for Adoption and Fostering.

Jonsen, A.R. (1991) 'Of Balloons and Bicycles', *Hastings Centre Report* 21: 14–16.

Kahan, B. (1994) *Growing up in Groups*, London: HMSO.

Kahn, W.A. (1992) 'To Be Fully There: Psychological Presence at Work', *Human Relations* 45 (4).

Kaplan, L.J. (1979) *Oneness and Separateness: From Infant to Individual*, London: Jonathan Cape.

Keats, J. (1952) *Letters*, ed. M.B. Forman, London: Oxford University Press, 4th edn.

Keenan, C. (1991) 'Working Within the Life Space', in J. Lishman (ed.) *Handbook of Theory for Practice Teachers*, London: Jessica Kingsley.

Kegerreis, S. (1995) 'Getting Better Makes it Worse', in J. Trowell and M. Bower (eds) *The Emotional Needs of Young Children and their Families*, London: Routledge.

Kennard, D., Roberts, J. and Winter, A. (1993) *A Workbook of Group Analytic Interventions*, London: Routledge.

Kennedy, R. (1987) 'The Work of the Day', in R. Kennedy, A. Heymans and L. Tischler (eds) *The Family as In-Patient: Families and Adolescents at the Cassell Hospital*, London: Free Association.

Kerfoot, M. and Butler, A. (1988) *Problems of Childhood and Adolescence*, London: Macmillan.

Klein, M. (1959) 'Our Adult World and its Roots in Infancy', *Human Relations* 12: 291–303.

Lacan, J. (1977) 'The Mirror Stage as Formative of the I as Revealed in Psychoanalytic Experience', in: *Écrits*, London: Tavistock.

Lampen, J. (1986) 'Aspects of Leadership', in D. Steinberg (ed.) *The Adolescent Unit: Work and Teamwork in Adolescent Psychiatry*, Chichester: John Wiley.

Lane, D.C. (1994) *An Independent Review of the Residential Child Care Initiative*, London: Central Council for Education and Training in Social Work.

Lanyado, M. (1991) 'On Creating a Psychotherapeutic Space', *Journal of Social Work Practice* 5 (1): 31–40.

Levy, A. and Kahan, B. (1991) *The Pindown Experience and the Protection of Children: The Report of the Staffordshire Child Care Inquiry 1990*, Staffordshire County Council.

Little, M. with Kelly, S. (1995) *A Life without Problems? The achievements of a Therapeutic Community*, Aldershot: Arena.

Loughran, J. (1996) *Developing Reflective Practice: Learning about Teaching and Learning through Modelling*, London: Falmer Press.

Lucas, M. (1992) 'Special Things: the Management of an Individual

Provision Within a Group Care Setting for Emotionally Disturbed Children', *Therapeutic Communities* 13 (4): 209–19.

—— (1993) 'Understanding and Working with the Symbolic Communications of an Eight-Year-Old Girl in a Residential Setting', dissertation for MA in Therapeutic Child Care, University of Reading.

Lucas, T. (1988) 'Holding and Holding on: Using Winicott's Ideas in Group Psychotherapy with Twelve- to Thirteen-Year-Olds', *Group Analysis* 21: 135–51.

Lyndon, P. (1997) 'The Median Group: An Appropriate Setting for the Negotiation of Hatred: An Elaboration of Ideas from the work of P.B. de Maré', *Group Analysis* 30: 131–7.

Maier, H.W. (1981) 'Essential Components in Care and Treatment Environments for Children', in F. Ainsworth and L. Fulcher (eds) *Group Care for Children: Concepts and Issues*, London: Tavistock.

—— (1985) 'Primary Care in Secondary Settings: Inherent Strains', in L.C.Fulcher and F. Ainsworth (eds) *Group Care Practice with Children*, London: Tavistock.

—— (1987) *Developmental Group Care of Children and Youth: Concepts and Practice*, New York and London: Haworth Press.

Main, M. (1996) 'Current Issues in Attachment', Emanuel Miller lecture, London: Association of Child Psychology and Psychiatry.

Main, T. (1990) 'Knowledge, Learning and Freedom from Thought', *Psychoanalytic Psychotherapy* 5 (1): 59–78.

Mason, B. (1989) *Handing Over: Developing Consistency Across Shifts*, London: DC Publishing.

Mattinson, J. (1975) *The Reflection Process in Casework Supervision*, London: Institute of Marital Studies.

Maturana, H. and Varela, F. (1987) *The Tree of Knowledge: The Biological Roots of Human Understanding*, Boston, MA: Shambhala.

McLennan, R. (1981) 'Action Research Consultancy: A Tavistock Approach', *Journal of Enterprise Management* 3: 25.

Menzies, I. (1977) *Staff Support Systems: Task and Anti-Task in Adolescent Institutions*, London: Tavistock Institute.

Menzies Lyth, I. (1988) 'The Development of Self in Children in Institutions', in *Containing Anxiety in Institutions*, London: Free Association.

—— (1988) *Containing Anxiety in Institutions: Selected Essays*, vol. 1, London: Free Association.

Miller, E.J. (1989) 'Towards an Organisational Model for Residential Treatment of Adolescents', London: Tavistock Institute.

—— (1992) 'The Therapeutic Community Approach: Does It Exist?', *Therapeutic Communities* 13 (2): 127–8.

—— (1993a) *From Dependency to Autonomy: Studies in Organisation and Change*, London: Free Association.

—— (1993b) *Creating a Holding Environment: Conditions for Psychological Security*, London: Tavistock Institute.

Miller, E.J. and Gwynne, G.V. (1972) *A Life Apart: A Pilot Study of*

Residential Institutions for the Physically Handicapped and the Young Chronic Sick, London: Tavistock Institute.

Millham, S., Bullock, R., Hosie, K. and Haak, M. (1986) *Lost in Care*, London: Gower.

Milner, D. (1983) *Children and Race: Ten Years On*, London: Penguin.

Milner, M. (1950) *On Not Being Able to Paint*, London: New Education Book Club, 2nd edn, 1957.

Mumby, T. (1975) 'Large Groups in Industry', in L. Kreeger, *The Large Group: Dynamics and Therapy*, London: Maresfield Reprints.

Murray, L. (1996) 'Winnicott: a Research Perspective', *Journal of Child Psychotherapy* 22 (3): 362–72.

Nelson-Jones, R. (1983) *Practical Counselling Skills*, Eastbourne: Holt Rhinehart and Wilson.

Newson, J. and E. (1968) *Four Years Old in An Urban Community*, London: Allen & Unwin.

O'Brian, C., Bruggen, P. and Dunne, C. (1985) 'Extra Meetings: A Tool for Decisions and Therapy', *Journal of Adolescence* 8 (3): 255–61.

Oaklander, V. (1978) *Windows to Our Children*, Utah, UT: Real People Press.

Obholzer, A. (1987) 'Institutional Dynamics and Resistance to Change', *Psychoanalytic Psychotherapy* 2 (3): 201–6.

Obholzer, A. and Roberts, V.Z. (eds) (1994) *The Unconscious at Work: Individual and Organizational Stress in the Human Services*, London: Routledge.

Ogden, T.H. (1983) 'The Concept of Internal Object Relations', *International Journal of Psychoanalysis* 64: 227–41.

Owen, P. and Curtis, P. (1988) *Techniques for Working with Children*, Euxton, Chorley, Lancs.

Pines, M. (1990) 'Reflections on Mirroring', sixth S.H. Foulkes annual lecture, *Group Analysis* 15 (2).

Preston-Shoot, M. and Agass, D. (1990) *Making Sense of Social Work: Psychodynamics, Systems and Practice*, London: Macmillan.

Rainer, T. (1980) *The New Diary*, London: Angus and Robertson.

Redgrave, K. (1987) *Child's Play – Direct Work with the Deprived Child*, Cheadle: Boys and Girls Welfare Society.

Redl, F. (1966) 'Just What Am I Supposed to Observe?', in *When We Deal with Children*, New York: Free Press.

—— (1966) *When We Deal with Children*, New York: Free Press.

Redl, F. and Wineman, D. (1957) *The Aggressive Child*, New York: Free Press.

Reed, J. and Procter, S. (1993) *Nurse Education: A Reflective Approach*, London: Edward Arnold.

Reeves, C. (1979) 'Transference in the Residential Treatment of Children', *Journal of Child Psychotherapy* 5: 25–37.

Rennie, D. (1992) 'The Unfolding Reflexivity', in S. Toukmanian (ed.) *Psychotherapy Process and Research*, London: Sage.

Richardson, E. (1973) *The Teacher, The School and The Task of Management*, London: Heinemann.

Roberts, J. (1993) 'Intervening to Establish and Maintain a Therapeutic Environment', in D. Kennard, J. Roberts and D.A. Winter, *A Workbook of Group Analytic Interventions*, London: Routledge.

Robertson, J. and J. (1989) *Separation and the Very Young*, London: Free Association; film series, *Young Children in Brief Separation*, 1967–71.

Rose, M. (1993) *The Trouble With Teenagers*, London: Positive Publications.

—— (1990) *Healing Hurt Minds: the Peper Harow Experience*, London: Tavistock and Routledge.

Rustin, M. and M. (1987) *Narratives of Love and Loss: Studies in Modern Children's Fiction*, London and New York: Verso.

Ryan, T. and Walker, R. (1993) *Making Life Story Books*, London: British Agencies for Adoption and Fostering.

Salvendy, L.T. (1985) 'Training, Leadership and Group Composition: A Review of the Crucial Variable', *Group Analysis*, 18 (2): 132–41.

Saltzberger-Wittenberg, I., Henry, G. and Osborne, E. (1983) *The Emotional Experience of Teaching and Learning*, London: Routledge & Kegan Paul.

Sartre, J.-P. (1967) *Words*, Harmondsworth: Penguin.

Schön, D.A. (1983) *The Reflective Practitioner*, New York: Basic Books.

—— (1987) *Educating the Reflective Practitioner*, San Francisco, CA: Jossey-Bass.

Segal, H. (1988) 'Notes on symbol formation', in E. Bott Spillius (ed.) *Melanie Klein Today: Developments in Theory and Practice*, vol 1, London: Tavistock and Routledge.

Semyonova, N.D. (1993) 'Psychotherapy during social upheaval in the USSR', *Group Analysis* 26 (1): 91–5.

Shapiro, E.R. and Carr, A.W. (1991) *Lost in Familiar Places: Creating Connections Between the Individual and Society*, New Haven, CT and London: Yale University Press.

Skinner, A.C.R. (1975) 'The Large Group in Training', in L. Kreeger, *The Large Group: Dynamics and Therapy*, London: Maresfield Reprints.

Skynner, R. with Pontatti, C. (1974) 'Report on Dr and Mrs Skynner's Seminar, Rome 1973, followed by comment from Dr Skynner', *Group Analysis* 12: 34–40.

Smale, G. (1977) *Prophecy, Behaviour and Change*, London: Routledge & Kegan Paul.

Social Services Inspectorate (1993) *Corporate Parents: Inspection of Residential Child Care Services in Eleven Local Authorities, November 1992 to March 1993*, London: Department of Health and Social Security.

—— (1994) *Standards for Residential Child Care Services: A Handbook for Social Services Managers and Inspectors, Users of the Services and their Families*, London: HMSO.

Spellman, D. and Scott, C. (1993) 'An Everyday Story of Systems Practice', *Journal of Family Therapy* 15: 23–34.

Stamm, I. (1985) 'The Hospital as a Holding Environment', *International Journal of Therapeutic Communities* 6 (4): 219–29.

Stern, D. (1985) *The Interpersonal World of the Infant*, New York: Basic Books.

Taylor, I. (1996) *Reflective Learning for Social Work: Research, Theory and Practice*, in N. Gould and I. Taylor, 1996.

Thomas, L. (1992) 'Racism and Psychotherapy: Working with Racism in the Consulting Room: an Analytical View', Chapter 9 in J. Kareem and R. Littlewood, *Intercultural Therapy*, Oxford: Blackwell.

Trampuz, D. (1993) 'The "Yugoslav crisis" Reflected in the Large Group in the Diploma Course in Zagreb', *Group Analysis* 26 (2): 183–8.

Trieschmann, A.E. (1969) 'Understanding the Stages of a Typical Temper Tantrum', in A.E. Trieschman, J.K. Whittaker and L.K. Brendtro, *The Other 23 Hours: Child-Care Work with Emotionally-Disturbed Children in a Therapeutic Milieu*, New York: Aldine.

Tripp, D. (1993) *Critical Incidents in Teaching. Developing Professional Judgement*, London: Routledge.

Trist, E., Higgin, G., Murray, H. and Pollock, A. (1963) 'The Assumption of Ordinariness as a Denial Mechanism', in *The Social Engagement of Social Science*, London: Free Association; repr. 1990.

Turquet, P.M. (1974) 'Leadership, the Individual and the Group', in G. Gibbard, J. Hartmann and R. Mann (eds) *Analysis of Groups*, San Francisco, CA: Jossey-Bass.

—— (1975) 'Threats to Identity in the Large Group', in L. Kreeger, *The Large Group: Dynamics and Therapy*, London: Maresfield Reprints.

van der Linden, P. (1988) 'How Does the Large Group Change the Individual?', *International Journal of Therapeutic Communities* 9 (1): 31–9.

Walker, D. (1985) 'Writing and Reflection', in D. Boud, R. Keogh and D. Walker (eds) *Reflection: Turning Experience into Learning*, Sydney: Kogan Page.

Ward, A. (1984) 'All you Can Do is Bring Your Own Self', *Community Care*, (March).

—— (1990) 'The Role of Physical Contact in Child Care', *Children and Society* 4 (4): 337–51.

—— (1991) 'Training for Group Care', *The Teaching of Child Care in the Diploma in Social Work*, London: Central Council for Education and Training in Social Work.

—— (1993a) *Working in Group Care: Social Work in Residential and Day Care Settings*, Birmingham: Venture Press.

—— (1993b) 'The Large Group: the Heart of the System in Group Care', *Groupwork* 6 (1): 63–77.

—— (1995a) 'The "Matching Principle": Exploring Connections Between Practice and Training in Therapeutic Child Care: Part 2: the Matching Principle – Concept and Application', *Journal of Social Work Practice* 9 (2): 189–98.

—— (1995b) 'Establishing Community Meetings in a Children's Home', *Groupwork* 15 (1): 4–23.

—— (1996a) 'Never Mind the Theory, Feel the Guidelines: Practice,

Theory and Official Guidance in Residential Child Care: the Case of the Therapeutic Communities', *Therapeutic Communities* 17 (1): 19–29.

—— (1996b) 'Opportunity-Led Work Part 2: the Framework', *Social Work Education*, 8 (1): 67–78.

Warren, B. (1992) 'Back to Basics: Problems and Prospects for Applied Philosophy', *Journal of Applied Philosophy* 9 (1): 13–21.

Westcott, H.L. (1992) 'The 1991 Criminal Justice Act: Research on Children's Testimony', *Adoption and Fostering* 16 (3): 7–12.

Whittaker, J.K. (1969) 'Observing and Recording Children's Behaviour', in A.E. Trieschman, J.K. Whittaker and L.K. Brendtro, *The Other 23 Hours: Child-Care Work with Emotionally-Disturbed Children in a Therapeutic Milieu*, New York: Aldine.

Whitwell, J. (1989) 'The Residential Treatment of Unintegrated Children', *The Journal of the British Association for Counselling* 68: 21–8.

—— (1994) 'Is There a Future for Long Term Psychotherapeutic Child Care?', *Therapeutic Communities* 15 (2): 87–97.

Wickes, F. (1977) *The Inner World of Choice*, London: Coventure.

Wilson, M. and Evans, M. (1980) *Education of Disturbed Pupils*, London: Methuen.

Winnicott, C. (1968) 'Communicating with Children', in R. Todd (ed.) *Disturbed Children*, London: Longman.

Winnicott, D.W. (1950) *Babies and Their Mothers*, London: Free Association; repr. 1988.

—— (1956) 'Primary Maternal Pre-Occupation', in *Through Paediatrics to Psychoanalysis*, London: Tavistock, 1958.

—— (1958) *Collected Papers: Through Paediatrics to Psychoanalysis*, London: Tavistock.

—— (1960a) 'The Theory of the Parent–Infant Relationship', in *The Maturational Processes and the Facilitating Environment*, London: Hogarth Press and the Institute of Psychoanalysis, 1965.

—— (1960b) 'Ego Distortion in Terms of True and False Self', in *The Maturational Processes and the Facilitating Environment*, London: Hogarth Press and the Institute of Psychoanalysis, 1965.

—— (1964) *The Child, the Family and the Outside World*, London: Penguin.

—— (1965a) *The Maturational Processes and the Facilitating Environment*, London: Hogarth Press and the Institute of Psychoanalysis.

—— (1965b) *The Family and the Individual*, London: Tavistock.

—— (1971) *Playing and Reality*, London: Tavistock.

—— (1988) *Human Nature*, London: Free Association.

Wolff, S. (1969) *Children Under Stress*, London: Penguin.

Worthington, A. (1990) 'The Function of the Community Meeting in a Therapeutic Community for Pre- and Young Adolescents', *International Journal of Therapeutic Communities* 11 (2): 95–102.

Wynne, L.C. (1984) 'The Epigenesis of Relational Systems: A Model for Understanding Family Development', *Family Process* 23 (3).

Yalom, I.D. (1975) *The Theory and Practice of Group Psychotherapy*, New York: Basic Books.

Yelloly, M. and Henkel, M. (eds) (1995) *Learning and Teaching in Social*

Work: Towards Reflective Practice, London and Pennsylvania, PN: Jessica Kingsley.

Zagier Roberts, V. (1994) 'Management at the Boundary', in A. Obholzer and V. Zagier Roberts (eds) *The Unconscious at Work*, London: Free Association.

Zinkin, L. (1983) 'Malignant Mirroring', *Group Analysis* 16 (2): 113–26.

Index